D1212634

WILDE TIMES

PATRICIA WILDE,
GEORGE BALANCHINE,
AND THE RISE OF
NEW YORK CITY BALLET

Joel Lobenthal

ForeEdge

ForeEdge

An imprint of University Press of New England

www.upne.com

© 2016 Joel Lobenthal

All rights reserved

Manufactured in the United States of America

Designed by Mindy Basinger Hill

Typeset in Garamond Premier Pro

For permission to reproduce any of the material in this book,
contact Permissions, University Press of New England, One Court Street,
Suite 250, Lebanon NH 03766; or visit www.upne.com

Hardcover ISBN: 978-1-61168-803-0

Ebook ISBN: 978-1-61168-943-3

Library of Congress Cataloging-in-Publication Data
available upon request

5   4   3   2   1

For my youngest and most arts-loving niece,

ADELAIDE FERSTEL LOBENTHAL,

who takes ballet and received encouragement from no less

an authority than Patricia Wilde!

CONTENTS

Illustrations follow page 146

INTRODUCTION

When New York City Ballet was founded in October 1948, a city that had lacked a resident large-scale company now became a place where ballet undertook one of the great adventures in its four-hundred-year history. Eighteen months later, twenty-two-year-old Patricia Wilde joined the company. She was ballerina there for the next fifteen years and was crucial to the developing troupe and its rising fortunes. Her story is essential to the history of this great company, which did so much to create an audience, a signature, for ballet in America.

In retrospect, Wilde's decade and a half with NYCB easily looks like a golden age. The creativity of these years is staggering. George Balanchine's repertory and aesthetic dominated the company, which also danced repertory by many other choreographers who weren't like Balanchine at all. Like many other NYCB dancers, Wilde had already worked for Balanchine in the émigré Ballet Russe de Monte Carlo, where he was chief choreographer from 1944 to 1946. But her experience and frame of reference were much broader than simply Balanchine's, and, indeed, such breadth was the hallmark of the company in the early years. Its emerging profile was defined by the diverse background, training, physical look, and kinetic temperament of the dancers.

Trained in Russia in the fundamentals of classical ballet, Balanchine added off-balance, hip-slung, syncopated "distortion" of purely classical equilibrium. And Wilde, trained in Ottawa, New York, and Paris mainly by Russian and Russian-influenced teachers, followed the same path. A solid grounding in the Old World gave her the secure foundation from which to follow Balanchine's neoclassicism in whatever form it might take.

At NYCB, Wilde and her colleagues performed in all kinds of ballets, from the most accessible to the most esoteric. Ballets of story, ballets of mood, and, of course, the works that would eventually identify the company internationally: the storyless ballets of Balanchine. This was movement set to music in the most intimate expression of Balanchine's conservatory training. It was ballet pared to its essence, but informed by the theatricality that Wilde and her colleagues had plied in different repertories. Ticket prices at Manhattan's City Center of Music and Drama made all these performance experiences accessible to virtually every income bracket.

The ballet world today, the ballet aesthetic, and the balletic instrument are in some ways very different than in Wilde's era. Today's dancers have generally superior raw material—superior by virtue of coming closer to the balletic ideal—but are also as a result more homogenized. Aerodynamically mandated, thinness as a prerequisite for the dancer did not originate with Balanchine but certainly was aggressively promoted by him—perhaps to excess. The emphasis on thinness made possible an increasing development of line, of long legs lifted high in space, which in turn demanded greater thinness.

Length and lightness were certainly desirable attributes in Wilde's time, but she and her colleagues embodied something rather different than today's ballet. In 1952, Edwin Denby described her "beautiful Veronese grandeur and plasticity of shape." Indeed, it was the light and shade found in paintings that ballet, born in the Renaissance, sought to emulate through its arrangements of the arms and torso. Wilde's colleague Robert Lindgren once told her about talking to Balanchine in the upstage wings of the theater during a performance in the late 1950s. Lindgren asked why he was watching from so remote a perch. The choreographer explained that it was because "you can see Pat Wilde from any angle." Wilde was well proportioned and her legs were shapely. She could lift her legs as high as she needed to. But above all, shape, tremendous speed, what ex-NYCB

Bruce Wells calls "a Mozartean precision," combined with fearless abandon made Wilde's dancing exceptional. "She was a force of nature," says Violette Verdy, Wilde's former NYCB colleague. "A beautiful tempest that was not dangerous to anyone, that was beyond the ordinary clouds."

Multidimensional in every sense, Wilde and her colleagues celebrated ballet as an art of fusion, an art form of many art forms. It was a way of moving that could be both elemental and the direct outgrowth of aristocratic refinement. It could also easily absorb the energies of contemporary society.

In Wilde's day, NYCB was small: around forty-five dancers. They were worked to the bone when they did work, for seasons were intermittent at first. Soon they were worked to the bone for longer and longer periods each year, grateful for every additional week of work and income. Vicissitudes and grueling schedules frequently pushed them to the breaking point, and dealing with their elusive, mercurial, often capricious and controlling resident genius was not always easy.

"The joy of it keeps you going," Wilde said. The audience's acclaim was, for her, icing on the cake. On stage, moving to music, enmeshed in a microcosm of poetically expanded horizons and magically supercharged space invariably put her "in another world." In the studio, Balanchine's creativity made choreography a voyage of discovery for the dancer. The end product always seemed to be stamped Balanchine as well as capturing and spotlighting the individual attributes of the dancer—challenging and expanding her talents as well.

Wilde and colleagues were soon showing major American cities and international capitals what they were doing in New York. They became emissaries of American cultural achievement potent enough to be sponsored by the State Department. In 1965, Wilde left the stage to begin a long and storied career as educator and administrator. By then, a dance and a ballet boom was in full swing in this country. Media interest, corporate and government funding were enthusiastic. Today ballet and dance have fallen on much tougher times. But when one watches tapes of Wilde and her colleagues made fifty and sixty years ago, their performances still live, still inspire; they make one wonder how ballet could not be something essential to the arts, to society, to life.

Wilde Times

EILEEN

SIMPSON

Patricia (née White) Wilde had an abbreviated youth. She was fourteen when she left her childhood home on the outskirts of Ottawa, and moved to New York. Before she was sixteen, Wilde was a professional ballet dancer. Looking back seventy years later, she believed that her upbringing had prepared her for life, but not particularly for a life in the theater. Although she and her older sister Nora were studying ballet at an early age, theirs wasn't in any sense a theatrical family. Nevertheless, her childhood gave her—by design as well as circumstance and vicissitude—qualities of resilience and drive essential for the rough, wild ride that is a career in ballet.

Her mother, Eileen Lucy Simpson, had grown up on a vast estate in Gloucester Township, southeast of Ottawa. Eileen's parents were of Scottish descent, their families having originally settled in St. Andrews, west of Montreal, before migrating southwest to the nation's capital. The Simpson estate was one thousand acres granted by Crown decree that lay between Montreal Road, formerly the King's Road, and the Ottawa River, descending to the water across several miles of hills and meadows. The family had holdings on the other side of Montreal Road as well.

Nora White's impression was that her grandfather Lester Simpson, Eileen's father, was both "very wealthy" and "very spoiled." Frequently he'd drive his horses into town, where he might spend hours drinking. When he arrived home, Eileen would be there to greet him, to try to prevent him from abusing the horses in a state of inebriated impatience. Horses were a passion for Eileen. At first she rode only sidesaddle, as was considered decorous for women at the turn of the century. But she was fully and expertly astride in her youngest children's earliest memories.

Nora came to know her maternal grandmother, Elizabeth Ewing Simpson, when she lived with them for a couple of years after Lester's death. She was quite different from what Nora would glean about her grandfather. Elizabeth was "very kind, and quiet. She'd been beautifully brought up, I think, so she was quite a lady. She read, and did a little painting."

Eileen's older brother was named for their mother; Wilde had a vague supposition that he hadn't gotten along that well with Lester. Ewing became an engineer and was killed in an accident on a job overseas well before Wilde was born.

Eileen received a good academic education at a convent in Ottawa. She also studied piano and voice there, and for the rest of her life she loved to sing. Her daughters remembered her being partial to love songs and ballads of Gibson Girl vintage: "By the Light of the Silvery Moon" was a favorite. She also rendered Scottish and Irish songs: "There's not a colleen sweeter / Where the River Shannon flows . . ."

Soon after graduating from the convent in 1908, Eileen married John Herbert White, the only man her father had let her date. He was fourteen years older and a good matrimonial prospect—an engineer who worked for the Ontario road commissioner, good-looking, established in his career, well educated. White was Irish, and for a while Eileen "said she was Irish, too," Nora recalled—her mother preferring its association with generosity to the traditional association of Scots with extreme thrift.

Was she more class conscious than her own father? He had no objections to White's pedigree, but Nora believed that "Mother would pooh-pooh" White's family. Eileen certainly retained a sense of seigniorial privilege. Nora remembered that when they'd make the twenty-five-minute drive into downtown Ottawa, Eileen would often go up to a policeman, tell him where she'd parked her car, and ask him to watch it. "Fine, Eileen," was the invariable answer.

Lester built Eileen and her new husband a spacious brick house at 61 Victoria Street, across from a tennis club in the village of Eastview, a recent amalgamation of three communities on the east side of the Rideau River. White subsequently owned a construction company, and from 1916 to 1918 was mayor of Eastview. He was entrepreneurial, buying a row of attached houses that he rented out.

The Whites' first child, born in 1910, was named Lester for Eileen's father; then came Herbert, whom the family eventually called "Barney," after a friend of Eileen's gave him that nickname. In 1915, Elizabeth was born. Ten years and one miscarriage later, Eileen gave birth to Nora on her own birthday, August 23, and not entirely by chance, it would appear. As Eileen's birthday approached, she became determined that she and her fourth child would share the same birthday. Eileen ventured out to buy castor oil and applied hot water bottles, claiming she'd been caught out in the rain. Dr. Nabery, the family physician, was bewildered and concerned, but what Eileen was going to do, she was going to do.

Three years after Nora, on July 16, 1928, Patricia Lorraine Ann was born in Rideau Hospital, one of the city's two main hospitals. In Eastview, Wilde recalled the big stairs that for her as a toddler were difficult to climb. Nora remembered more, remembered her father, "a very calm sweet, man," putting her to bed every night. "We'd kneel down in front of the bed and say, 'Now, I lay me down . . . ' Then he put me in bed, put my hands under my head." Before she drifted off, there would be "the whistle from the train, that wonderful sound."

Because there were eighteen years between the eldest and youngest White children, it was Wilde's brothers' children who seemed contemporaries to Nora and Patricia. But both girls were close to their older sister Elizabeth, whom they called "Bet." As a teenager, Bet was a whiz at mechanical repair: "She could do anything," Nora said, sitting in her Vermont home at a kitchen table her sister had built out of a tree she felled herself. On occasion Eileen would drive Bet to the local dump, where she'd pick out a derelict vehicle, drive it home, and retrofit it herself. Like Lester and Barney, Bet became an engineer.

Eileen often took the girls to visit Wilde's godmother, "Aunt" Hattie, who lived across the Ottawa River in Quebec. She was married to a very successful wholesale florist who also farmed. They had a beautiful home surrounded by greenhouses. Hattie, too, loved to ride and kept a stable. Her children were around the age of Wilde's eldest siblings; like Eileen, she probably married right out of high school. The White sisters recalled Hattie as very intelligent and active. Nevertheless, some of Eileen's other friends, probably women she knew as students, were of a different ilk—"half the time they were having nervous breakdowns," Nora said, "and couldn't get out of bed."

From her daughters' point of view, Eileen was certainly not the kind to have a nervous breakdown—"she was too busy managing everybody," Wilde said. But after twenty years of marriage to the man her father had selected, she experienced a dissatisfaction that led to the Whites' separating permanently, although neither husband nor wife ever initiated a divorce.

Eileen left Eastview and took her three daughters—Elizabeth, sixteen, Nora, six, and Patricia, three—back home to what was by now a diminished Simpson family estate, reduced to around three hundred acres. On Eileen's part, the separation was acrimonious, so much so that she refused to let her two youngest children have anything to do with their father. "She didn't take any time to tell us what had happened," Nora complained. "I was just told I couldn't get in touch with my father, and that he was a bad man." Wilde recalled her mother driving her sister and her downtown: "Turn your head, turn your head! There's your father!"

Around this time, Nora began sleepwalking. If she spent the night at a friend's, "I'd tie myself to the bed." The separation was traumatic for John White as well. He stayed alone in the big house in Eastview, but rented part of it out to what turned out to a petty criminal gang that used it as a gambling den. "He should have known better," Nora said. "But I think he was so depressed." Finally White, perhaps with the assistance of his son Barney, was able to eject them. Where Nora was concerned, Barney and his wife Helen stepped into the breach as well, spending extra time with her, doing things like taking her on camping trips. But Wilde, three years younger than Nora, was hardly aware of the breakup at the time.

Exactly why Eileen nursed so much animosity remains a mystery to Wilde. Bet continued to be close to her father and, since she had her own car, could see him whenever she wished. Sometimes she took Nora with her. Bet told Nora some of what had happened and told her even more as the years went on. According to her, in a gesture of condescension and enmity, "Mother left him in the house in Eastview with a dollar pinned on his jacket."

Wilde retained almost no memories of her father from childhood, although on occasion he would send his two youngest presents and Bet would drive Patricia as well as Nora in for a brief visit. But she became acquainted with him as a young adult. Over the years they developed a fond if not close relationship. "There was nothing wrong with my father," Wilde said. "I think Mother just didn't think he was potent enough." Compared to Eileen's strength "he was not weak, but not pushy, certainly. Not demanding for himself a lot."

Three years older, Nora had a much more pronounced sense of deprivation. "I've worried about it, and I've thought about it, and how I really felt about my mother," Nora said. "I maybe didn't love her any less, but I lost faith in her, I guess, is probably what happened." When White died in 1960, she cried continually for days, until her five-year-old son, who had also spent some time with him, began wetting his bed.

With Eileen and her three daughters went Dolly, a British woman who had cooked for them in Eastview. Bet helped her mother, and then the household expanded to include a local teenager, Evvie, roughly the same age as Bet, who was raised by her grandparents. "Mother knew them," Nora recalled, "and they were having a very hard time. Mother kind of adopted her, but she certainly did more work in the house than Bet."

The move to Montreal Road represented rupture as well as a new beginning for the two youngest Whites. Soon after, Eileen enrolled six-year-old Nora in ballet class at the school directed by Gwendolyn Osborne on Sparks Street in downtown Ottawa. And soon after that, three-year-old Pat started studying there too.

Perhaps Eileen saw ballet class was a way to steer her two youngest girls into more traditional incarnations of femininity than her eldest. She didn't try to dampen Bet's enthusiasm for cars and construction, but as Nora said, "I think that Mother decided, we'd better have these little girls learn something that isn't to do with cars!"

Both White sisters would come to know any number of stage mothers—among them the almost legendary Edith Le Clercq, mother of Tanaquil, later a close colleague of Wilde's in New York City Ballet. In the recollection of classmate Joy Williams, Edith was a daily spectator at her eleven-year-old daughter's lesson at the School of American Ballet in Manhattan.

That was certainly not Eileen White. It was usually she who drove them to class in her Dodge: weather permitting, they liked to ride in the rumble seat and let their skirts fan out in the breeze. But she didn't sit in and watch their class. Instead she shopped, went to the nearby bank, or visited friends.

Osborne's school on Sparks Street was located several flights above a beauty parlor. There were two studios, both very well equipped. The larger had mirrors all across one wall, the smaller one mirror only at one end of an elongated space. All told there were perhaps fifteen students. At first there were only girls; later came the welcome arrival of a single boy student.

Osborne, the daughter of a prominent Ottawa attorney, was in her mid-thirties. She had studied ballet in New York. Osborne herself danced sometimes in her school recitals; Wilde thought she was very good and remembered her pretty feet. Ballet didn't support Osborne, however; her day job as secretary to a judge usually left her free by midafternoon.

Osborne's hair was cut short; looking back, Wilde thinks she may have been gay, although such a thing didn't occur to her over the decade that she studied with her. But Osborne certainly stood out as a maverick in the generally more staid atmosphere of Ottawa, a city without a visible bohemian culture. As she taught she moved around the studio a lot, not touching the students so much a pointing out to them what they should be doing and what they weren't. In her mind's eye Wilde still sees Osborne's strong face, one that "looks interested, always interested in whatever you were doing," in or out of ballet class. Osborne wanted to know what she was reading, wanted to tell her students what she was reading.

For both girls, it was love at first sight where ballet was concerned. For Wilde, it was strictly about her own enjoyment. She used to dream through class, leaning on the strategically low barre, until it was her time to execute a combination in the center of the studio, at which point her energy and attention came to life.

During her adult career, Wilde would become exceptionally quick at learning choreography. Even as a beginner, a certain amount of analytic facility was in play. When Osborne taught them combinations, it was easy for Wilde to see how the combination reversed from one side to the other. "Some people were so slow getting it."

An important contribution was made by Osborne's pianist, Evelyn Williams. Sometimes she would improvise, and sometimes she would accompany them with noted classical compositions, identifying for the students whatever it was she was playing.

Osborne staged rather elaborate recitals every spring. White family or Osborne studio lore retained the story of Wilde's behavior at her first recital, a little story ballet that Osborne put together. The plot dictated that Wilde, then four years old, had time before her appearance. She was told to wait before her entrance in a bassinet-like cradle on stage behind the scenery. She was to stay put until she heard her music cue, then execute a polka around the stage before exiting. She had embarrassed her older sister, several months more advanced than she, because initially, "I didn't know how to polka."

Nora was wracked with fear that her younger sister would fall asleep and never make it onstage. But just the opposite occurred: Wilde appeared eagerly, grinning from ear to ear. The audience loved the sight of her, and their applause told her as much. So she went around and did her entire number again before receiving the proverbial hook. The future ballerina was commanded back to her bassinet.

THE ESTATE

High ornamental gates led from Montreal Road to the imposing stone home Eileen had grown up in. While living in Eastview for twenty years, she and her ex-husband, John White, had stayed involved in her family's property. Eileen kept horses there and sheep for shearing, while John built the family a vacation cabin. He also augmented a stand of apple trees: they now commanded an orchard numbering two hundred trees of many different varieties, guaranteeing a long harvest season beginning in June.

By the time Patricia was a girl, Eileen had sold the venerable stone house and with that money bought some rental properties around Ottawa. An elderly couple was living in the stone house during Wilde's childhood; nevertheless, Pat and Nora freely picked blossoms from the hedge of lilacs screening their family's former seat—"We considered them ours," Wilde said. But they themselves lived first in what they called "the bungalow," reached by a separate driveway, situated on what everyone around the estate called "Skid Road," so designated because in the nineteenth century logs had once been skidded from there to the water to be shipped east to Montreal.

Clad in wooden shingles, the bungalow had been built by Eileen's father as a present for his wife. A big veranda commanded a sweeping view of the river. It was a large house with large rooms and a wide staircase. Downstairs there was a small bedroom off the kitchen for their live-in helper and companion Evvie. On the second floor were spacious bedrooms for Eileen, for Bet, and for Nora and Pat.

The five took care of practically everything on the estate themselves. Bet helped with the animals. Mornings before school it was Nora's task to walk the hundred or so feet to the barn, throw out the manure, and feed and pump water for the horses. During lambing season, Wilde was assigned stable duty; if there was a problem with a delivery she could run up to the house and get help. Many times the sheep would stray. Discovering a hollow under some fencing, the flock would crawl under it until the pen was empty. Eileen would send the girls out to retrieve them. A telltale tuft of wool let them know where the migration had begun and put them on the trail of the errant flock; by the time the girls found them, the sheep usually seemed content to conclude their excursion and be driven home again.

The bungalow sat in the middle of the apple orchard, which Eileen now managed as an additional source of revenue. Together they picked the perfectly ripe apples, packed them in baskets, and took them to the Ottawa city market, a combination of stores and open-air bazaar that hosted a lot of extra traffic on market days. Green apples were stored and eventually made into applesauce for the household. The least-choice fruit went to the horses.

Years later, Wilde and Balanchine were each surprised to find that the other knew about a particular type of mushroom, a puffball, that Wilde had picked on her mother's estate. It is large, ripens overnight, and then must be eaten immediately—delicious when sliced and fried in butter. Puffballs, too, were sent by the Whites to the Ottawa market. Wilde rarely saw them in the United States, but Balanchine knew them from Russia: St. Petersburg and Ottawa are on a comparable latitude, with comparable frigidity.

Eileen assigned the girls chores that were obligatory and established routines that structured their lives. But the estate was theirs to explore. And whatever Wilde and her sisters wanted to do, Eileen's preference was that they do it outdoors. "What are you doing inside?" she would ask. "It's a beautiful day out." Eileen was "a good sport," Wilde recalled, "up to doing anything that you asked her to do: go fishing or take a boat rowing." A cherished memory remained walking with her mother late one summer afternoon down a tree-covered hillside overlooking the river, everything aglow with the sunset. Her mother responded to the beauty by singing one of her favorite old ballads.

Eileen never claimed that her vocalizing was of professional caliber, but she insisted that her younger son's might have been. "Mother always said, 'Oh, Barney could have had a career!' He had a nice big, full voice," Wilde recalled, "and seemed to have a good ear." But an actual career the way Eileen envisioned it would have seemed the remotest of possibilities. Wilde didn't think that Barney even sang in a chorus. Ottawa was the capital of Canada, but it was not a theatrical capital. There wasn't an opera company. It was as yet too early even for the Metropolitan Opera broadcasts, which Wilde and her sister would later listen to after transmissions began in the early 1930s. Barney, Lester, and Bet had amassed a large collection of 78 rpm disks, ranging from popular to opera to symphonic. Wilde and Nora would spend many a rainy day or after-dinner evening listening to them.

Eileen's own performing instincts centered on equestrian display. She won silver cups for hackney carriage driving; at the big horse exhibition held annually in Ottawa, she made a dashing impression. She'd wait strategically on a plinth just outside the ring. Once the conductor's downbeat sparked an enthusiastic trot, Eileen entered with reins held high. From an early age, Wilde herself was riding a Welsh pony named Baby. "She hated to jump but I made her: she would just buck over the jumps." Baby had been in the family many years, throwing off riders since Wilde's elder brother Lester was a boy.

The estate was almost, but not quite completely, free from the ravages of modern congestion and industry. Across the Ottawa River to the west were big paper mills and factories making wood products, among them matches, which sometimes brought a noxious stench of sulfur.

Baby hills just across a meadow from the bungalow were the perfect junior slopes on which to learn to ski. It was Bet who began teaching Wilde, when she was three. She made her own makeshift skis—not much more tailored than a barrel stave.

"We were rough," Nora said of the games she and her sister played with local children. Cops and robbers or cowboys and Indians required a tied-up prisoner. Wilde confounded her sister and friends by being able to extricate herself, Houdini-like, from anything, even when they tried tying her tight around her stomach (not a very good idea, Nora considered in retrospect). A combination of dexterity, slightness, strength, and determination enabled Wilde to quickly and easily extricate herself. Eventually, however, Nora came up with a new and most effective idea. They pulled down branches from two saplings, and tied Wilde spread-eagled to both trees. Once they let go of the supple branches she was lifted up into the air, seemingly immobilized, and they retreated from the scene of the crime. That was one trap Wilde could not get out of; but she was soon released by her captors: "Thank God we did not stay away very long," Nora said.

A favorite playground on the estate was an abandoned quarry—the area had once been known as Gloucester Quarries—full of huge shattered rocks. The children impressed each other with displays of fearlessness, leaping across sizable gaps from one rock to the next. "We were silly kids," Wilde recalled—a fall could have produced major injury.

Ottawa's high northern latitude meant short nights during summer. In the brightness that lingered long after dinner the girls liked lying on a hillside, the perfect spot to watch the northern lights flash their different densities—sometimes white only, sometimes continually shifting hues.

On occasion, the winter temperature in Ottawa could drop as low as fifty degrees below zero. But in winter the property turned into "an absolute fairyland." Winter rain turned to sleet, then wound up sheathing the trees in ice. On brightly moonlit nights, Wilde and her sister would ski down an allée of glistening sumac trees.

North of their property, overlooking the shores of the River, was a Canadian Air Force base. When opportunity arose to rent the bungalow to servicemen and their families, Eileen seized it. She moved her own household into another very small house on the property, originally built for a single man. Then they moved into the vacation home that John White had built—the family called it "the cabin." Like the bungalow, it sat on a hill. It was spacious, all on one floor, with a big main room, and a dining room with fireplace. Adjacent to the kitchen was a small bedroom for Evvie, while Bet had her own large bedroom. The girls slept in a sunroom off their mother's room that opened onto a veranda; outside was an apple tree with a carpet of raspberry bushes. Their sunroom had a separate side door so that they could slip in and out without having to go through the house or their mother's room.

Wilde loved the way the walls of the cabin felt, the chinking between the thick cedar logs. In the fashion of early log cabins, the bark was removed, but the knots and knurls left in. For optimum heat retention the cracks between the logs were filled with cloth soaked in oil. Then mortar was applied, then tar. Drifting off to sleep, Wilde focused on the patterns in the wood and let her imagination freely associate resemblances to plants, animals, insects.

The cabin was heated by a number of wood stoves. In the winter, Eileen was up through the night keeping them going. In the morning, they were sometimes greeted by snow that had sifted through cracks in the walls. At night the girls piled their covers up high, sometimes wearing the next day's clothes so they wouldn't have to dress in the morning cold.

There was an outhouse attached to the cabin, but it could only be reached by an outside entrance. Nor was there running water. Instead they drew from their pump located five hundred feet away. A tub of water was kept in the kitchen, to be heated in pots and kettles as needed.

The rigors of cabin life didn't bother Wilde, however. She loved living there. She felt like a frontier homesteader. That she could survive buttressed her sense of self-worth and her self-confidence; the cooperation and mutual consideration needed for the household's joint survival drew them together.

The White children had been baptized alternately in accordance with their parents' different faiths. It fell to Wilde to be Anglican like her mother rather than Presbyterian like her father. But the family was not particularly religious. Eileen claimed that attendance at church services made her nervous and that instead she went for private consultations with a pastor. Nevertheless, she enrolled her daughters in Ottawa's Notre Dame convent on Gloucester Street, which would give them a good academic education and also train them in the ways of proper and polite behavior. An H-shaped compound, Notre Dame dated back to the 1880s but had recently filled out its intended footprint by adding a new wing. It was a posh neighborhood near a large park. The convent had also taken over several old nearby mansions.

Wilde's impression was that her mother preferred keeping her at home with her as long as possible, so her entrance into school was delayed. She had some homeschooling with a family renting the bungalow, who were homeschooling their daughter. The father was an officer in the air force, and the little girl was storybook pretty, with blond ringlets, while Wilde was lanky and muscular, with a wide, open face and smile, light blond hair, and blue-green eyes.

She entered Notre Dame rather late and by then lagged behind the other students. Sister Nora was consistently an excellent student, but "I was always behind."

The nuns were generally quiet and pleasant, and she "loved" most of them. Deportment was strict: she still finds herself folding her hands one open palm on top of the other, she way she was instructed eighty years ago. Hands could be rapped with rulers—but that was a punishment she never experienced. Yet "I was never totally sold on the convent," largely because of daily chapel attendance. Some of the girls would take communion, having confessed the day before. Not being Catholic, "I just sat there." Twelve stations of the cross were reenacted by students. Wilde's faith again meant that she could not participate, but she was instructed to remain on her knees throughout the entire ceremony. She balked to no avail—until one day she fainted while kneeling. After that she was allowed to sit.

Some disenchantment resulted as well from the nuns' attitude toward dance. When she was six, Osborne had created a solo for her to perform wearing a short little costume. The nuns wanted her to perform it, but when she brought the costume, they decided it was too short. They tacked on long petals of crepe paper so it would come down to her knees.

Deficient in the basics, she felt insecure in school. "I never wanted to get up and say anything in class." But she read on her own voraciously. Apart from the Bobbsey Twins mysteries and the standard canon of children's books, adventure and the outdoors was the keynote to both sisters' reading. "I read all my brothers' adventure stories," Nora recalled, "mostly about the North, the Yukon, and all this kind of stuff." Wilde also loved adventure and mystery, including Arthur Conan Doyle and Jack London: "That fitted in with the way we were living. Mountains, sleighs—that was our kind of stuff!"

Indeed, as a girl it was the solitary experience of reading that Wilde preferred to most others. Perched alone in a tree, she was inclined to resist the insistent invitations of Nora or friends. Often as not, her response was "Let me alone, I want to read!"

Despite Wilde's adult lifetime of smoothly negotiating numerous public duties and social exchanges, a core part of her identity remained the solitary girl perched on a high branch. "I've always been shy," she says today. "I really am not that confident person that's out in front of everything. I make myself do it. I make myself talk to people as best I can." All the more compelling, then, became the ballet stage, a place where any and all inhibitions could be banished.

DEPRESSION

AND WORLD WAR

Wilde and her family struggled, but they stayed afloat. All around them, though, were much more dire and, to Wilde, frightening demonstrations of what the Depression had wrought. In downtown Ottawa people waited in breadlines, and Wilde saw homeless people who looked as if they were at death's doorstep. Closer to home, a "relief camp" for homeless men on the air force base perched on the north shore of the Ottawa River. The men were fed and boarded in a big shed and paid twenty cents a day in return for laboring on public works.

Eileen hired men from the camp to do odd jobs around the estate. Once during the mid-1930s both Wilde and Nora, sick with measles, were forced to lie in a dark room to protect their eyes. A man living at the camp came to read to them. Eventually he presented them with a beautiful book about the two Windsor princesses, Elizabeth and Margaret, who were their own ages. "I don't know how he managed to bring us this book," Wilde said. "He pinched his pennies somewhere." He was shabbily but always cleanly dressed and spoke as beautifully as one of her teachers. He seemed to know as much as they did, too. To her he appeared to be a great age, though he was probably no more than forty. Distinguished as he seemed, he had been shunted to the margins of existence. It dawned on her that something was very wrong with the world's equation; life did not fit together neatly.

However, when it came to the family's hard-earned fruit of the land, Wilde was less charitable, at least in the heat of battle. One summer the Whites had planted an entire field with melons. Near harvest time, Nora and Pat were lying on a hillside when they looked down to see the melon field swarming with men from the camp, each intent on carrying away a melon. The girls sicced their Doberman pinscher down to the field. The men quickly dispersed.

Two men from the relief camp became regular guests at the White estate. Andy and George were cowboys from Canada's Northwest Territories. They were wooing Evvie and Bet, who were good friends. George eventually married Evvie. Bet, however, went off to McGill University in Montreal, where she majored in electronic engineering. Her tuition was in all likelihood paid for by her father, with whom she remained close. Bet's studies enabled her to install both telephone wires and electricity in the cabin. No more kerosene lamps, and no more, for Wilde, the daily nuisance of cleaning them out.

Eileen continued to sell more parcels of land; they now had new neighbors, as two more houses were built between their land and the stone house. Living outside the Ottawa city limits, the Whites did not receive the benefit of municipal maintenance. A heavy snow could make the roads impassable. The local governance would eventually clear Montreal Road, but the Whites and their neighbors had to take care of their own Skid Road themselves. Driving back home after ballet class, Eileen and the girls, together with the new neighbors, would often have to shovel to get down the driveway.

Girls from all income brackets were attending the Notre Dame convent, but as non-Catholics, the White sisters didn't qualify for subsidy. Wilde had been at the convent two years when Eileen transferred both girls to the local public school, a picturesque two-room stone cabin housing combined grades in each room. Officially titled the Quarries School, it stood on Montreal Road a ways west of the Simpson estate. Appropriately enough, an old quarry was just behind it.

Transferring came just at the moment that Wilde was beginning to feel comfortable at Notre Dame. She now took combined third and fourth grades, then fifth and sixth together. Wilde loved the old schoolhouse, but the compressed curriculum again made her aware of gaps in her education.

When the snows came it was easier for the girls to travel together on skis. The one-mile trip to school took a good half hour, as they crossed their own property, then a cow farm, then continued uphill past another home with a big pond. They wore scarves around their mouths, so that the wind didn't take their breath away, but sometimes wind and snow meant they could hardly see in front of them. Each girl would shoot off on her own, then they'd meet up at certain fences, navigating as much by intuition as anything else.

In retrospect, Wilde saw Nora as the more even-tempered. Wilde herself received frequent scoldings for losing her temper. Certainly the two, as close as they were, did their share of squabbling. Once they were fighting on one of the twin beds in their room. Wilde was scratching and kicking—"She was good at kicking." Nora got on her back and, legs bent under her sister, used legs and arms to heave her off the bed. Wilde went sailing onto the floor. "I don't think she cried." In fact, Nora didn't recall any instance of seeing her sister in tears during childhood. Wilde attributed that stoicism to "sheer determination" not to give her sister the satisfaction of victory. However, Wilde also said she was "in tears all the time." Kid-stuff taunts stung her—accusations of "fraidy-cat" about something she didn't want to do when she wanted to read instead. But before bursting into tears she'd run off on her own so as not to be seen with her guard down.

Age six was when her sense of injustice pitted her against Vincent Fletcher, the same age, the son of a family renting the bungalow. He and Wilde were in the barn, watching a bantam hen sheltering eggs about to hatch, when Vincent grabbed the eggs and threw them against the wall. Livid, Wilde took after him, ambushed him by the water pump, and banged his head against the pump support, her thumbs in his mouth. His mother saw them from her kitchen window. "You're killing Vincent!" "I'm *going* to kill him!"

His mother subsequently came up to the cabin to complain to Eileen but instead received an earful: "Well, what a horrible thing for him to do!"

Eileen lectured. "You should have him better disciplined. If he's going to do that kind of thing, what is he going to grow up to do?"

Wilde was also about six on a day when she and ten-year-old Nora were once again fighting. Walking away with Eileen, Nora tossed a snippy remark over her shoulder and went blithely off down the orchard path to the barns. Wilde picked up an old dog bone, threw it, and hit her right between the shoulder blades. Nora screamed and Eileen took after Wilde, who lit across the field, then snuck back into her room to get a book before making herself scarce for several hours. Most of the time Eileen would spank with her hand, but when she said she was "going to get the measuring stick," she usually meant it. Worst of all punishments meted out to Wilde, however, was no ballet class—that would bring on tears she wouldn't try to contain.

Ballet came easier to Wilde than to her sister. Nora recalled Osborne teaching pirouettes, making her come closer and closer to the studio mirror, so that she could study and improve the way she was "spotting," spinning her head around ahead of each pirouette to preserve orientation, whereas "Pat had a head that could turn on its own! I used to try to see what her secret was." "They always made fun of me," Wilde recalled: her head was set on backward, so she was going to meet herself coming around. Later on, as a professional dancer, Wilde's pirouettes would be widely admired.

The girls loved Osborne, who was just "Gwen" to them outside class. Eileen and Gwendolyn became friends as well. "Mother was not interested in gossip at all," Wilde said, and Osborne was "always learning something"; at one point she studied German. "She was interesting to be with." Osborne didn't drive, and Eileen loved to; on several occasions she drove Osborne, Nora, and an older student, Clare Pasch, to New York, where they'd take class with Osborne's old teacher Konstantin Kobeloff. Pasch was one of the few students in Osborne's studio who was interested in dancing professionally. Later she would join the White sisters in Sergei Denham's Ballet Russe de Monte Carlo.

At times, Osborne came and stayed with the Whites—"I think that was in lieu of paying her," Nora recalled; certainly Eileen resorted to barter when necessary. Friends of Osborne's from New York came to visit her there; they struck Nora as distinctly different than the run-of-the-mill Ottawa population.

Osborne often choreographed pas de deux for the White sisters in which Nora—older, taller, and stronger—would assume the man's traditional role. During their convent days, they sometimes walked at lunchtime the ten blocks from Gloucester Street to Osborne's studio on Sparks and rehearsed with her. She worked them hard. They were in demand around Ottawa and environs, once performing at a museum opening.

A tricky lift in one of the pas de deux had Wilde jumping into her sister's arms, folded across her chest. When she slammed hard into Nora's chest, Nora responded with retaliatory pinches timed rhythmically to Johann Strauss's "Blue Danube" waltz as they circled the stage in pirouettes and more lifts. "And everybody thought we were just so sweet!" Nora chuckled wickedly.

Osborne was calm in the studio when teaching class, but her behavior as spring recitals approached made clear that she could never have withstood the stress of a professional performing career. She was "hell" at those periods. "You knew that everything meant so much to her," Wilde recalled. Typically Osborne's lungs would become congested at these times and she would temporarily lose her deep voice. Any little thing that went wrong upset her, but it was not so much mistakes by her pupils, it seemed to Wilde, as the onus of living up to her own exacting standards. Adding to her stress was the responsibility of performing. Osborne herself was frequently onstage. Given the absence of men, it fell to her to dance male roles. "I can't get the door open!" Osborne panicked at one dress rehearsal. "I can't get the door open!" Osborne's hysteria on occasions like this could be frightening to her students.

They frequently performed at Ottawa's Little Theater, a converted church on King Edward Avenue, a major thoroughfare. The Little was used for visiting attractions as well as local amateur dramatics and recitals. Usually Osborne's recitals featured her own ballets set to children's stories. Wilde didn't remember details of the choreography, but looking back she thought it was well done, well constructed. Eileen was frequently involved organizing the costumes, sometimes sewing them herself.

As Nora approached high school age, her educational career and Wilde's diverged for the first time. Given the hazards of ballet, the constant possibility that an injury could suddenly end Nora's career, Osborne thought that Nora needed a fallback. It was advisable, too, because Canada offered so few opportunities for professional dancers. Nora was duly enrolled in a high school where she could learn typing and shorthand as well as the standard academics. Secretarial work had made Osborne's own teaching career in Ottawa possible.

An Ottawa insurance executive, Mr. Burden, was someone Eileen trusted when she needed financial advice. Burden's daughter was an only child Nora's age, and Nora frequently stayed over at the Burdens. They lived in one of Ottawa's loveliest neighborhoods, close by the Rideau Canal that connects Ottawa to Lake Ontario.

Eileen's finances, ever in flux, did permit her to move Wilde back to the Notre Dame convent. The convent conducted grade school classes separately in both French and English, but older students had to be bilingual. Wilde was now fluent in the patois that is Canadian French.

ON SEPTEMBER 1, 1939, France and Britain declared war on Germany after Hitler refused to withdraw his troops from Poland. For ten-year-old Wilde, British prime minister Neville Chamberlain's announcement was solemn and sobering. Travel, foreign countries, and global events had already begun to exert a fascination on her. Over the radio, Chamberlain's declaration seemed like a sad admission of failure—self-indicted above all. This was so patently not what he had been hoping for.

Ten days later Canada joined the Allied cause, and wartime shortages began to mandate even more steadfast conservation on the White household front. Bacon fat was saved, then submitted to a transport depot. Bits of string, odds and ends—they were needed for the war effort, too.

On May 10, 1940, Winston Churchill succeeded Chamberlain as prime minister. His speeches stirred Wilde; his voice throbbed with a command that Chamberlain's lacked. At the end of that month, Osborne and her students performed in the auditorium of the Glebe Collegiate high school in Ottawa. In an adaptation of *Swan Lake*, Osborne was a prince in pursuit, while Wilde, according to the *Ottawa Evening Citizen*, was "a picturesque Robin Hood companion," and another student, Aline Dubois, was the Swan. To the Intermezzo from Bizet's second *L'Arlésienne Suite*, Osborne danced a solo that was described in the program as a "tribute to conquered nations of Europe." The Farandole from the same suite was a showcase for Pasch, Nora, and Louisa MacDonald, Osborne's assistant at her studio. A medley of popular music sung by Elise Ralston included "Wish Me Luck as You Wave Me Good-Bye," made famous in Britain by Gracie Fields, as well as "Mademoiselle from Armentières," which had been a camp favorite during an entire century of wars. This last song was also a solo for Wilde.

During these early years of the war Osborne and her students took their popular music routines to Canadian army and air force bases, where troops were billeted before shipping out from Halifax to the European front. Speakers and a sound system replaced the live singing that Glebe Collegiate had heard. "Armentières" had once been considered risqué; ten-year-old Wilde appeared just when "all the guys were expecting something gorgeous, voluptuous." Nevertheless, they were highly appreciative of her solo.

4

LEAVING OTTAWA

Looking back, Wilde is not sure that she would have become a professional dancer had her life not changed dramatically. Soon after war was declared, Eileen received notice that her family's estate was to be appropriated by the government's National Research Council, which was looking to expand its experimental farm system. Proximity to the air force base likely had trained the government's sights their way, while the stone house in which Eileen had grown up had earlier been sold by its current owners to the government. It built a windmill for aerodynamic research on that part of the former Simpson family property.

Eileen was not one to take such a thing lying down: she angrily contacted General Andrew McNaughton, director of the National Research Council, whose daughter was a convent classmate and friend of Nora's. He told her there was nothing he could do. Eileen was suspicious, telling her children that the government really intended to provide itself with new vacation homes commanding views of the river. She strategized by making a show of preparing to build a new house on her land. That way, she thought, she might be allowed to keep a parcel or could command extra compensation. But her subterfuge was futile. In the end she wasn't allowed to keep any land at all, and the purchase price settled on her was "measly," Wilde claimed, "not anything as much as it should have been."

It was around that time that Osborne decided that the two White sisters were ready to hone and test their talent in a much more competitive forum. She announced her intention to take them to audition at the School of American Ballet in Manhattan, which had been founded in 1934 by George Balanchine and Lincoln Kirstein. Having seen Balanchine's choreography in Europe, Kirstein, a young aesthete who was heir to the Filene's department store fortune, had invited the choreographer to resettle in the United States. Together they would undertake the formidable task of establishing an American beachhead of classical ballet. Balanchine had insisted that, before anything professional could be attempted, it was essential to establish a school, modeled, at least in theory, on the Imperial Ballet School in St. Petersburg, where he had been trained. He began his American Ballet, forerunner of New York City Ballet, later that same year as well.

Older students of Osborne's had joined the Ballet Russe troupe, but it was a surprise to the White girls that she considered them advanced enough to chance Manhattan scrutiny. Osborne herself was also undergoing a transition: she had decided to close her studio. Perhaps that was another reason she wanted the Whites to move on. Wilde speculates that her teacher did not feel up to the task of rearing a new generation of beginners.

Nora turned sixteen in August 1941. "You know, Nora, you don't have to go," Eileen told Nora. "You could stay here and go to college." Did Eileen think that Osborne was pressuring the girls prematurely? "I don't think so," Nora said. "I just think she gave me the possibility, in case I hadn't thought of it." Nora didn't tell her mother that she had already considered pursuing an entirely different career path: someday owning her own horse farm. But both White sisters were sufficiently dedicated to ballet to be willing—if given a little push—to see where and how far they might pursue it.

Eileen might have been mulling the sudden adjustment to an empty nest. Certainly the girls' decamping for New York was going to leave her lonely, but looking back, Nora didn't think Eileen was trying to keep her close at hand. Wilde thought her mother was "very brave" and knew that it was a great opportunity for her daughters, an opportunity greater than anything available at home. And there was always the possibility that it might not come again.

In fact, Eileen supported her girls' ambitions in the face of her friends' opposition. Wilde remembered that her mother "got hell" from them for letting her daughters go off on their own. "'How can you let two young girls go and turn out to be God knows what?'" The implication was, above all, the likelihood of sexual exploitation. But Eileen "had faith in us" and stood up to her friends. Her girls were going to be fine. They were intelligent; they would take care of themselves, not fall victim to snares.

Not that the specific nature of the snares was something Eileen could easily broach. "I don't think she used the word 'rape' in her entire life," Wilde said. Indeed, Eileen had found it impossible to discuss menstruation with her daughters. Instead she asked Osborne to explain it to Nora. Eileen "never told me nothing!" Wilde recalled. "Just expected me to be a good girl."

As much as Wilde loved to dance, professional ballet remained a mystery. Wilde had never read any books about dance; she'd seen hardly any performances except those staged by Osborne. One of the few shows she could remember took place when Anna Pavlova's ex-partner Mikhail Mordkin brought his little company, later the nucleus of Ballet Theatre, to the Capital Theater, the city's largest movie palace and, as well, a venue for visiting live attractions. The Whites also went there to see modern dance choreographer Kurt Joss and had been swept away by his antiwar piece *The Green Table*.

Eileen took charge of the move and didn't involve her two youngest. But they were certainly aware of their mother's nervous distress as she managed the logistics and coped with the move's emotional toll, weighing decisions about what she should or could now do with her life.

The abrupt and irrevocable termination of their earlier life made both White sisters eager to seek out an entirely new environment. Losing the estate was "part of the reason why I left," Nora said. "It was very sad." "We didn't have any roots anymore," Wilde laments. "I was ready to go."

The trip to Manhattan in October 1941 took most of the day. They left early in the morning, driving south to cross into the United States at Ogdensburg, New York. "Knowing Mother we probably barely stopped—only for gas." On the drive they feasted on peanut butter sandwiches, sang songs carried away by the wind. They made up games—counting cars, how many of this color or that—while Osborne rode up front with Eileen.

Wilde's sharpest first impression of the city was its teeming traffic, so much more congested than Ottawa. On the way into Manhattan they stopped in Riverdale to visit the Kindalls—the daughter of Ottawa friends of Eileen's, her professor husband, and their two small boys. Downtown they registered at a hotel near Carnegie Hall, across town from the school, located at Madison Avenue and Fifty-Ninth Street. Wilde and her sister were auditioned by Muriel Stuart, one of the school's leading teachers, an Englishwoman who had danced with Pavlova's company. "I wasn't nervous," Wilde recalled. "I didn't have the sense to be!" They were both placed in the advanced class. But the school's administration decided that at thirteen Wilde was too young to be living on her own in New York. To her disappointment, she had to return to Ottawa for the time being.

Nora remained in New York, excited about making her own independent life. She immediately began studying full-time at the School of American Ballet, living with the Kindalls in their comfortable house on a circular drive. When needed, she could babysit their two children. In the morning, Nora took the bus east to Broadway and caught the subway downtown. Eileen was paying for Nora's classes, but the curriculum was mandatory for all full-time students, whether on scholarship or not. It was quite diverse. Nora studied not only ballet technique but also different forms of character dance, a special class in Spanish dancing, and some form of modern. Nora wrote home frequently, sending her sister descriptions of the combinations she'd been given in class, which Wilde then tried out on her own. Indeed, Wilde, encouraged by being placed in the advanced class at SAB after her audition, now worked harder than ever in ballet class.

A year later, Wilde and her mother came down from Ottawa to watch Nora make her professional debut. In 1942–43 Balanchine was choreographing for the New Opera Company, which performed opera in English translation. That fall they were mounting Rimsky-Korsakov's *Fair at Sorochinsk* on a bill with Balanchine's *Ballet Imperial*, set to Tchaikovsky's second piano concerto. Balanchine drew freely upon the advanced students at his school; Nora was dancing both in the ensemble of *Ballet Imperial* and in a Russian folk dance in the opera.

Ballet Imperial starred sixteen-year-old Mary Ellen Moylan, a new favorite interpreter of Balanchine's, one of a by now considerable lineage of teenage dancers he showcased in ballerina roles. She was partnered by the much more experienced William Dollar, who had danced for Balanchine in the American Ballet, including its appearance in Hollywood's *Goldwyn Follies* in 1938. Onstage at the Broadway Theater, both Moylan and Dollar gave performances that the White sisters to this day remember as spectacular.

Osborne's former pupils Betty Low and Nesta Williams were dancing in Sergei Denham's Ballet Russe de Monte Carlo. That month it was sharing the Metropolitan Opera stage on alternate weeks with the newly formed (now "American") Ballet Theatre—impresario Sol Hurok was handling both companies. During Wilde's visit Low and Williams invited the White sisters to be extras in Ballet Theatre's production of Mikhail Fokine's haunting and eerie *Petrushka*, part of a memorial tribute to its legendary creator. Fokine had been working for Ballet Theatre when he had died two months before, at age sixty-two.

The sisters might have stepped into the epicenter of elite ballet as well as into a time capsule of momentous cultural history. Diaghilev's company had premiered the ballet in 1911, performed to a score commissioned from Stravinsky. Vaslav Nijinsky's portrayal of the oppressed puppet Petrushka had passed into legend, as had his entire career, curtailed by insanity by the time he was thirty. Now, at this Ballet Theatre performance, Petrushka was to be Léonide Massine, who had been Nijinsky's successor as Diaghilev's lover, star dancer, and choreographic protégé.

The Whites would appear in the crowd scenes that opened and closed the ballet. They reported to the Met's wardrobe room to get their costumes, Wilde wearing a street dress made by her mother. Eileen made most of their clothes, made them well and to last, patronizing an Ottawa seamstress when special finesse was required. Wilde's dress was heavy wool, rust-colored, hand smocked around the sleeves and neck. "That's perfect!" the wardrobe mistress said. "I'll just give you a skirt"—and she lengthened Wilde's hemline to make it appropriate to the St. Petersburg of 1830. Wilde was quite disappointed to be wearing her own clothes rather than a full costume as she went onstage at the Metropolitan Opera for the very first time. Nevertheless, she and Nora were agog.

"You saw all the people wandering around," Nora recalled, "and you were out there and you were a part of it!" Making cameo appearances in the crowd were not only some of Ballet Theatre's young stars, but impresario Hurok as well.

In *Petrushka* individual destinies, human archetypes, and collective fate all find devastating personification in the public and private lives of three fairground puppets. *Petrushka* can be a shattering theatrical experience, and it was that night for the two sisters. Massine's articulation of Petrushka's raggedy, hinged physique as well as his angst "enthralled" Wilde. André Eglevsky was the Moor who brutalizes Petrushka; later Wilde would dance frequently with him at New York City Ballet, but the Moor stayed in her mind as one of the best things he ever did. The Ballerina doll, love object of both pathetic Petrushka and the braggart Moor, was Irina Baronova, an idol of Nora's. Baronova, another teenage discovery of Balanchine's, had been a star since she was Wilde's age a decade earlier.

The Whites went back to Ballet Theatre that month and enjoyed Baronova's versatility. They saw her dance Princess Aurora in a suite of excerpts from *Sleeping Beauty.* They also saw her in another creation of Fokine's, the peasant Boulotte in *Bluebeard*, which Ballet Theatre had premiered a year earlier. For Baronova and Anton Dolin's Bluebeard, Fokine made a duet that combined elements of virtuoso Soviet adagio and earthy Apache dance combat. "Dolin would swish me around," Baronova recalled, "and I would hang around his neck with my legs out. And he would turn-turn-turn, and I would let go my arms, and fly through the whole stage. . . . I was covered with bruises—and I loved every minute of it!" The girls, too, would have considered every bruise worthwhile, so memorable was that duet. Every ballet that Wilde saw seemed to reveal new possibilities of the art form and of what she might possibly do one day.

Back in Ottawa, Osborne's studio was now closed. Wilde took class instead with her assistant, Louise McDonald, who taught in the gymnasium of the Ottawa YWCA. Wilde recalled practicing piqué turns in a circle around the entire vast gym space. Eileen continued to drive Wilde to and from classes but was now spending most of her time managing the farm of an old family friend. Wilde sometimes stayed there, but more often at her sister Bet's in Aylmer, on the Quebec side of the Ottawa River. Bet had married Norman Rudolph, a member of the Royal Canadian Mounted Police. He went into the service, and Bet went into Red Cross Transport.

In spring 1943, Wilde left Ottawa permanently. At the School of American Ballet, Nora had become friendly with Todd Bolender and Mary Jane Shea, both young veterans of Balanchine's American ballet ventures and both natives of Canton, Ohio. Each was beginning to choreograph as well as dance. They were planning to take up residence in an old hay barn they'd been loaned in Pennsylvania's Pocono Mountains. They had invited Nora to join them and were happy to let Wilde participate as well.

5

BIG CITY

AND BARN

Eileen and a friend, an American woman who worked in the consular delegation in Ottawa, drove Wilde down to Ogdensburg, where she boarded a sleeper car for the overnight trip to New York. The next morning, as the train made its way downtown through the Bronx and Upper Manhattan, Wilde acquainted herself at close range with inner-city ecology, something she hadn't seen much of in Ottawa. She peered into tenement windows, studied laundry drying on clotheslines suspended from them. The fourteen-year-old was apprehensive as she got off the train at 125th Street, which she had heard was the epicenter of New York's famous and infamous dance halls and nightclubs. But as her mother had told her, the Kindalls were waiting to drive her to much more sedate Riverdale.

Nora continued to study at the School of American Ballet, where Wilde now auditioned once again. This time her audition was given by the faculty member Anatole Oboukhoff, a veteran of St. Petersburg's Imperial Ballet. In her letters home, Nora had remarked on how difficult the class was, but Oboukhoff placed Wilde in the advanced class, just as Muriel Stuart had done after her previous audition eighteen months earlier.

Most of her summer was spent with Nora in East Stroudsburg, Pennsylvania. The barn Bolender and Shea had secured was owned by the Harritons, a family who lived in Kew Gardens, Queens. A decade earlier the Harritons had purchased an old farm outbuilding nearby for use as a vacation cottage. David Harriton owned a successful New York mirror business, and he and his wife Helen were both interested in the performing arts. A niece, Maria Harriton, was dancing on Broadway in *Oklahoma!*, while daughter Carol was studying at the American Academy of Dramatic Arts. The Harritons had met Bolender and Shea in South America in 1941, where the dancers were on a four-month tour with Balanchine's American Ballet Caravan. The Harritons offered them the use of their barn — provided daughter Carol be allowed to take class with them.

The barn — at the end of a lane, surrounded by woods, adjoining a stream — had already been semiconverted to residential use and had a kitchen downstairs, as well as bedrooms upstairs. Electricity, however, didn't arrive in East Stroudsburg for two more years, and kerosene lamps were used instead. Bolender had transformed the wagons' entrance downstairs into a dance studio.

The White sisters paid their own room and board, which meant that they had a bedroom upstairs rather than being relegated to a tent in the woods. There were half a dozen young women participating. Like Shea and Bolender, Adelaide Varicchio was already a veteran of Balanchine's U.S. enterprises. Another girl, Jodi Williams, was currently a student of Bolender's first teacher, Phyllis Knoll in Ohio.

Work at the barn was by no means punishing. Morning class was "not too early," Nora recalled. "We spent a lot of time at breakfast," usually prepared by Bolender, while over the course of the summer, "Pat and I did a lot of sunning up on the roof." During work hours, inspiring piano accompaniment was provided by composer John Colman, who also played for classes at the School of American Ballet.

Bolender "always had his head on his shoulders," Nora recalled, while Shea, five years younger, was "kind of a wild kid." Bolender remembered her as "a very dramatic character." Teaching class in the barn one day, Shea was exhorting the dancers into the air when she herself leapt with such enthusiasm that she hit her head on a beam. For a while thereafter she claimed that her thoughts were too scattered for her to be able to work. She perched on a large rock near the barn and insisted that anyone walking by announce his or her appearance. "You'd say, 'Mary Jane, I'm going to walk by the rock!'" Wilde recalled. "So that you wouldn't startle her."

The Whites made friends with the Harriton children—Carol had a younger brother, Lewis—and with Carol's best friend, Jacqueline Kilgore. A few years earlier, Kilgore's family had been neighbors of the Harritons in Sunnyside, Queens, when each decided to buy outbuildings on the remains of the same East Stroudsburg farm. The Whites were "lovely girls," Kilgore said. "Exceedingly nice." Kilgore's mother was friendly with the dancers as well. Like so many Sunnyside residents, Mrs. Kilgore was politically progressive, but she was not a cultural sophisticate. As was Balanchine, she was of Russian Georgian descent, but when Balanchine came down to visit East Stroudsburg, he and Kilgore's mother had less to say to each other than it was presumed their common heritage might have warranted.

Kilgore's brother Robin, ten years younger, often wandered over to the barn. There was a dearth of men in American ballet at that time; very few began studying early enough to become first-rate technicians. In addition, World War II had certainly diminished the professional ranks. Robin was long-legged, and Bolender wanted him to begin studying, but the boy's interest was strictly confined to spectating.

Bolender would later tell Wilde's NYCB colleague Robert Barnett how impressed he was with both White girls' technique. Looking back, Wilde realized that she was "capable," but thought it was her enthusiasm above all that made her attractive. "I was ready and involved, and obviously enjoying the work. Anything they asked me to do I would work on and do. A very willing body."

When the summer ended, the Harritons invited the Whites to move in with them in their house in Kew Gardens. "We loved them," Harriton recalled. "They were very, very special," both sisters exuberantly and intensely "involved in what was going on." Much of Nora's time would now be spent on the road, however, since she was joining the Ballet Russe de Monte Carlo. She was now almost eighteen, and Oboukhoff had insisted that she audition.

As summer dwindled, Wilde was working in the afternoons in a studio at the School of American Ballet with Bolender and Shea, who had followed up their country workshop by announcing the formation of the American Concert Ballet, a company seventeen dancers strong. They were preparing a program that included their own choreography as well as Balanchine's 1941 *Concerto Barocco*, today considered one of his greatest works. Pianist Hazel Scott's Baroque breakdowns were the rage at jazz clubs in Manhattan. Reportedly inspired by Scott, Balanchine's choreography drew right angles as well as parallel lines between Baroque and boogie-woogie. His choreography used classical steps, but their timing and accents made the music sound as though composed that very moment.

Two years earlier, *Concerto Barocco* had been previewed at Hunter College in an invitation-only dress rehearsal before being taken to South America on the American Ballet Caravan's lengthy tour. American Concert Ballet would therefore be giving *Barocco* its first actual public performance in America. Together with Marie-Jeanne Pelus, Shea had created the two lead women's roles in the ballet. They were repeating their performances at the ACB premiere. Wilde was dancing in the eight-member corps of women. William Dollar would also repeat his partnering role in the slow central movement. Lillian Lanese was alternating with Marie-Jeanne (who shed her last name professionally) in the first ballerina role. Fifteen-year-old Wilde was being taught Shea's role by both her and Marie-Jeanne with an eye toward her performing it in a future ACB program.

Dancing closely together throughout much of the first and third movements, Shea and Marie-Jeanne provided an intriguing contrast. Shea was small, "very sharp and precise," Wilde recalled—"a neat little technique, everything in proportion"—whereas Marie-Jeanne was also small but had unusually long legs and feet. They looked spectacular in the many supported passages of expansive stretching on the ground and in the air she did during the slow second movement.

In addition to dancing, Dollar was company ballet master. He had also started to choreograph; as dance colleague and choreographer he would figure prominently in Wilde's future career. "Bill was such a sweetheart," Wilde recalled. "Very quiet, but fun, a really good sense of humor. I enjoyed working with him always. I think everybody did."

Also dancing was Edward Bigelow, destined to be a fixture in Wilde's later career with New York City Ballet. He started ballet very late but was nevertheless "usable" as a dancer, but had a much more enduring career as indispensable factotum to Balanchine. Even in 1943, Bigelow was "always around and helpful if you needed to know where somebody was."

Wilde decided that she would now try for a scholarship at the School of American Ballet. Another disappointment was in store, however. According to Wilde, only one scholarship was to be awarded to the advanced class. Another girl trying for it was sixteen, which was the cutoff age. At fifteen, Wilde would presumably have time to try again, but she couldn't be enrolled in the school for a more than a certain period of time before applying the next year. With the eventual goal of receiving a scholarship the following fall, she stopped taking class at SAB. Instead she followed Bolender and Shea's recommendation that she study with Dorothie Littlefield, who was teaching at Steinway Hall on West Fifty-Seventh Street.

The Littlefield family of Philadelphia was a pioneering dynasty in American ballet. Dorothie, her elder sister Catherine, and their brother Carl had all gone routinely to Paris to study with ex-Russian Imperial Ballet teachers. Catherine founded her own ballet company in the mid-1930s; in 1937, it put on the first full-length *Sleeping Beauty* in America. Bolender had danced with the Littlefield Ballet in the late 1930s.

Balanchine had met the Littlefields in Europe, and after he arrived in New York in the fall of 1933 his personal and professional paths immediately entwined with them. He went regularly to Philadelphia to woo Dorothie, who became one of the charter teachers at his school when it opened January 1, 1934. Littlefield company dancers began studying there, too, and Balanchine borrowed them for his early companies. "They were very good dancers," recalled Elise Reiman, a member of Balanchine's American Ballet. "They were all pretty. I thought they were fabulous."

Now Dorothie was teaching independently, perhaps because at SAB she had been paid drastically less than Mariinsky veteran Pierre Vladimiroff, also with the school from its inception. Her mother came in every day from Philadelphia to play for class, sitting on a dais above the studio, "watching everything we were doing." Mrs. Littlefield was a dance instructor as well.

Neither White sister was born with pronounced arches, but Dorothie Littlefield's beautiful feet inspired Wilde to work extra hard on making hers more flexible, more shapely. In class, Dorothie emphasized using the whole foot, working through the feet. In Ottawa, Gwendolyn Osborne had also been concerned with that, but Wilde now worked with added determination.

The following spring, Dorothie was guest artist with Ballet Theatre, dancing in her sister's ballet *Barn Dance*. In the merciless way that dancers have, Wilde judged her teacher's feet weaker than ideal—a common drawback to the beauty of pronounced arches. Nevertheless, Littlefield was "a lovely performer—alluring, slightly voluptuous."

Dancers from the Littlefield Ballet also came in to take class with Dorothie. "I was the only kid in there," Wilde said. Dorothie took class together with her students, but that didn't in any way diminish her pedagogical vigilance. Littlefield was tough on her: "She had her eagle eye on me all the time."

Once she ordered Wilde to leave the studio center and "go to the barre and stay there until there's no wiggling in your sixes!" When the dancers' legs cross in beats, the hips are not supposed to flail. Using the barre for support would enable her to make sure her hips did not respond too strenuously to the strain of remaining airborne. "All right, let me see," Littlefield said after several days. "OK, all right, now you can do them."

In between class with Littlefield and rehearsals with Bolender and Shea, Wilde was now enrolled at the Professional Children's School near Columbus Circle in Manhattan. She reported every day for a study period, taking her homework assignments home to Kew Gardens.

American Concert Ballet made its debut at the Central High School of Needle Trades on October 13, then repeated its program on November 14 at the 92nd Street YMCA, where Balanchine came to see his ballet performed.

Wilde still recalls the mishap that occurred during her first professional performance. In Bolender's *Mother Goose Suite*, to Ravel's score, she was a bird in the Hop o' My Thumb episode. Her entrance—perhaps lifted from Balanchine's 1934 *Serenade*—had her walking behind the dancer Aaron

Girard so closely that they practically merged, with her hands covering his eyes. As they walked out, she stepped on his heel, and when he stepped ahead to perform a solo he was forced to do so with one shoe missing. Wilde was certainly unnerved but, as she would have to do so many times in her career, simply carried on with the show.

Critical reception for the two performances was not overwhelming. It is interesting to note that *Concerto Barocco* received nothing like the praise that it has enjoyed since. But in 1945, it entered the repertory of Sergei Denham's Ballet Russe, and it has been a constant in New York City Ballet repertory since its opening season in 1948.

THE MARQUIS

It was difficult to keep together a troupe that offered only part-time work without pay. After only a few months of existence, Bolender and Shea's American Concert Ballet was now effectively over. Eileen sent Wilde as much money as her finances and wartime restriction would allow. Wilde also found work in the popular-priced opera stagings that were pursued across New York City. The New Opera company in which Nora had danced was one manifestation, as was the New York City Opera, which opened in 1944. In and around New York City over the winter of 1943–44, Wilde danced in several opera productions choreographed by Mikhail Fokine's niece Irine, or by Lillian Moore, who was a pioneer author in the field of dance studies as well.

Wilde continued to study with Littlefield; in class one day, Adelaide Varicchio, who had danced both in East Stroudsburg and the ACB, told her that she had just joined a new company, the Marquis de Cuevas's Ballet International. Other ACB alumni—Marie-Jeanne, Mary Jane Shea, William Dollar, Yvonne Patterson, and Zoya Leporsky—had also been hired.

The marquis was a Chilean, who was serving as secretary in the government's legation in London, when in 1927, age forty-two, he married the Rockefeller heiress Margaret Strong, granddaughter of John D. She was twelve years younger than he, and they had two children. The marquis was believed to be gay, but their marriage could have been described as a success of its kind. He was a passionate admirer of ballet and now, after becoming a naturalized U.S. citizen in 1940, was determined to become an active creative propagator as well. And his wife was willing to pay to make it happen.

Varicchio suggested that Wilde take class with the company, taught by Anatole Vilzak, a veteran of the Mariinsky and of Diaghilev's Ballets Russes. Vilzak's class "wasn't dry exercises," Wilde said. "You felt prepared after the class," and his corrections were helpful. Class and rehearsals were being held in Carnegie Hall's famous Studio 61, a hallowed dance space. It was on the eighth floor of the Carnegie studio tower, a floor boasting studios with specially sprung floors designed for dance. Isadora Duncan had once conducted rehearsals in that studio. Plans for Ballet International to open its own school were also being mentioned.

Watching class was the marquis, together with Salvador Dalí, a close adviser who would also be designing for the company. They called Wilde over. Would she like to be in the company? Their invitation could not have been more propitious. The company survived in New York for less than a year before moving to Europe. But dancing in the corps brought her into initial contact with some of the greatest, most individualistic figures in ballet. In years to come she would work more closely with many of them.

Rehearsals began in May 1944. The Rockefeller inheritance meant that the marquis could bankroll a rehearsal period as long as five months— something virtually unheard-of in this country. The marquis's inexperience, however, produced a kind of artistic profligacy that did not make for coherent policy. Over the ten months Wilde danced for him, he signed off on no fewer than three different versions of *Giselle*. None of them, however, was actually performed by the company in New York, although the staging done by Bronislava Nijinska was eventually taken into the company after it moved to Europe. Wilde's own role, as a member of the sisterhood of ghostly Wilis in act 2, was expanded in a version staged by Boris Romanoff, a former Mariinsky soloist who had started to choreograph in prerevolutionary St. Petersburg. In 1938, he succeeded Balanchine as resident choreographer at the Metropolitan Opera. Romanoff added extra music to make possible an additional ensemble for the Wilis. There were also going to be black- as well as white-clad Wilis, perhaps a reference or evocation of the original 1841 *Giselle*, where they were different nationalities. Since then they had merged into a homogeneous community of white wraiths.

Then there was a *Giselle* put on by Anatole Oboukhoff of the School of American Ballet and his wife, Vera Nemchinova. She had been a star in Europe for twenty years and now was planning to dance the title role. A ballerina of redoubtable authority, Nemchinova was not the first whom one would readily think of as fragile Giselle. Nor was she still in her prime. Nevertheless, she regularly took company class, where Wilde admired her "wonderful back, strong and open. And lovely feet."

Less than two years after seeing *Petrushka*—still imprinted with the stamp of its creator, Vaslav Nijinsky—Wilde was now working with his sister. As exciting as the prospect was, the reality proved rather trying. Nijinska's *Giselle* was one of many assignments on which she was working more or less simultaneously. There was also *Swan Lake*, act 2, as well as modern ballets of her own. *Pictures at an Exhibition* used an orchestration of Mussorgsky's piano score. *Brahms Variations* was also a full-company work.

Nijinska "wasn't wasting a second," Wilde recalled, except when it came to her *Bolero*, on which she seemed to get stuck over the course of the 1944 summer. "More heavy," she'd say, hammering Ravel's rhythm on the dancers' necks, her cigarette dropping ashes on them. Nijinska's hearing wasn't very good, which tended to increase her impatience. Her husband and manager, Mr. Singayevsky, was more intimidating still. In the studio, he insisted that the dancers pay strict attention to whatever Madame was doing, even if they weren't involved; when sitting on the sidelines, they couldn't just darn toe shoes or knit tights.

A happier experience was being rehearsed by Fokine's widow, Vera Fokina, when she came to stage his *Les Sylphides*, his 1908 tribute to the filmy phantoms of the nineteenth-century romantic ballet, seasoned with the earthier influence of Isadora Duncan, who had made several tours to Russia.

Wearing high heels and a veil, she walked around the studio, her husband's rehearsal book in her hands. Each member of the ensemble was required to wear numbers to ensure that she could track their movements as recorded in his book. In the corps, Wilde felt inspired by soft-spoken Madame Fokine's remark about the opening of the ballet, when the dancers turn out of their tableau to bourrée downstage toward the audience. "You are like *les papillons*," she told Wilde and her sister sylphs. "You come out of your chrysalis."

Léonide Massine, whose impersonation of Fokine's Petrushka had so impressed Wilde two years earlier, was also now choreographing for the marquis. Massine's new *Tristan Fou* used excerpts from Wagner's *Tristan und Isolde* to conjure Tristan's act 3 delirium. Dalí's costumes and setting were naturally hallucinogenic. Wilde went for a costume fitting to Barbara Karinska's atelier on Fifty-Sixth Street just east of Fifth Avenue. There she tried on a rather normal type of tutu. But then Dalí himself appeared with something that fit over her head and sat on her shoulders. He proceeded to arrange petals dangling on wire bars, apparently meant to suggest the ribs of a lampshade. Wilde was mystified but thrilled; she stood up very straight as he fiddled.

Massine had sponsored a leading fashion model, Toni Worth, to dance a barefoot duet with Francisco Moncion, a young dancer who would later become a frequent partner of Wilde's at New York City Ballet. But onstage it was Dalí's surrealistic designs, not Massine or Wagner, who dominated. Wilde's ensemble duties included pushing a wheelbarrow around the stage. "We are moving the shit around," the laborers joked. Wilde was still close enough to her upbringing to blush if and when she uttered the taboo epithet.

The marquis himself was ever-present and thoroughly engaged. Elegant and affable, his manners were solicitously Old World even to the lowliest in the company, Wilde among them. For his company he purchased what had been the Majestic Theater on Columbus Circle, built in 1903, when the boundaries of the Theater District extended farther north and south than they do today. To renovate it, De Cuevas commissioned architect and set designer Joseph Urban. Urban had designed the Ziegfeld Theater on Sixth Avenue in addition to sets and costumes for many theatrical genres, from the *Follies* to the Metropolitan Opera. As Broadway houses go, the stage of the now-renamed International was expansive enough for ballet. Even in some of the big-cast ballets with scenery, Wilde didn't feel cramped.

A "packed and resplendent audience" filled the lavishly renovated theater to greet the company's debut on October 30, 1944, the *New York Times* reported the next day. The season was to run through Christmas; even allowing for the fact that the theater was a third the capacity of the Met or City Center, a run of this length was then unheard-of in the New York ballet. Although Wilde recalled full houses, undoubtedly above and beyond ticket sales, it was the De Cuevas / Rockefeller subsidy that made so long a season possible. De Cuevas's wife was often at performances, a pleasant, distinguished-seeming presence. As a young woman she had studied chemistry. Marriage to the marquis brought her into an aesthetic wonderland that she embraced.

Traveling to and from the Harritons in Kew Gardens got to be burdensome, and Wilde was happy to accept Mary Jane Shea's invitation to share her walk-up apartment on Fifty-Fifth Street just east of Second Avenue, a streetcar ride away from the theater. Shea's orbit was bohemian and intellectual, and it enhanced Wilde's experience of the city. Shea's painter boyfriend, Paul Valtetich, sometimes took Wilde to visit art galleries on Fifty-Seventh Street. Both of Shea's parents were psychiatrists. When Wilde came upon Freud's treatises in Shea's apartment, she read them with fascination and attempted to use them to decipher the flamboyant personalities she now routinely encountered in the ballet world.

Wilde had turned sixteen the previous July, but she was determined to remain in school as long as she could. Since most of her work at the Professional Children's School was correspondence, she had decided to transfer to Lodge's Tutoring School in Manhattan. Then she switched to a high school in the east Eighties where she could take classes very early in the morning. There she studied pattern-making and typing, the only classes available at that time of day. Most of the students were just arriving as she left to go to ballet class.

Extremely ambitious and eclectic, full of novelties, de Cuevas's repertory piqued Wilde's curiosity throughout the long season. She enjoyed *The Mute Wife*, choreographed by Antonio Cobos, who also danced the title role.

Onstage in a medium that customarily proscribed speech, Cobos signified her voice's restoration by manipulating a set of castanets. Caton's *Sebastian*, danced to a commissioned score from Gian Carlo Menotti, was a lurid melodrama in which Moncion came to the fore as an outstanding dance actor. He portrayed a slave whose affections were disputed. Also planned was a new ballet by William Dollar, *Last Flower*, with a scenario by James Thurber, but it was postponed when Thurber became ill.

Sentimental Colloquy, led by Marie-Jeanne and André Eglevsky, was choreographed by Balanchine but credited to Eglevsky. Because Balanchine was at the moment chief choreographer for Denham's Ballet Russe de Monte Carlo, he did not want his name used. The ballet was titled after a poem by Verlaine and was intended to represent isolation in the midst of a crowd. The music was by avant-garde composer and author Paul Bowles. Once again, however, it was Dalí's stage design that had the last, outlandish word. The two leads were veiled in white velvet; they entered perched together on a bicycle, draped to match.

De Cuevas's troupe was billed as "New York's only resident company." Presumably the Rockefeller sponsorship would prevent it from the incessant touring necessary for Ballet Theatre and Ballet Russe. Nevertheless, after the season closed at Christmas, they embarked on a short tour, opening in Newark. On tour Massine staged *Le Beau Danube*, one of his most popular works, much less obscure than *Tristan Fou*. The company also saw the arrival of Ballet Russe husband-and-wife stars Tatiana Riabouchinska and David Lichine. The war had brought them to Los Angeles, where they opened a school. Lichine brought several of his students to the company as well. For the marquis, Lichine now began staging Fokine's *Paganini*, which had premiered in Europe in 1939.

Together with Irina Baronova and Tamara Toumanova, Riabouchinska was one of the three teenage "baby ballerinas" launched by Balanchine in 1931. Since then she had created any number of unusual roles in the works of Massine and Fokine, as well as Lichine, who had turned to choreography. *Paganini* gave her one of her greatest roles, which she was now planning to re-create. She was the Florentine Maiden who becomes delirious under the influence of Paganini's virtuosity.

Riabouchinska was "a gorgeous person," Wilde recalled, in rehearsal "a little dynamo." Noted for her jump, she "had a lot of bounce." Wilde was appointed her understudy, a distinct honor and promotion.

In March 1945, however, the marquis disbanded the company, announcing that he had decided to return to Europe. His farewell to the corps de ballet was as courteous as the little bows with which he customarily greeted them in theater or studio corridor. He paid the balance of their contracts and let them keep new pointe shoes that had already been ordered. If they were interested, they had jobs waiting for them in Europe. That was where his aesthetic heart lay and, now that the Allies had declared victory, the idea of starting a ballet company there was once again possible. He directed his company in France and Monte Carlo until his death in 1961.

As she had done so often in her early years, Wilde once again that spring followed in her sister's footsteps when she joined Ballet Russe de Monte Carlo. Nora was now finishing her second year with them. Wilde today has no recollection of how or when she was hired, but is sure that she was offered the job without having to audition. By mid-May the company was writing her, care of Nora, requesting that she return to Madame Karinska's to be measured for costumes for the upcoming season.

7

SCHOOLING

AMERICAN BALLET

Not only was Wilde joining Ballet Russe, but Balanchine also invited her to join a small group of dancers he was taking to Mexico City that summer. They would dance in the opera season at the Palacio de Bellas Artes and put on an all-ballet program there as well. Wilde didn't remember taking Balanchine's class at the School of American Ballet, but he was in and out of the school all the time, "always peeking his head in" to classes, and he certainly talked to the teachers. He had also watched her dance in the corps of his *Concerto Barocco* with the American Concert Ballet. On top of the strong classical foundation she'd acquired with Gwendolyn Osborne in Ottawa, Wilde now could boast experience with an extremely wide spectrum of choreography.

At SAB, admission to class was free for "professionals." At sixteen, Wilde did not quite see herself as yet worthy of that exalted classification, but to SAB she indeed was. Consequently she was now taking class there whenever she could.

The school was on the top story of the Tuxedo Building on Madison Avenue and Fifty-Ninth Street, which was stacked with floors of studio and showroom space. SAB's floor had once been used by Isadora Duncan. A big square studio faced Madison Avenue, and a smaller rectangular studio ran along Fifty-Ninth Street. At its founding in 1934 the school was directed by Vladimir Dimitriev, who had made it possible for Balanchine to leave Russia in 1924. Dimitriev was an opera singer who also thrived as a croupier in postrevolutionary years, after private enterprise was partially restored in 1921, ushering in a half decade of the "New Economic Policy." He had included Balanchine and several dancers close to him on a small touring program of music and dance that appeared in German summer resorts.

Balanchine remained grateful to Dimitriev, but many others considered him an avaricious troublemaker. He was finally forced out of the school in 1940, when Lincoln Kirstein was appointed director. Dimitriev's wife, Kyra Blanc, remained on the faculty, which she had just joined. Blanc had an interesting background, having danced in Moscow in the 1920s with Kasyan Goleizovsky, the avant-garde choreographer whom Balanchine always named as a major influence. She was much better liked than her husband, treating beginning students, the most difficult to teach, with gentleness.

Indeed, everyone at the school had an interesting background, usually tracing back to Russia. The school was administered by two émigrés, Eugenie Ouroussow and her assistant, Natalia Molostwoff, who shortened her name to "Molo" for professional use in the United States. Looking back to the 1930s and '40s, Molo recalled in 1981 that "the school was much smaller and we had more contact with the kids than we now do." Molo was, for example, particularly close to Tanaquil Le Clercq and her mother Edith. But for those not in the privileged circle, the two Russian administrators could be formidable. In later years, Wilde was friendly with both women, but at the school early on, "we were scared to death of them." It was Molo who went into classes to check that every girl who was supposed to be there had shown up. Ouroussow more often remained burrowed in her back office, yet both women could lay down the law when they had to.

Both Pierre Vladimiroff and Anatole Oboukhoff, with whom Wilde studied in the advanced class, had been Mariinsky stars who emigrated after the Revolution. Wilde would hear stories of jewelry presented to dancers by admirers among St. Petersburg's aristocracy and haute bourgeois. Ballet in its remote czarist manifestation seemed like a very glamorous profession indeed.

To disguise a stammer, Oboukhoff would pretend that he was coughing, and perhaps for the same reason he was prone to yelling. Yet Wilde believed that "in his gruff and bluff way," he "really loved me." He often asked Wilde to demonstrate his center combinations. Both Wilde and her sister Nora were entertained at home by Oboukhoff and his wife, Vera Nemchinova. They presented Wilde with little gifts after important performances well into her years with New York City Ballet.

Oboukhoff would demonstrate beautifully with arched back and lovely arms, but Vladimiroff danced more in class. He was elegant and flamboyant. Watching him, Wilde was sure that onstage at the Mariinsky, he "would have always done that extra pirouette!" Despite his intermittent yelling, Oboukhoff was much quieter. His class was "more complex," Vladimiroff's "freer and more flowing."

She still remembers some of Vladimiroff's combinations: they were very kinetic, with "lots of pirouettes, lots of waltzes." Indeed, Vladimiroff was "the turn person," and good also for *fondu* exercises, in which the sporting leg remains in plié.

The length and complexity of Oboukhoff's center work became famous. There would be a long *tendu* section, perhaps including pirouettes, then a lengthy adagio with strength-building promenade, grand pliés down to the ground, finishing with traveling *piqué* and *chaîné* turns. "The only thing you didn't do was jump." Otherwise, contained within his adagio "was a complete class!"

A favorite pastime of Oboukhoff's was fishing on Long Island. "We all laughed," Wilde recalled, "because we said, 'Mr. Oboukhoff is sitting in his boat now concocting his adagio.'" Sometimes he would toss in the odd character dance step as a punctuating flourish. It was perhaps the inventiveness of these adagios that vainly prompted Balanchine to urge Oboukhoff to try choreography. Both Vladimiroff and Oboukhoff stressed batterie: Oboukhoff often used to finish class with batterie and fast turns across the floor.

Vladimiroff's body structure was more free and Oboukhoff more placed. "Finding the movement from your back and clear down to your waist I learned from Oboukhoff; he put you in place," said Wilde's NYCB colleague

Robert Barnett. SAB's Muriel Stuart, an Englishwoman who had danced with Pavlova's company in the 1920s, asked for a different alignment again. She didn't seem to embody the Russian school, even allowing for how that school incorporated elements of French and Italian ballet. What she asked for was very personal. Stuart "had this great thing about lifting up, and 'the soul,'" recalled Pat McBride Lousada (not to be confused with later NYCB star Patricia McBride). "We should be very lifted," Wilde recalled. "Kind of stretched out over and above."

Although the advanced classes weren't standardized, all the SAB teachers subscribed to a training philosophy emphasizing strength, stamina, and control. The priority in today's training on developing high, light, extremely flexible and turned-out legs was not nearly so pronounced in Wilde's day. "The number of slow grand pliés that we used to do!" Wilde exclaimed. Slow pliés and exercises in *fondu* enabled dancers to develop a softly cushioned quality of landing. Enormous stamina was generated at the barre by circling the knee away from the supporting leg in sixteen *ronds de jambe en dehors*, then sixteen turning *en dedans*, toward the supporting leg. At the end of class the students were given sixteen *entrechats six* and then again sixteen more. This amount of repetition is out of fashion today because of its tendency to build muscle bulk. Wilde says she wouldn't assign them today, but she wonders if something has been lost as a result. Perhaps, she thinks, it might be a good idea to reinstate some of what has been excised, since those exercises did so much to develop strength and control.

In addition to ballet technique, the curriculum offered to students at SAB was extremely eclectic, as Nora White had discovered earlier. José Fernández taught Spanish dance. Yurek Lazovsky, a leading character dancer in the Ballet Russe, taught character when he was in New York. The Dalcroze school was down the block on Fifty-Ninth Street. Émile Jaques-Dalcroze had pioneered a system of music education called "Eurythmics," which sought movement analogues to musical concepts. In the early 1940s, Balanchine imported a teacher from Dalcroze, because, Muriel Stuart recalled, "he felt that most of the girls didn't have a musical sense, a natural musical sense."

Modern dance and ballet were often warring camps at the time.

Then-director Dimitriev, however, had understood during the 1930s that it behooved the school to begin incorporating the new techniques. Stuart herself had studied with Martha Graham. Dimitriev approached her about the possibility of her teaching the Graham syllabus, but he didn't want to use any name resembling "modern." Instead he wanted to call the class "plastique." Plastique was a particular school of dance that emphasized the shape-making capacity of the whole, integrated body. Graham was much harsher and more percussive than anything contained within the plastique category. Stuart refused to teach counterfeit Graham, but did fashion some type of modern synthesis that Nora enjoyed taking. It "wasn't Graham, although we were down on the floor," she said. "It was great to have that kind of possibility, to use our bodies that way." Later, modern dance was taught by Dorothy Bird, still later by Janet Collins. An experimental edge, too, was provided by the avant-garde composer John Cage, who taught a music appreciation class at SAB.

Although there were almost no black dancers in ballet companies at the time, black students at the school were something of a regular occurrence after the appearance of Betty Nichols in 1943. She was dancing on Broadway in the musical *Carmen Jones*, choreographed by Eugene Loring. He had made ballets for Lincoln Kirstein's Ballet Caravan, established in the late 1930s, to make American subject matter the stuff of which a ballet repertory could be built. Loring advised Nichols to study at SAB. "I knocked on the door, presented myself," Nichols recalled. "I thought there was considerable surprise! But the door was opened and that was it." She was eventually offered a scholarship. The school was certainly generous, frequently releasing from financial obligation students who were thought to have promise.

Balanchine himself taught when he was available. During her years attending SAB full-time, Nora White recalled one season when he taught frequently. When she'd taken his class earlier, it seemed to be similar to the school's other teachers, but now he seemed to be working on a new structure—explicitly, a progression. Each part built on the preceding part, and he played with the rules, giving the dancers things to do at the barre on half-toe usually reserved for later parts of class or for full pointe.

Pat McBride had entered the school in 1941. Later a charter member of NYCB, she recalled that Balanchine's class was becoming more complex, more experimental, by the late '40s. The relation of movement to music became asymmetrical. "He used four against five, and three against four. It wasn't just on the beat. He often wanted the accents in different places." The structure of class became unpredictable as well, Balanchine varying the number of repetitions in different directions. "You had to listen hard and think hard."

SAB was a place where Wilde could not only work with great teachers, but also see and study talented students—younger, older, contemporary—as well as current stars of ballet and Broadway. She was frequently in class with Balanchine muse Marie-Jeanne, who had started at the school when it opened in 1934. She was intimately familiar with what each teacher wanted to see, and she shared that knowledge freely with Wilde. "I adored her," Wilde recalled. "She was so alive. Lots of fun. She was smart and she knew her way around."

Also frequently in class with Wilde was Balanchine's wife, Vera Zorina. They had married in 1938 while she was dancing his choreography on Broadway in Rodgers and Hart's *I Married an Angel*. Then twenty-one, Zorina was already a veteran of musical comedy in Europe, as well as three years with the Ballet Russe. Following their marriage, Balanchine choreographed for her in a succession of movies and Broadway shows. "She was gorgeous," Wilde said; the German/Norwegian's bone structure was remarkable. "And I liked her: she was really nice, open and welcoming."

And there were legends from the recent past. Not only Nemchinova, who frequently took her husband's class, but Alice Nikitina, icon of the final, outré years of Diaghilev's Ballets Russes prior to his death in 1929. Nikitina was forty and had not danced professionally in several years, having turned instead to opera singing in Europe. Nevertheless, she was now in New York and now in class, and although "she wasn't in great shape, she was doing everything." Nikitina continued to epitomize ballet's adoption of the unisex look in 1920s fashion and culture, her hair still cut short, and Wilde found her intriguingly exotic. There was no hierarchy of celebrity in class, however. Instead, Wilde recalled compliments and suggestions exchanged between her and her as yet much more celebrated elders.

Most helpful to Wilde was Marie-Jeanne, who provided microscopic inspection; her corrections were "fantastic." The older dancer would remind Wilde when she wasn't developing full control of her foot by articulating the landing into the floor, when her line wasn't attractive, when she didn't keep her feet together skimming across the floor in a chassé.

Vladimiroff would stop Wilde and make her finish pirouettes just the way he wanted—with a little lift: "You almost landed with a little jump; it was lovely." But she didn't get from him—or, in fact, anyone at SAB—the extensive individual corrections that Marie-Jeanne gave.

BALANCHINE'S TRIP TO MEXICO that summer of 1945 was something in the way of occupational therapy. He was now mourning the end of his marriage, which had always been troubled. For one thing, Zorina and her mother were inseparable. Years later, Balanchine would recall to Wilde that once he had presented Zorina with two Siberian huskies, then a fashionable breed. Zorina had just purchased new couches for their apartment. Coming home from a performance, she and Balanchine discovered that the dogs had shredded the sofa cushions. Zorina and her mother sent the dogs packing, and eventually Balanchine too.

Now Zorina had met Columbia Records executive Goddard Lieberson and "had suggested a divorce" to Balanchine, Molo recalled. The divorce was decreed the following year, in January 1946, and Zorina married Lieberson immediately. In years to come, however, Zorina would be a regular attendee at New York City Ballet premieres and a backstage visitor.

"Balanchine talked to me once very personally about love," Nora White recalled. They were rehearsing at Carnegie Hall when Balanchine suddenly told her that "he'd only had love once in his life: Vera Zorina."

And so the offer from Mexico City came at the right time for Balanchine, and was certainly eagerly awaited by the small group of students he invited. They would dance alongside several established dancers: Marie-Jeanne;

William Dollar and his wife, Yvonne Patterson; and Nicholas Magallanes, a young soloist with Ballet Russe. "The rest of us were just kids," Wilde recalled—twelve in all, among whom Joy Williams, Shirley Haynes, and Bernice Rehner were also headed for the Ballet Russe corps de ballet; Marie-Jeanne would join as a principal dancer. Balanchine didn't tell Wilde yet, but he may have already decided that—newest corps member or not—she would be dancing ballerina roles in Mexico over the summer and on opening night of the Ballet Russe's New York season in September.

8

MEXICO CITY,

1945

A decade later, Wilde would recall to the dancer Joy Williams that she thought the individual attention Balanchine had lavished in Mexico on each of them, on all the dancers present, was unique and unrepeatable. In years to come, he would be so busy with many responsibilities at New York City Ballet that, as Wilde recalls today, "I always felt that his time was so valuable that I couldn't take any more of it than was absolutely necessary—from his point of view."

It was slow going on their train trip down: wartime travel was never easy. Sometimes their train was shunted to a side track so that a troop train could pass. When they reached Mexico, the border was not terribly well administered. The teenagers were chaperoned by SAB's Natalia Molo. "She had us organized: what we could do . . . when we could go to the dining car." Trips to the dining car were particularly regimented because of their possibilities for flirtation. Molo later recalled that the Mexicans were "very impressed" with the girls' "blond good looks."

They were receiving "some pittance of pay," Wilde estimated, but unlike with most ballet touring at the time, room and board were provided. Molo settled them into various apartments in a complex at 139 Avenida Niños Héroes, near the theater, where they had rooms to themselves. They all ate together at one apartment. A local woman cooked, but Molo oversaw the menus and ensured that they had box lunches to take to the theater every day.

Balanchine taught class every morning at ten o'clock and conducted rehearsals into the late afternoon—without, unlike most of the city, a siesta break. But once at work the dancers didn't want to leave. It took many flights of stairs to get to the ballet studio. Outside the streets were hot, but inside the old stone theater was cool.

Balanchine had choreographed for opera as far as back as Russia, but extensively for Diaghilev's company while in winter residence in Monte Carlo during the 1920s, and again for the Metropolitan Opera during the three years his American Ballet was in residence there.

Either dancing or filling in crowd scenes, the girls appeared in Gounod's *Faust*, Verdi's *Aïda* and *Rigoletto*, and Saint-Saëns's *Samson et Dalila*. The Palacio's opera seasons featured international guest stars, this year including Lily Pons—whose "Caro Nome" impressed Wilde—as well as up-and-coming singers who soon afterward made good in New York. For June and July the conductors were Jean Morel, later with New York City Opera and the Met, and Karl Alwin, whose twenty years with the Vienna State Opera had ended with the Nazis. Conducting the ballet evening would be distinguished composer Eduardo Hernández Moncada.

Balanchine and William Dollar collaborated, as they had when Nora danced with the New Opera company in New York in 1942–43. Early in June, their season began with *Aïda*, a joint effort. The little company's all-ballet program was scheduled as Dollar's *Constancia* flanked by Balanchine's *Apollo* and *Concerto Barocco*. Dollar began rehearsing *Constancia* in New York; Wilde was one of four semi-soloists who would be partnered by local men hired in Mexico. Balanchine didn't do quite that kind of long-range preparation, and the ballet program was going to come at the end of their stay. Nevertheless, in Mexico City he immediately began rehearsing his ballets, too. Balanchine assigned Wilde the role of Polyhymnia, muse of mime in *Apollo*, as well as the second ballerina lead in *Barocco*.

She was one of the youngest members of the group, but if Balanchine believed she could do it, she believed that she could. And the casting made sense: it played to strengths that she had. Polyhymnia has many pirouettes, and she turned easily — "You do so easy," Felia Doubrovksa, the role's originator, would tell her years later, when Wilde performed the role at New York City Ballet. *Concerto Barocco* she'd known since American Concert Ballet, when she danced in the corps and was taught the second violin role by its creator, Mary Jane Shea.

In *Faust's* "Walpurgisnacht" ballet, Balanchine choreographed a solo for her — the first of many. He was friendly and businesslike as he showed her what to do, she repeated what he did, and instantly, the solo was finished — with his astonishing gift for apparently spontaneous and painless invention. Osborne, Littlefield, and Oboukhoff's emphasis on footwork had paid off — Wilde's beats were now something to be showcased. The solo was filled with *entrechats six*.

In *Samson et Dalila*, Balanchine's Dance of the Priestesses in act 1 and his Bacchanal in act 3 went fine, but "we just about got killed" at the premiere. After the Bacchanal they remained onstage through the temple's collapse, at which point bigger chunks of scenery than anyone had envisioned rained down. But adjustments were been made by the second performance. As the season continued, Molo began spending frequent evenings out on the town, and the girls she was chaperoning could themselves enjoy new friendships. Backstage was an abundance of floral tributes; Wilde and another dancer, Ethel Van Iderstine, were pleased to receive flowers from two Mexican brothers. Amesqua and his brother were determined that the girls have a grand time. They drove them to the town of Cuernavaca in the hills, thirty miles south of Mexico City. It was where many of the city's elite owned vacation homes, and their travel to and from was an apparent provocation to highway robbery. Amesqua showed Wilde the revolver he kept in his glove compartment, which for her only added to the adventure. Before returning to Mexico City, they danced at an open-air café, to live accompaniment from the guitars played everywhere in Mexico. Wilde hadn't ballroom danced before, but she picked it up quickly following his lead.

The brothers took the girls to bullfights on Sundays, which Wilde found thrilling. Her sympathies were with the horses, which wore some padding but usually got roughed up nevertheless. She found the toreadors' stylized provocations elegant. The tradition fascinated her, and she began reading up on it.

On Sundays they also went frequently to the water park at Xochimilco, where on wide canals expensive boats served as floating restaurants and floating gardens. On Sundays the whole city flocked there. It was here that Wilde celebrated turning seventeen in July.

Looking at Balanchine's relationship to his ballerinas, it seems significant that frequently their own relationships with their fathers were problematic, or, as in Wilde's case, nearly nonexistent. Interviewed by Tobi Tobias in 1976, forty-eight-year-old Wilde would say that "one of my problems . . . was that I'd been so close" to Balanchine "so young, that he really replaced . . . a father in some respects to me. So I never could give him too much argument." Asked about this in 2009, when she was eighty-one, Wilde reflected, "I wouldn't have known how to treat a father."

Certainly Wilde at seventeen, despite having several of Freud's treatises under her belt, was not capable of understanding exactly how this transference might occur. But she was grateful for Balanchine's attention when she suddenly became incapacitated by stomach gas and cramps. Perhaps it was the altitude, or perhaps, she thought, it could have been the amount of bread she consumed when she had sandwiches for lunch day after day. "I certainly didn't miss any performances," said Wilde, who would, over the course of her career, take show-must-go-on responsibility to extraordinary lengths. But after taking to her bed one day, she woke up to find Balanchine sitting by her side. "Oh, you're all right, Pat, you're OK. The doctor came and you're going to be all right." The mayor of Mexico City was inviting the dancers to a party at his hacienda in Cuernavaca. "Am I going to be able to go?" Wilde asked Balanchine. "I'll check. . . .Yes, the doctor said the mayor will definitely have goat meat for you, and that's what you should have to eat. You must have baby goat meat."

Wilde did as she was told at the lavish party, replete with mariachi players and all the trimmings. Food seemed to be everywhere; baby goat did turn out to be easily digestible.

But Wilde flouted Balanchine's quasi-parental as well as artistic authority when the two Mexican brothers took her and Ethel to play pickup games of soccer as well as to the Mexican equivalent of American baseball (running to two rather than three bases). Balanchine objected to sports that could injure a dancer or hinder her figure—which really meant any sport. Wilde knew he wouldn't have been pleased but, then again, "he didn't have to know about everything."

"I can't do *Barocco*!" Marie-Jeanne suddenly announced not long before the ballet program was due to premiere. "I'll never get through *Barocco*." Wilde thought that the ballerina's legs were cramping painfully. "Her legs always killed her in *Barocco*." They would subsequently dance it together at Ballet Russe. "Her calf muscles just used to get too knotted" by the ballet's abundance of tight, fast movement. Apparently Mexico City's altitude didn't help.

Wilde didn't doubt that she was genuinely in distress, but Marie-Jeanne was prone to lapses of discipline that, despite extraordinary talent, caused her career to sputter prematurely. During American Ballet Caravan's tour of South America in 1941, she was pursued by Balanchine but nevertheless remained in Argentina to marry her first husband, who by now was absent. And in Mexico City the twenty-five-year-old was certainly capable of going out, having a ball, and not being ready for what had to be done at work the next day.

Balanchine decided that Fokine's *Les Sylphides* would replace *Barocco*. It was a work he admired. Dollar had originally studied with Fokine and had danced the ballet with de Cuevas the previous fall. He staged the ballet very quickly, reducing the corps de ballet. He again danced the poet's role and cast Wilde as first sylph. The son of an East St. Louis grocer, Dollar could be soft and moonstruck here without seeming effete. A deeply cushioned plié helped him in his solo, filled with sighing landings and poses in arabesque. His coaching was also authoritative, as was his partnering. In their duet there were many different lifts that required the illusion of utter effortlessness, and Wilde was perfectly relaxed in his arms. For her solo, he assigned her the Waltz, affording her a great sense of liberation as she leapt across the stage. Patterson, who had the streamlined shape of today's dancers in an era when few women did, danced the equally airborne Mazurka.

Balanchine went to Mexico City's Follies Theater to see Yvonne Mounsey, who had worked for him in the de Basil Ballet Russe four years earlier. She had been stranded in South America in 1941 when the de Basil troupe went on strike. Now she was dancing ballet and acrobatic turns with a vaudeville troupe, using the Russianized stage name Irina Zarova. He invited her to perform *Sylphides'* hushed, meditative Prelude, bringing her back into the ballet fold. She would eventually spend the final decade of her performing career as ballerina with New York City Ballet.

Mounsey was involved with a wealthy Mexican banker, and Balanchine sometimes accepted their invitations to go nightclubbing. But, as always, the ballet studio would be his primary vehicle for overcoming the emotional distress of his breakup with Zorina.

Balanchine considered his 1928 *Apollo* a landmark in his creative evolution. It charts Apollo's progress from embryonic emergence to full consciousness and mobility. *Apollo* was created for Diaghilev's Ballets Russes, where it conformed to a major theme of the company's late years: antiquity revisited by classical Baroque, then seen through a lens of postwar modernism. It is Balanchine's earliest work to survive, in part because it was one of the choreographer's favorites, perhaps because of the Greek god's connection to the arts. Apollo's trajectory from youth to maturity parallels the journey that twenty-four-year-old Balanchine himself was then experiencing. Balanchine believed that this ballet enabled him to learn to distill the most economical statement. Stravinsky's score, composed exclusively for bowed strings, undoubtedly helped to point the way.

Since Diaghilev's death in 1929, Balanchine had programmed *Apollo* wherever he found himself. Up to the very end of his life, he took special care rehearsing the role and the ballet. Wilde watched closely as Balanchine showed Nicholas Magallanes, who danced Apollo in Mexico City, exactly what he wanted.

During the course of his career, Balanchine had intermittently danced classical and romantic roles when required. But his own special affinity was for movement outside the academic canons of classical harmony and grace. In his first solo, Apollo begins awkwardly to explore and understand the capacities of his body. Balanchine's demonstration of it was "incredible," Wilde recalled. He was ungainly, reminiscent of a child's awkwardness, the movement sampling something of the balletic genre of grotesque. The role is difficult technically as well as interpretively, and Magallanes was not a technician. But with Balanchine's guidance "Nicky did wonderfully."

Marie-Jeanne was Terpsichore, muse of dance. In her adagio with Magallanes, her body and proportions suited the many leaning arabesques perfectly. In her variation, she transmitted something of a French sexuality, a sense of humor that made itself felt all the way down to the way her feet articulated the frequent brushing and pawing the ground.

Teaching Wilde her solo, Balanchine, as was his wont, left it up to her to formulate any thoughts about the identity of Polyhymnia. *Apollo* made her aware of how many variations on the steps learned in class were possible in the hands of a great choreographer. A finger pressed to her lips, as befit the personification of mute eloquence, Wilde danced a circle of *relevés* in attitude—a twist in the body made it almost like a truncated arabesque. As so often with Balanchine's choreography, rhythm and momentum took precedence over a conventional expression of a step. During rehearsal, his hands on her shoulders, Balanchine steered her through the rhythmic evolution.

In the Coda, Marie-Jeanne and Wilde, together with Williams, who was Calliope, muse of eloquence and epic poetry, gamboled playfully with Apollo. "It's a game," one that Wilde and sister muses had fun playing. Then came the gravity of the Apotheosis, when muses and Apollo make their way in a procession to Parnassus. After the exertions of the Coda, it was a chance for Wilde to catch her breath, to experience a calm grandeur that was also highly dramatic.

Billed as a "Ballet Spectacular," their program was performed successfully on July 19 and 26. Soon after that, their two-month stay was over. During those months Wilde had continued to write her mother every week, as she had since leaving Ottawa. She was more than ever grateful that Eileen had defied her friends and allowed her to go to New York. Amesqua had been "not a big love affair," but the first time she dated.

Rather than take the train back to New York, Wilde flew to New York with Ethel Van Iderstine. Time was short before Ballet Russe was to begin rehearsals for a two-week season at City Center. Van Iderstine's father, a lawyer, was the Republican mayor of Tenafly, New Jersey. As she would do frequently in months to come, Wilde went to stay with the family. Together they all went for a week to their vacation home in Skaneateles, New York, on the Finger Lakes, a full day's drive. Ethel was an only child, doted upon by her parents, and the Van Iderstines were almost like a second family to Wilde.

Ethel was good enough for Balanchine to have selected her, but she wasn't going to pursue ballet. Unlike Wilde, she had graduated from high school. To Wilde's chagrin the Ballet Russe's touring schedule was going to make further formal education impossible. Ethel was dating a West Point student, and Wilde went with her to see him graduate. Soon thereafter, she was a bridesmaid at their wedding.

Shortly before leaving Mexico, Patricia Wilde was born as a professional and personal moniker. The Ballet Russe director Sergei Denham did not like multiple family names on his roster, so Nora White's presence meant that it was Patricia who had to find a new last name. It so happened that Eileen had just given her a monogrammed suitcase, so she wanted the new name to begin with "W." She told Balanchine. He had her run through the names of family members. Nothing propitious turned up. Balanchine came up with a few suggestions of his own before hitting upon "Wilde—like Oscar Wilde." "Oh, I like that!" She was from that moment, onstage and off, Patricia Wilde.

OPENING

NIGHT

At Manhattan's City Center on September 9, 1945, opening night of the Ballet Russe season, Wilde warmed up at the back of the stage. This was her debut with the company, and ahead was a very full program. She was dancing a solo role in Balanchine's *Danses Concertantes* and a lead in his *Concerto Barocco*. In the closing ballet, Massine's *Le Beau Danube*, she would resume her official rank as newcomer to the corps de ballet.

Danses Concertantes was opening the program, and she was more nervous about it than *Barocco*. *Concerto Barocco* was just entering the repertory of Ballet Russe, and the company had worked on it over the past several weeks. Furthermore, Wilde had already rehearsed it with American Concert Ballet in 1943 and with Balanchine in Mexico a month earlier. By now, she was eager to finally get onstage in it. But *Danses Concertantes* had been premiered by Ballet Russe a year earlier, and performed continually. With rehearsal time at a premium, it hadn't been given a lot of attention as the company prepared for its fall season.

Everything about *Danses Concertantes* was deluxe, chic, prestigious. It was performed to a new acerbic and mercurial score for chamber orchestra by Stravinsky. The great Eugene Berman—painter, commercial artist, and theatrical designer—created the scenery and costumes. He was a personable

Russian émigré, frequently around the theater and interested in how his work functioned for the dancer.

The leads were Ballet Russe's star couple, Alexandra Danilova and Frederic Franklin. Danilova went back a long, long way with Balanchine. They were students together in St. Petersburg, had left Russia together, and had joined Diaghilev's Ballets Russes together immediately after. They shared an apartment together in Paris after Balanchine's marriage to Tamara Geva, who had left Russia with them, dissolved. He made many roles for Danilova with Diaghilev; she was a prototypically Balanchine ballerina: not primarily lyric—quicker and more staccato. She was tall, with long, beautiful legs, an almost animalistic physical intensity as well as an inimitable effervescence.

But in 1931, after he broke up with Danilova, Balanchine joined the de Basil Ballet Russe, convened as self-styled successor to Diaghilev. In the throes of launching the "baby ballerinas," Balanchine told Danilova that at age twenty-seven she was "too old" to join his company. Not long thereafter, however, he was replaced by Léonide Massine, and Danilova was hired. Since then, however, mutual convenience had brought them together as colleagues. Now she was forty-one, still at her peak but entering an age when fighting to stay on top could become a matter of diminishing returns. Between Balanchine and Danilova, "there was nothing left of what must have been," Franklin recalled. Wilde said that Danilova "was funny with him"—inconsistent, that is: although there was no question that "she did respect him very much," in the studio would sometimes come out with an exasperated "Oh, George!" over a correction he'd given. (At other times she addressed him as "Mr. B.")

Although Danilova had danced *Danses Concertantes* for a year, in rehearsal she frequently had trouble staying connected to the complicated music. It was much less comprehensible played by the rehearsal pianist than delineated with orchestral coloration in performance. Together Franklin and Balanchine made up a song, melody lifted from the popular hit "Marietta," but with appropriate rhythm and admonitory lyrics: "If you do it right, you can't go wrong..."

Supporting the two leads in *Danses Concertantes* were four trios, each costumed in a different color and each distinctly characterized by Balanchine. Following the classic pattern of nineteenth-century ballet, each trio was two women and one man. Wilde was dancing the red trio, together with Maria Tallchief and Nicholas Magallanes. This trio was pedigreed. Her role had been created a year earlier for Mary Ellen Moylan, who was now leaving to dance on Broadway. Both Moylan and Tallchief had joined Ballet Russe in 1942, and they were two of the young Ballet Russe dancers Balanchine was most interested in. Red was the jazziest, the fastest, the most virtuosic and audience-catching of the four trios. There was a step practically on each note, and a lot of Balanchine's signature hip-jutting, off-balance movement. There was no time or place for a single wrong move or musical miscue.

Wilde was discomfited to realize that there was a little bit more to the role than she'd learned. Balanchine came by as Wilde warmed up for the opening. "So, Pat, how are you?" "I'm OK, Mr. B., but doesn't something happen before that olio goes up?" *Danses Concertantes* began with a short passage before the olio, the front curtain, in which the cast introduced itself, establishing a flavor of strolling players and commedia dell'arte. Then they'd run behind it and get into formation; when the olio rose, it showed the entire cast standing in a semi-circle with one leg extended forward in a *tendu*.

"Oh, yeah, oh, yes: you go across in front of the stage," Balanchine informed Wilde. "Nobody showed me what do to," she confessed. He wasn't worried. "You just do *sauté*, step, glissade, *entrechats cinq*, and then you bow to Nicky and he will come on." "But when do I come on, and what's the music?" Her experience of Stravinsky had begun with *Apollo*. "Oh, well, Nicky will push you out," Balanchine assured her, and went about his business. His mind, unlike hers, was on *Barocco*.

Balanchine liked juxtaposing contrasts. Fair-haired Wilde and dark Tallchief provided one. Nora thought that she and Gertrude Tyven paired in the lavender trio was another. "Gertie was the most natural dancer in the world," Nora recalled. "She didn't have to work to do anything. I had to work like crazy. In *Danses Concertantes* we were a couple of characters. We must have been!"

Wilde's costume was magenta-red printed in black, while the man's jacket picked up the same print in black jet beads. Balanchine "always had something to say about the costumes," Wilde recalled, and Berman's designs represented a true collaboration. The tutus were extremely short, layer upon layer of printed tarlatan. They were in line with Balanchine's desire to impose a strict classical standard by exposing the "how" of the way the dancer accomplished her steps, the quality of her line, the degree of turnout. Wilde liked showing her legs. She was turned out, she was very thin at that time, and her legs were nicely shaped.

Berman had designed butterfly-wing headdresses in the same fabric as the women's skirts, and Wilde and Tallchief pinned them elaborately so that their headpieces couldn't resist, even microscopically, their frequent, lightning-fast changes of direction. Onstage before the curtain, Nora gave her younger sister ballet's ritualistic "Merde," together with knee tucked into her rear end.

Although the red trio was renowned, neither it nor the full ballet was ever preserved. Balanchine rechoreographed it entirely in 1972. The music was pounding and raucous; the three dancers up in the air on the music's opening thump, leaping downstage in tandem. Then "Maria and I were doing fouettés and double pirouettes and all this wildness was going on." Both women were in the same key of virtuosity but not always heeding the same musical cue. The score was syncopated and so was their relationship. They turned together; they turned in opposite directions; they moved on alternate beats.

Wilde related to Balanchine's neoclassicism as an "extreme" presentation of the academic vocabulary and positions she had now studied for more than a decade. If she was all the way up in a fifth position on pointe, it was an overly crossed fifth position preceding an earthier lunge and chassé slide. There were dynamic contrasts between explosive turns and "lots of little steps across ourselves." In some of the trios the women interacted with the man, but here Magallanes "practically didn't touch us—he had to stay out of our way!"

Tallchief was step- and note-perfect in the role she'd created; her clarity made it easier for Wilde to get through the pas de trois without mishap. It was with a sense of relief that she went to prepare for *Concerto Barocco*, which was always for her sheer pleasure, no more so than this night.

At its 1941 premiere the ballet had also been dressed by Berman, but his sets and costumes were now going to be jettisoned by Ballet Russe. They were later reinstated, however, for New York City Ballet's debut performance in 1948, when cast member Barbara Walczak thought they were "the most beautiful I ever saw." The set was gray and white, suggesting ocean waves, relating, Walczak felt, to wave patterns in the movement. In the slow second movement the dancers create many complicated formations, including one they called "the snail." The women's costumes were short, but scrolled and frilled in a Baroque fashion.

At Ballet Russe, the ballet was performed without set, dressed in spare leotards and short skirts suggestive of women's athletics as well as contemporary jitterbug attire—not inappropriate for the ballet's many colloquialisms. This kind of slightly theatricalized practice wear would become Balanchine's default costuming at New York City Ballet during the fifteen years Wilde danced there.

It was exciting for Wilde to finally dance opposite always-supportive Marie-Jeanne in the role she had created in *Barocco*. The ballet seemed to have been built directly out of her physique. To Wilde, she seemed in this ballet a quintessential demonstration of Balanchine style and technique.

Rehearsing Wilde in the part for American Concert Ballet two years earlier, Marie-Jeanne and Mary Jane Shea had been specific about the recurrent exposition in which the two ballerinas revolve around each other, often in arabesque: "You had to really be in contact, conduct a dialogue."

Nora was a member of the eight-member ensemble, who were constantly on the go throughout all three movements, their steps as intricate as those the two ballerinas did. Onstage too was Joy Williams, who recalled Marie-Jeanne and Wilde being "almost on top of each other, they were so close." It was a unique density and intimacy paralleling the relationship of the two violins. Today, as Wilde notes, the relationship has "opened up" differently, as a result of being performed by New York City Ballet on its large home stage at Lincoln Center.

Wilde "loved every moment" of *Concerto Barocco*. As was his habit, Balanchine said nothing, which Wilde had by now learned meant that he thought what she'd done acceptable.

Massine's 1924 *Le Beau Danube* couldn't have been more of a contrast to the two Balanchine works. For one thing, there was a story line: on the eve of marrying, a Hussar meets the Street Dancer who was once his mistress.

In it, Danilova and Franklin danced a lovely, nostalgic duet to the famous waltz, an entirely different encounter than the astringent duet Balanchine had made for them in *Danses Concertantes*. Massine was dynamic in rehearsal, demonstrating not just steps but acting reactions so necessary to incidents of street life in old Vienna.

Eileen had come to New York for her youngest daughter's debut. She was thrilled at both of her dancing daughters' success. She also enjoyed the chance to sample the art form they pursued: Eileen had seen as little professional ballet as her daughters had before they left Ottawa. Balanchine and she got along well. She was one of the few mothers he knew who was not overly solicitous, not disgruntled, but felt only appreciation. Her daughters' achievement provided all the rebuttal she needed to her friends' disapproval.

Any jealousy Wilde's sister corps members may have felt about the opportunities she'd been given so quickly were not expressed to her. But they would have been "understandable always," she says today.

Soon after the two-week season closed, Anatole Chujoy wrote in *Dance News* that "Patricia Wilde was nervous opening night but found her composure in subsequent performances. She has a tendency to wear a quasi-tragic expression in most things she is doing, and it does not go well with Concerto Barocco. However, she is a brilliant dancer and Ballet Russe de Monte Carlo was wise in adding her to its ranks."

Reviewing the season, Edwin Denby in the *Herald-Tribune* praised Wilde's "fine clean style," noting as well that "her charm is a little lanky as yet." Any youthful gaucheness that the debutante may have manifested would only have increased her appeal to Balanchine. It was a question of showman's instinct as well as personal attraction. Balanchine certainly understood how the youngest performers transmit a vulnerability that is always appealing to an audience. In something of the same way, he was drawn to impressionable human material that could be molded. Today Wilde explains that Balanchine preferred it when "you were an open book—and he was going to turn the pages!"

ON TOUR

Wilde's career onstage would extend into the 1960s, when regional companies began springing up around the United States. But back in the 1940s, there was far less opportunity for employment. "If you made it to a company, you really had been fighting to get there," Wilde says today. "'I'm going to do this or die trying!' was the way we felt." But the real struggle only began with the dancer's professional career—and one of the most grueling struggles was the battle against the rigors of touring. With Europe as well as most of the entire world closed to them, the Ballet Russe routinely gave two New York seasons a year, but spent most of its performing weeks on marathon tours of the United States under conditions unimaginable to today's ballet dancers.

Given the Ballet Russe's itinerary, the White sisters were out of New York as much as they were in. Nevertheless, they rented a one-bedroom apartment on Second Avenue between Fifty-Sixth and Fifty-Seventh Streets, where they slept in bunk beds. Although there were more small, independent studios on the West Side, the School of American Ballet at Madison Avenue and Fifty-Ninth Street made the East Side an attractive place for ballet dancers to live. Nikita Talin from the Ballet Russe lived downstairs. Zoya Leporsky, with whom Wilde had danced in the American Concert Ballet and the marquis's International Ballet lived next door. Sometimes the Whites were able to sublet before going out on the road.

A seventy-nine-city tour immediately followed Wilde's Ballet Russe debut in New York. Chicago, Houston, Los Angeles, and San Francisco could each sustain a season of one or even two weeks, but most of the stops were much briefer. One-night stands heavily stamped the company's itineraries. Wilde recalled one tour when she danced no fewer than twenty-eight of them consecutively. For the corps, however, one upside was that they were onstage so routinely that, when they had a solo to perform, nerves didn't get the better of them.

The company paid for their transportation, but it was frequently substandard. Traveling in Texas, they once left a train to board an old school bus that had broken windows. It was freezing, and an older musician put his coat over the shivering Wilde's shoulders. As they were getting off, a younger horn player named Johnnie Bishop fainted. They arrived at their hotel at dawn but were told that the rooms would not be ready until noon. They protested that afternoon rehearsals were scheduled to break in replacements for that night's performance. Finally Wilde, together with five other corps women, was shown to a room. They took the mattress off the springs, and it was three sharing the mattress, three on the box springs. Almost the moment they turned off the lights, Sonia Tyven screamed: a bedbug had seized its opportunity. Lights went back on, and the dancers got as much rest as they could.

The dancers were responsible for food, accommodations, and incidental travel expenses, but were given a small allowance. Whenever possible, they would try to reserve single rooms across the country before they left New York. Otherwise they would have to find a hotel when they got off the train in the morning. On one-night stands, however, they would simply go straight to the train after the performance. They were all pinching pennies, and one in the corps was secretly doubling up in their rooms. "The hotels knew what we were doing," Nora said: "'ghosting.' Playing the army game."

Personal hygiene suffered on the road. "Cologne was much in use," Wilde says. Most of the time there were no showers at the theater. They hoped they'd get one at the hotel, if they were spending the night. One ballerina was seen to do her hair in the classic over-the-ears style on a Monday and leave it undisturbed for the rest of the week.

Cooking in the hotel rooms was also against the rules, but many dancers traveled with Sterno stoves and used some subterfuge to disguise the smell. Nevertheless, the liberal use of garlic by some Russian mothers traveling with the company often permeated the hallways. Wilde's diet, however, become sporadic. It just wasn't possible to eat regularly or properly. She would consume a big breakfast and get whatever she could on the train. After the performance, often there were few places open. It could take a while to find someplace to eat and a while to get served, so she found herself ingesting a great deal of bread. Often she went to bed with a knotted stomach.

Tour stages were often treacherous. Once the company was performing at a parochial college that wanted to welcome them in high style. Unthinkingly, it had waxed the school stage. Stagehands slipped and slid as they tried to tie on backdrops. During Balanchine's *Mozartiana*, soloist Robert Lindgren foundered as he tried to get offstage after leading the Gigue movement. Later, when Wilde entered with the corps in a big jump, bodies went *splat* all over the stage.

Not only the dancers but also the costumes they wore were subject to extra strain on the road. Pittsburgh's dust and grit was all but proverbial. It covered the stage of the Syria Mosque, built for the Shriners thirty years earlier. Wardrobe mistress Sophie Pourmel pleaded with Frederic Franklin—who was ballet master as well as premier danseur—not to have the two white-tulle-clad demi-soloists in *Les Sylphides* position themselves on the stage floor as they were supposed to. He wasn't willing to shortchange Fokine's precise design, however, and the costumes did become so soiled that Madame Pourmel had to wash them in her hotel bathtub.

Company class on tour was almost unheard-of. "When we'd go on the road, we fended for ourselves," Franklin recalled. Sometimes Danilova and he "would take a group; we'd separate and take the kids. But there was nothing organized." Wilde and a group of corps members would often conduct their own class or warm-up in whatever space was available. They took turns leading the class; often it was Sonya Tyven who taught. There was no actual music, but they would sing internally. "Edwina, can't you hear the music?" Tyven asked corps member Edwina Seaver, who was a little late in the unilateral rhythms they were able to preserve.

Touring gave Wilde an upsetting introduction to the country's racial divide—something she never imagined growing up in Ottawa, where blacks were rarely to be seen at all. The United States in the 1940s was, of course, strictly segregated throughout the South. On tour there, Wilde along with a couple of other company members hopped onto a bus and took seats at the back, where they could all sit together. It never dawned on them that they were someplace they shouldn't have been—until a black woman asked them to move forward.

On the road, prima ballerina Danilova functioned as self-appointed ombudsman. She set an inspiring example. Alongside the rank and file, she coped with difficult traveling conditions. Only on very rare occasions did she and Franklin take a flight rather than endure a grueling train and bus hop. Wherever and whenever they were onstage, no matter how obscure the locale, Danilova invariably "gave a performance full out," Wilde recalled. "The audience always knew that they were going to get the best that she could give."

She was seemingly omniscient and frequently censorious. "You couldn't get out of there early enough in the morning," Nora recalled, "'cause she was always down in the coffee shop and she'd see what everybody was doing." She was a stickler for impeccable professional deportment. In 1944, the entire company had spent two weeks in Los Angeles dancing Balanchine's choreography for the new musical *Song of Norway*. At one point Nora and a few others had to exit, run behind a backdrop, and reappear onstage from the opposite wing. Danilova noticed her slightly fluttering the backdrop, and later "gave me holy hell: 'That was terrible. Don't do it. It's not theatrical.'"

As queen bee, Danilova did allow herself some liberties. One night when the conductor was going too fast for her comfort, she yelled "Slower, slower!" from the stage, which was hardly standard protocol. By this point, Danilova's performances sometimes aroused anxiety among her colleagues. The act 3 pas de deux in *Coppélia* could be "Oh, God!" for Wilde as she watched Danilova wobble through her balances. But the best performance she ever saw her give in that ballet was at a slightly tipsy Sunday matinee in San Francisco. The prima ballerina had gone to brunch and evidently enjoyed at least one Bloody Mary. She was "gay and giddy" as she arrived; by the time the third act rolled around, "she was just blowing it off!"

Wilde had no doubt that Danilova truly "cared about the company," not simply about her own success. But where its younger women were concerned, she wanted to nurture, and then again, she didn't. When in New York, Danilova taught a variations class at the School of American Ballet. "She was wonderful," Nora recalled, with the caveat that Danilova "held things a little close to the chest. I think she might have been a little more helpful." In the studio, part of her was still onstage and not relinquishing the limelight.

In the Ballet Russe, Danilova frequently made helpful suggestions to both White sisters. But each also had the experience of Danilova personally making her up for a performance with indifferent results, due not to malice but to a certain narcissistic blinkeredness. Early in Nora's career, Danilova announced that, like her, Nora had heavily lidded "bedroom eyes" that should be made up as hers were. Nora submitted to her attentions, although she didn't think their eyes were similar. Ballet Russe director Sergei Denham was not pleased. During the performance, he suddenly appeared backstage: "Get that girl offstage! She looks like she has two black eyes!"

Certainly Danilova believed that the company's mystery and allure should be preserved at all times. She insisted that the corps women dress elegantly during any public appearance connected to the ballet: arriving in a city, leaving the theater. Slacks were taboo. Wilde conformed to Danilova's dress code and believed that it benefited the company's mystique. But she ignored injunctions against athletic exercise; on days off she went bicycling and bowling. Once on a bike trip she and some colleagues stopped by a stream and used whatever was at hand to go fishing. They took their haul back to their hotel, where the chef prepared it and served it to them.

Word from on high was that horseback riding was strictly forbidden. Nevertheless, during one season in Phoenix, Nora and Wilde, company members Maria Tallchief and Alexander Goudovitch, as well as the company's music librarian, all decided to go riding. Danilova somehow got wind of their outing. That night the music librarian was walking downstage to put the music on the stands when he tripped and the scores flew down all over the pit. Danilova fumed that their riding excursion was to blame. The first ballet was Balanchine's *Serenade*. Tallchief in the final Élégie movement went zooming upstage to jump into Nicholas Magallanes's arms. After zooming, however, she started slipping upstage and wound up on her back. Danilova did more fuming. But then Danilova came out for the final ballet, *Danses Concertantes*, and now she too fell flat on her rear end. Magallanes, standing behind her, made some derogatory sounds, loud enough for her to hear. Either she realized she had been insufferable, or the wind had been taken out of her sails, because neither White sister, both of whom were onstage, remembered any further comments from Danilova that night.

BALANCHINE'S

BALLET RUSSE

In the fall of 1945, Balanchine was choreographing two new works for Ballet Russe to augment the seven they currently performed. *Night Shadow* was a one-act ballet, set to Vittorio Rieti's arrangement of themes from the bel canto operas of Bellini. It was a Gothic horror story that could have been lifted from the literature of the period. The three-act *Raymonda* was entirely different. Performed to a sumptuous score by Glazunov, it had premiered in St. Petersburg in 1898. Its plot concerned a noble's daughter whose affections were divided between, and disputed by, a Crusader and Moor. Both Danilova and Balanchine had danced children's roles in it, and now they were going to jointly stage it. It was all but completely unknown in the United States. Both of Balanchine's new ballets turned out to be important achievements; Wilde had roles in each—indeed, in *Raymonda* she had multiple roles.

Balanchine routinely joined the company on tour during its stays in large cities. He would make a point of conducting a full class—a rarity on their tours—which was a treat for Wilde and colleagues. He was with them in Chicago when Ballet Russe opened its 1945–46 tour with a two-week season there at the end of September. A backstage notice summoned Wilde and three other women to a rehearsal with him, scheduled on a Saturday night after matinee and evening performances. They went to a studio up-stairs at the opera house, which turned out to contain yet another waxed floor. Balanchine gave them hoops, and he choreographed a dance to the cabaletta from "Mira, o Norma." They had to learn to turn the hoops and strike arabesques as they held them. They rehearsed following the next day's performances as well. The hoop dance was going to be one of the entertainments offered guests in the Baron's castle where *Night Shadow* would be set.

After Chicago the company made its way west and south. Balanchine joined them in San Francisco mid-November, and then in Houston shortly before Christmas 1945. Wilde was staying in a two-bedroom suite, with the customary two dancers in each bedroom. Danilova's secretary/companion Gertrude Twysden invited the dancers in for the plum pudding she made every year—a British holiday tradition. After the performance, Balanchine often went back with Wilde and her friends to one of their rooms, where they laughed and talked.

It was Balanchine who had installed Frederic Franklin as chief ballet master at Ballet Russe. "Oh, Fredinka, what it means," Danilova inquired mischievously. "You're going to be my boss?" Franklin had spent years studying piano in his native Liverpool. His musicality was a great help in remembering choreography; in those days very little was recorded on film.

As a balletic consort, Franklin was unfailingly solicitous of Danilova, whose energy could sometimes flag. Franklin "pulled her through a lot of things," Wilde said. "He really took that responsibility." In addition, he was able, when needed, to exert administrative/artistic authority over her by virtue of diplomacy and humor. But problems arrived during *Raymonda*.

By 1946, certain performance practices of the Russian Imperial Ballet could seem very odd indeed to contemporary balletic sensibilities. In the Imperial Ballet, sometimes the principal male role had been divided be-tween two lead performers: one for the mime scenes, which were quite elaborate, and another for the technical solos. Sometimes, too, the man was only there to support the ballerina. Apparently that had been the case in St. Petersburg's *Raymonda*; in any event, that was how it was going to be perpetuated at the Ballet Russe. When Franklin realized that his role as Raymonda's victorious suitor was not going to have any solo, he went to Balanchine. "Mr. B., I'm not doing this." "I know," Balanchine told him. "We fix." Balanchine then made a solo for him to music originally danced by a men's quartet in the final act.

Franklin tried out his new solo at a stage rehearsal. Expostulations in Russian issued from the auditorium: Danilova was miffed at not being alerted to this new interpolation. In the immediate aftermath, Franklin advised Danilova to "talk to Mr. Balanchine. It's his ballet too." Danilova relented: "No, Freddy, OK. You do good. Lovely solo."

Though willing to comply with Franklin's demand, Balanchine didn't make it easy for him. The solo contained of a series of jumps that taxed what he could do; it never became anything other than a "struggle" for Franklin as Wilde watched him in performance after performance.

Naturally, Danilova was starring in *Raymonda* as well as collaborating in its staging. Balanchine had no choice but to continue to choreograph starring roles for her, and they were great roles. As surviving amateur footage shows, she was still an extraordinary performer. But her highly ornamented style, enchanting to audiences and critics alike, was not as clean and economical as what he looked for in younger dancers. For Balanchine, the future lay with them.

Marie-Jeanne was proving problematic. She was prone to put on weight, prone to anxiety about whether she could survive a demanding ballet, and prone to canceling performances. That represented a great inconvenience, particularly on tour. The company numbered only forty dancers, reduced from the sixty employed when it was founded in Europe in 1938. As the *Herald-Tribune*'s Walter Terry would write in January 1946: "The leading dancers are excellent, but there are not quite enough of them."

Mary Ellen Moylan was on Broadway dancing the choreography of Balanchine's rival Antony Tudor in Lerner and Loewe's *The Day before Spring*, but it was twenty-year-old Maria Tallchief who was increasingly attracting the master's attention. Tallchief represented both challenge and inspiration to Balanchine. Like him, she was a trained musician: she had studied piano well into adolescence. "She was different with the music," Ballet Russe's Vida Brown recalled. She wasn't at all four-square in her musical response—"She didn't go bum-bum-*bum*," Brown said. "It was on the end or the beginning of the note."

Trained principally by Nijinska in Los Angeles, Tallchief embodied strengths the teacher espoused. Her equilibrium was rock steady: "Get on your leg and stay there," as Wilde described it. Tallchief was a good turner and used her arms beautifully. She was a unique expressive presence. In the Nijinska works danced by Ballet Russe, Wilde admired Tallchief's "wonderful enveloping quality, a kind of expansiveness." But lacking from Tallchief was refined articulation of the foot and turnout of the legs, both essential to the neoclassicism Balanchine was developing.

She was also very arresting-looking; at this particular point in Balanchine's life, however, on the rebound from Zorina, creative inspiration rather than romance seemed to be his overriding pursuit. Too, Balanchine was infatuated with her Native American pedigree. Her father was a full Osage Indian who had struck a windfall selling his oil rights, leading him to take his family from Oklahoma to Beverly Hills. In Balanchine's *Le Bourgeois Gentilhomme*, set to Richard Strauss's suite based on Molière's 1670 comedy, he created an American Indian dance for her and Yurek Lazovsky, a star character dancer. The company found Tallchief's typecasting amusing, but "I don't think she was very happy about it," Wilde recalled.

Tallchief was part of a group of inveterate poker players in the company, who sat up playing late into the night on the company's train trips. "I can still see Nora sitting with her poker face," Joy Williams recalled. "I thought it was the height of sophistication." Musicians and stagehands also participated avidly. Wilde, however, had no interest in cards or gambling. That was fortunate for Nora. Her younger sister's circumspection enabled her to advance money to cover Nora's poker losses. But Nora says today, "I think I still owe a hundred dollars to one of the stage crew."

Tallchief thought that Balanchine's was the most musical choreography she had ever danced. Her head was a little big for her body, potentially a bar to the highest reaches of classical ballet. However, she believed that Balanchine could choreograph so as to disguise this drawback.

In New York, Tallchief shared an apartment with Ballet Russe colleagues Vida Brown and Helen Kramer, each of whom was astonished when Maria suddenly brought up the possibility of marrying Balanchine. "We talked about boys all the time," Kramer recalled, and Balanchine as a potential partner had never been even mentioned. But for Wilde the marriage was not unexpected. She had watched the symbiosis between muse and creator intensify in the ballet studio.

Tallchief sometimes relaxed by playing a free piano in the ballet studio. Wilde envied Tallchief's ability: "I was very lacking in that." Nora studied piano and Bet played violin, but Eileen had not been intent on providing music instruction for her youngest. Wilde did eventually acquire some ability to read music, but strictly on her own. She was, as always, acutely aware of any shortcoming and determined to overcome it. One night at Ballet Russe, exiting the stage a few seconds too soon, Wilde was heard saying to herself, "I must work harder on my music."

It was also somewhat on the fly that Wilde became practiced in the mechanics of being partnered. Nora had been taught the man's role in partnering by Gwendolyn Osborne in Ottawa, as she prepared her for pas de deux with her younger sister. Facility in the woman's role she acquired in Oboukhoff's adagio class at the School of American Ballet. Wilde as an adult learned anecdotally at rehearsals, fed instructions by partners: "Plié and jump and sit on my shoulder — stick out your ribs!"

Despite a great deal of overlap, the two White sisters led their own lives. "We didn't keep track of one another," Nora recalled. Nora had a strong technique, but pointe work didn't come easily to her. Wilde was always going to be more of a classical technician, and White more of a character dancer — leading the Czardas and Mazurka, starring as the Cowgirl in Agnes de Mille's *Rodeo*.

"I don't think we're competitive," Nora says today, but "I may have been a bit cold about Pat. I often wonder." Certainly, Wilde was once again following a path trod by her older sister. Nora was not smoothing the way, but, on the other hand, her younger sister "didn't seem to need any help."

Ballet Russe returned to City Center on February 17, 1946, for a six-week season. February 27 was the premiere of *Night Shadow*. Danilova was the Sleepwalker, variant of the "madwoman in the attic" of Romantic novels — the Baron's prisoner in his castle turret. Franklin and Magallanes alternated in the role of the Poet who has a life-altering encounter with her. Tallchief was the Coquette, the Baron's current mistress. A little dalliance with her costs the Poet his life at the hands of the jealous Baron.

Danilova's Sleepwalker was haunting. "When she came walking on, you felt that presence: it was eerie," Wilde recalled. Most of Danilova's role consisted of bourrées as she drifted across the stage, apparently impervious to the fascination of the poet. Danilova's bourrées were exceptional—"They had their own tremble," Wilde remembered, that was unique to this ballet.

The suite of entertainments played before the Baron and his guests included Wilde's hoop quartet and a Pastorale, also a quartet, in which Nora danced. For Marie-Jeanne, Balanchine created a Harlequin solo that seemed to spoof her propensity for frequent indispositions. It began with steps that showed off her striking long legs and line, but then veered toward the ballerina's simulated aches and pains. Nora thought Marie-Jeanne realized the comment Balanchine was making. Certainly she "made the most of it," and was as funny as she was beautiful.

To the accompaniment of "Ah, non credea mirarti," one of Bellini's most unearthly melodies, the entertainers at the Baron's fête mourned their fellow artist, the Poet. Then the haunted figure of Danilova's Sleepwalker appeared—she had not, it now turned out, been oblivious to his attempts to penetrate her trance. The entertainers transferred the Poet's corpse into her arms; she cradled him as she backed off the stage—a sensational theatrical stroke. A spotlight high in the sky suggested their progress into the castle and toward some kind of apotheosis.

Night Shadow was received with a good deal of boredom and bafflement by the critics, who found the ball entertainments protracted. Wilde's hoop dance was eventually cut. The entire ballet lapsed from Ballet Russe's repertory after three years, but reached Europe soon after when the Marquis de Cuevas, Wilde's former employer, took it into his company. It was revived in 1960 by New York City Ballet, which continues to perform it today, retitled *La Sonnambula*. It is now considered a major work.

Raymonda opened on March 12, when the audience included "just about every Russian dancer and teacher in New York," Jack Anderson writes in his history of the company. As an expression of Russian Imperial inheritance, it would have proved heartening to the international émigré community. Scenery and costumes were designed by the venerable Alexander Benois, who had been one of the principal creative forces in the early years of Diaghilev's Ballets Russes. Balanchine and Danilova also consulted the memoirs of a musician in the current Ballet Russe orchestra who had once played for the St. Petersburg Mariinsky.

Balanchine and Danilova achieved an extraordinary feat of historical recall and reclamation by introducing one of the enduring products of the Imperial Ballet to America. They also shortened and modernized the original ballet. Mime passages were streamlined, although retained was the entirely mime role of the White Lady, a statue that comes to life to guide young Raymonda. The role was a kinetic descendent of tutelary archetypes in medieval literature such as Lady Wisdom in the thirteenth-century *Roman de la Rose*. She was enacted alternately by Nora and by Joy Williams.

Raymonda takes place in a Middle European duchy, somewhere perhaps in Hungary. The ballet is permeated with steps and accents derived from the Czardas, thus the pretext for the "Grand Pas Hongrois" at the act 3 wedding celebration. Marius Petipa, whose choreography dominated St. Petersburg's ballet in the final decades of the 1800s, fashioned a superb mixture of Czardas and classical vocabulary. But Balanchine typically left his stamp on what was one of the hallowed inheritances from Petipa. He took music from other parts of the ballet to provide new solos for four women leading the Grand Pas Hongrois. At the premiere, the new solos were performed by a stellar roster: Marie-Jeanne, Ruthanna Boris—one of the company's most prominent younger ballerinas—and Maria Tallchief, as well as very young Yvonne Chouteau, who like Tallchief was of Native American descent.

The Imperial as well as Soviet state ballet companies of Moscow and St. Petersburg numbered two hundred dancers apiece, but Ballet Russe's ensemble had to double and triple up. In act 1, Wilde and Gertrude Tyven were demi-soloists in the Waltz following Raymonda's entrance. In the second act Wilde was a member of the infidel Saracen's retinue. She performed a Moorish stick dance, one of a number of divertissements climaxing in a madly whirling coda and then armed combat between Crusader Jean de

Brienne and the Saracen Abderachman. For the wedding celebration of act 3, Balanchine created a fast trio for Wilde, Gertrude Tyven, and Leon Danelian, in which they were dressed as pages.

The three-act ballet was performed with only one intermission, following act 2. Nevertheless, its running time of one and three-quarter hours was still considered too long by critics, perhaps because the Ballet Russe administration thought fit to program it together with an entirely separate one-act ballet. Indeed, after *Raymonda*'s premiere, Wilde, Ruthanna Boris, and Nicholas Magallanes all reappeared to dance *Concerto Barocco*.

Perused today, the reviews seem as blinkered as the critical reception to *Night Shadow*. Anatole Chujoy, editor of the monthly *Dance News*, was one of the few critics to write about the production with perception. Chujoy would have seen the Mariinsky production in St. Petersburg. For him, *Raymonda* was "a superlative ballet," and its spectators needed to understand that it was the product of an aesthetic entirely different from the contemporary world of ballet: "Whether you stage a classic ballet, write about it, or just watch it, you must make up your mind whether you accept it as a definite art form withal [*sic*] its shortcomings and conventions, or reject it—approach, form, and content."

Rejected by the critics, *Raymonda* apparently excited the less tutored audiences who showed up on Saturday nights—the "popcorn" audiences, as the company called them. They gasped when the statue of the White Lady came to life in act 1. They delighted in booing the Saracen.

Raymonda's production values made it a difficult ballet to tour. It was performed only during Ballet Russe's longer stops. Soon the production began to dwindle. In February 1947, a year after the premiere, the *Herald-Tribune*'s Walter Terry reported that "generous cuts" had been made. Eventually only the festive Grand Pas Hongrois was retained as a freestanding piece; Wilde now took over one of the new solos that Balanchine had created for it. But Balanchine would return to Glazunov's score no fewer than three times over the next thirty years. In 1961, his *Raymonda Variations* for New York City Ballet was a showcase for Wilde and his final ballet made for her.

NO SAFETY NET

During a Ballet Russe rehearsal period, the White sisters played host to their father when he made a surprising but very welcome visit to New York. The reunion was masterminded by their brother Barney, who "realized that Mother had not really told us the truth," Nora said. Barney had written a letter to his siblings, decrying a "family divided." His wife Helen brought John White to New York and then went to stay with her son, who lived just outside the city.

The medium-height man with an abundance of wavy gray hair who appeared was not a complete stranger. Back in Ottawa, White had sent presents to his two youngest from time to time, and elder sister Bet had driven them to pay a quick thank-you visit. If it was now too late to construct the relationship they could and should have had, it was nevertheless a pleasant and comfortable stay for all three. Nora remembered taking the Manhattan bus with him; whenever a woman boarded, he'd get up and offer her his seat. Both White sisters were busy rehearsing, however, and couldn't spend too much time, so he went on sorties around the city by himself.

"What did you do today, Dad?" "Well, I walked up to 125th Street, then I went across the Park and then I went down to 42nd Street. Oh, it was wonderful. It was really interesting!" He spent four or five days with them, and in years to come they would see him whenever they could.

Eileen, who went to see her daughters perform in Boston and Montreal, also came down to New York from time to time, although she usually stayed in a hotel. She easily made her way around New York, but wasn't overly fond of the city, finding Ottawa more manageable. And as far as the natives were concerned—"I don't like these Americans much," she told Nora. "They smoke cigars and put their feet on the table."

Frequently the two sisters double-dated boys from the company after a Sunday night performance or when invited out by someones-who-knew-someone when they weren't working. They were together on the night in 1946 when Nora met her future husband Roger Shattuck, an author and a professor of French literature. He was then working for publisher Harcourt Brace. Nora was friendly with Harvey Shapiro, a poet and longtime *New York Times* editor. Shapiro was around the company, "madly in love," Nora said, with Tallchief, who was not yet married to Balanchine. "He used to write Maria poems on paper bags." Shapiro wanted to introduce Nora to Shattuck, and the two young men dropped in unannounced to City Center one evening, where Ballet Russe often rehearsed from seven to ten. Nora had been strenuously rehearsing *Rodeo* and was not feeling very presentable. Nevertheless, she fixed herself up, and together with her sister they accepted an invitation to hear Billie Holiday that same night at a jazz club on Fifty-Second Street. Holiday was late for her show, and while they waited, all four hungrily ingested such nibbles as the club offered. Finally the singer appeared, two large dogs in tow. Once she hit the stand with her combo, however, the Whites and their dates forgot hunger, thirst, and fatigue. After Holiday's set, the four went on to dinner.

There was an immediate spark between Nora and Shattuck. A serious relationship, however, was a difficult proposition while she remained on tour much of the year. They continued to see each other when circumstances permitted. Three years later, Nora retired from performing to become his wife, a marriage that lasted until he died in 2005.

Fifty years old in 1946, Sergei Denham was a Russian émigré whose love of the arts was avocational until he left his banking career and began his company together with choreographer Léonide Massine in 1938.

"Denham was terrible," Vida Brown said. She recalled his habit of bringing honored guests backstage to watch from the wings. Once he asked

Brown to slightly modify her position in a line of corps de ballet so that his guests would have a better view of the principal dancers onstage. She refused, since the audience would have seen her misaligned in a strict geometric formation. This did not go over well—"He didn't like me."

Neither White sister recalled Ballet Russe director Denham with fondness. Certainly their relationship with their boss did not become any easier after Nora became company head of the emerging dancer's union at the instigation of principal dancer Ruthanna Boris. She was something of an intellectual mentor to both White sisters. Years later she studied psychotherapy and became interested in the therapeutic possibilities of dance itself, but already in the 1940s she was absorbed into the widespread dissemination of psychological exploration. Today Nora describes her as "psychologically involved with everything." Rooming with her on tour, Nora recalled that Boris kept the bathroom light on and a typewriter at the ready. Awakened from a dream, she'd head straight to the typewriter to record what she could recall.

Boris was a decade older than Wilde. She had joined Ballet Russe in 1943; her future husband Frank Hobi joined two years later. Hobi was also intellectual. Boris "wanted me to be literary and knowledgeable," Nora recalled. "I probably had never talked to anybody like her before, and nobody like that had spoken to me." It was the beginning of a literary self-education that would accelerate after she married Shattuck. Wilde herself was acutely aware that many people of college age were receiving an education that she was not. She gratefully received both Hobi's and Boris's suggestions about which books to read, which museums to visit in cities on tour.

Nora found Boris a bit trying at times. "Ruthanna expected quite a bit of you." And she now expected Nora to take her place as dancers' advocate. Boris was herself involved, while Nora was already convinced of the need for a much more muscular union presence. She was popular with the dancers and with the musicians as well. Indeed, Nora described herself as a "kind of a mother figure to the orchestra players. Not really, but all these older men from Europe—they'd tell me all sorts of things. I'd listen. They did have difficulties."

Boris may have realized that Nora had already attracted Denham's roving eye and that perhaps it would give her some extra leverage. Denham "wanted to dance with me at parties," Nora recalled—company gatherings to which patrons and possible patrons were invited. The administration considered dancers' attendance a definite encouragement to charitable contribution, and it was mandatory. But abundant food and drink ensured their enthusiastic appearance. On one occasion a dinner invitation from Denham was conveyed to Nora via someone on the administrative staff: "You be very careful," she was advised by sister members of the ensemble. Nora thought it was Denham, rather than ballet master Frederic Franklin, who cast her as the Cowgirl in *Rodeo*, a favorite role for her and one in which she received particular critical praise.

Certainly, Nora had her union work cut out for her. The American Guild of Musical Artists (AGMA), into which the dancers' fledgling union was slotted, offered exceedingly lax protection at that time. In Los Angeles for *Song of Norway* in the summer of 1944, the dancers' salaries were paid for by the Light Opera companies of San Francisco and Los Angeles, which were jointly producing the musical. Ballet Russe took advantage of their freedom during the day to schedule rehearsals with Balanchine, who was creating *Danses Concertantes*. But they received no pay for these rehearsals. The dancers were resentful but at that point powerless.

Every once in a while in a major city Ballet Russe would put on all-Balanchine evening, frequently consisting of *Ballet Imperial, Danses Concertantes*, and *Concerto Barocco*. "We died!" Wilde recalled, her feet hurting her more than anything. All three ballets demanded pointe work that was more extensive than anything known in ballet to that time. Customarily a Ballet Russe triple bill included one ballet not on pointe but instead danced in character shoes, boots, or soft slippers. One of them was Fokine's 1910 *Scheherazade*, which remained a repertory staple in Denham's company. Wilde danced a harem musician and recalled the bacchanalian pounding she gave her metatarsals in the culminating, full-cast Bacchanal: "I didn't know about taking it easy."

But their task on the Balanchine nights was not made easier by the fact that their pointe shoes were frequently in parlous condition. Balanchine had insisted when he staged *Concerto Barocco* for the company in 1945 that after every five or so performances, each woman in the ensemble received an extra pair in her allotment from management. Yet on tour new shoes were frequently in scarce supply and the corps often told that an expected shipment hadn't arrived. The dancers resorted to stiffening their old shoes by spraying them with shellac and stuffing them with newspaper.

Nora did not believe the company's excuses and was convinced that this was just another instance of its pinching pennies. Denham himself was "making all kinds of money, and building a lake for his wife and his girls in Connecticut."

One time in Texas, where the company usually toured in December, it narrowly averted a work stoppage. They had just gone through a harrowing stretch, in which even the principal dancers slept in coach seats on all-night trips. The administration responded to the dancers' complaints with the explanation that sleepers were impossible to obtain due to priority given returning troops. Ruthanna Boris called AGMA in New York and told them they were not going to perform that night. They stayed at the train station and also threatened to cancel the balance of the tour if accommodations weren't improved. It didn't take much to mollify them, however. The administration offered to pay for a handful of club chairs in the lounge car to be placed at their disposal. Naturally, Danilova received one, as well as ballerina Nathalie Krassovska, who had been with the company since its inception in 1938, like Danilova, and ranked second to her in company prominence. To her surprise, Wilde found herself by consensus a lucky recipient of an individual chair after discussions about which corps members had the heaviest workload. "It was really nice of the company," Wilde recalled. "It was honest: 'Pat's in all three ballets.'"

Nora was initially bewildered by the fact that during company meetings on tour she could not organize a majority to approve resolutions for which she knew there was widespread support—ground rules about working hours, about days off, about traveling arrangements. Eventually she figured out that Denham was informed by spies in the company once she posted advance notice of a meeting. On occasion he suddenly appeared on tour and conducted private meetings with the dancers, threatening to take parts away if they approved a pending resolution. But once she'd gotten wise, she stopped calling meetings ahead of time, posting a notice only on the morning of the meeting pending. Progress picked up considerably. Nora considered AGMA a "hopeless place" in terms of advocating for the dancers; nevertheless, "they reacted once I got the thing organized."

Nevertheless, Denham directed threats to Nora that hit home: the many lead roles that Wilde danced could be retracted at any moment. She had no statutory right to them, since officially she remained a member only of the corps de ballet. Nora insisted through tears that she was speaking for the company and that personal considerations were immaterial. Their sessions across the negotiating table apparently dampened Denham's earlier affection.

Nora recalled with some incredulity that her mother "thought Mr. Denham was wonderful." Perhaps Denham's Continental manners apparently impressed her—he neither smoked cigars nor put his feet on the table. After Nora left Ballet Russe in 1948, Eileen on a visit to New York dropped in to see Denham. "Nora was such a lovely young woman when she first came," he told her. "But something happened to her, and she changed."

NEW VOICES

The 1946–47 season brought an influx of new choreographers into Ballet Russe and a series of interesting and expanding new roles for Wilde. Balanchine's marriage to Tallchief in the summer of 1946 also marked the end of his association with Ballet Russe. The company's perpetual touring was both an inconvenience for him and a detriment to maintaining the company in optimum condition. He and his longtime patron Lincoln Kirstein were now embarking on Ballet Society, a subscription-only organization in New York that would feature new works by him and other choreographers. For Ballet Society's first season he made four ballets—among them, *Divertimento* and *The Four Temperaments* are still performed.

In addition, that fall the Paris Opera offered him a six-month contract, to begin March 1, 1947. He would rehearse, stage, and create in the absence of ballet director Serge Lifar, Balanchine's old colleague from the Diaghilev company. Lifar had been relieved of his post after being accused of collaboration with the Nazis. Balanchine loved the prestige and the pedigree of the Paris Opera, its magnificent old theater, its enormous institutional resources. But before he left for Paris he also found time to choreograph *The Chocolate Soldier* on Broadway.

Sergei Denham cast a wide net for new Ballet Russe repertory; he was willing to commission a work from a twenty-six-year-old modern dancer, Valerie Bettis. Bettis choreographed for herself and a small group, but had never created anything for a ballet company before. Also in the pipeline was a piece by the concert dancer Phyllis Nahl, who gave herself the masculine stage name Antonio Cobos. Cobos's *The Mute Wife* had been a favorite repertory item for Wilde in the Marquis de Cuevas's company three years earlier.

Ruthanna Boris had already choreographed for summer resorts and on Broadway. Repeatedly she asked Denham if she could create a piece for his company, but he was resistant. "Why should I allow you—an unknown American—to choreograph?" At a party given by Richard Hammond of the Hammond Organ company, Boris was so upset about it that, most uncharacteristically, she burst into tears. Within a few days, she had a commission from Denham. Unbeknownst to Boris, Hammond had gone to bat for her. A director of the Hollywood Bowl association, he had insisted that a new work by Boris be seen during Ballet Russe's season there the following summer.

Boris envisioned a humorous little ballet performed to Gounod's venerable "Walpurgisnacht" music from *Faust.* Her *Cirque de Deux* drew parallels between the often-derided circusy nature of classical ballet virtuosity and the performance practices of actual circus acts. Boris herself and Leon Danelian were the headliners, and Frank Hobi and Wilde were their attendants.

Denham's acceptance remained equivocal; Wilde and her colleagues had to rehearse the ballet on their own time before he eventually put it on the company schedule. In New York, they worked at the Upper West Side ballet school owned by Audrey Hitchens, an Englishman who had partnered Pavlova in her company and frequently reminisced about the legendary ballerina. They continued to work together when Ballet Russe launched its tour later in the fall.

On February 16, 1947, Ballet Russe opened at City Center for a six-week season. Bettis's *Virginia Sampler* was given its first performance March 4. The ballet was about an American town at the time of the Revolution, through which a series of mysterious strangers passed. Music was by Leo Smit, who like Bettis was under thirty. In rehearsal she had a hard time getting the dancers to relax out of their regimented ballet technique. But finally she seemed to be satisfied. Unfortunately, the critics were not. Most considered *Virginia Sampler* an uneasy truce between two genres, and it left the repertory almost immediately. But Wilde loved her role—enjoyed it, in fact, almost more than anything else she danced with the company.

It gave her a real opportunity to act as well as dance. Wilde was the malevolent mother of Marie-Jeanne, trying to force her daughter to make a loveless but advantageous marriage. Both of them thought the lopsided stage relationship was hilarious: Marie-Jeanne was eight years older, and offstage it was she who was the voice of experience counseling Wilde. The choreography intrigued Wilde: Bettis gave her strong, sharp steps, entrusting her with the responsibility to maintain a flinty, domineering presence from her first entrance. Her back was kept ramrod-straight and authoritarian. Despite her youth, critics found her convincing.

In Cobos's *Madroños*, which premiered March 25, Wilde danced a solo with castanets, one of a suite of individual numbers to music by individual composers, united by a Spanish theme. Her own particular provenance was to be Moorish: she wore what in those days was a not particularly inflammatory blackamoor costume, complete with blackface makeup. Unlike *Virginia Sampler*, *Madroños* was liked by the critics and was included in the repertory every season over the next five years.

After closing in New York, the company began a tour of upstate New York, Canada, and New England. On April 1, they opened a ten-day season in Toronto, where Wilde injured her ankle in *Ballet Imperial* on the closing night. From there the company was proceeding to a week of one-night stands in no fewer than six different cities in New York and New Hampshire, before opening a week's season in Boston on April 21.

Wilde spent her Sunday off teaching Sonya Tyven her part in *Concerto Barocco*. Tyven and she were roommates. Usually, as Tyven recalled, "a lot of laughing went on" between the two of them. This day was only about work, but it went easily. Tyven had less natural ability than her sister Gertrude but a more surgically applied focus and intelligence. She learned fast—Wilde was an excellent teacher, Tyven recalled—and had already danced one of the corps parts. Then Wilde went to Frederic Franklin and explained the situation. He gave his consent.

Tallchief was soon leaving Ballet Russe to join Balanchine at the Paris Opera. In Boston, she was scheduled to dance the first ballerina role in

Concerto Barocco. Looking back, Wilde thinks it may have been Tallchief's debut in the role, and for all Tallchief knew, she was never going to dance *Barocco* again. Apparently she had her heart set on Wilde dancing the second lead.

In Boston, Wilde wanted to see Tyven dance with Tallchief. Arriving early at the theater, at the stage door she bumped into Tallchief, who told her, "You're going to dance." Tallchief insisted: "You can dance." To Wilde, Tallchief seemed to be channeling a stone-faced and implacable-voiced ancestral chief. Nevertheless, Wilde insisted that it was simply impossible. Tallchief replied that she herself had danced with a sprained ankle, which Wilde found dubious. There are of course different degrees of sprain, but it would be impossible to bend a severely sprained ankle. Tallchief had no choice but to accept the unavoidable—later, however, at New York City Ballet, they did dance the ballet together.

Boston proved to be a booby-trapped engagement. Wilde took advantage of her downtime to get the smallpox vaccination she needed to accompany the company on their upcoming visit to Mexico City. She had a terrible reaction: her fever spiked to 104 degrees, and an abscess on her leg opened. But since her ankle was better, she forced herself to go back onstage. In *Ballet Imperial*, she had to will herself not to collapse as she stood with the corps on the side of the stage, framing the principals.

She continued on to New York. The Whites were subletting their apartment and so went to stay with the Tyven sisters and their parents in Morningside Heights. Mrs. Tyven took one look at Wilde's leg and insisted that she go with her to the doctor. He diagnosed that the inoculation had precipitated an actual case of smallpox and that she should have been in the hospital. But he cleaned out the abscess and told her that she was now on the road to recovery.

On May 19, Ballet Russe opened in Mexico City. It was good to be back at the Palacio de Bellas Artes, but the three-week season was less fun for Wilde than her first visit, two years earlier, had been. Dysentery assailed the company, and she was filling in for a number of afflicted dancers. Wilde didn't remember running into Amesqua, who had squired her around two years earlier. However, she saw him once twenty years later, when he visited

New York and looked her up. He was now an executive with Coca-Cola in Mexico.

In late July 1947 Ballet Russe arrived in Los Angeles for a season at the Hollywood Bowl. Together with most of the company, Wilde stayed in one of many small, inexpensive hotels and motels near the Bowl. As she always did when in Los Angeles, Wilde went to take class with Nijinska at her studio on La Brea Avenue. Nijinska was always formidable, but welcoming to "Petrushka." She taught a very strong class that was worth the bus trip.

On August 1, day of the premiere of *Cirque de Deux*, Hammond brought Ramon Novarro and Judith Anderson backstage with him to congratulate Boris on bringing to fruition the ballet he had brokered.

Immediately after returning from Los Angeles, the company gathered in New York to rehearse for a two-week season at City Center opening September 7. One of its most illustrious members was gone: Marie-Jeanne had left the company. She would spend 1948 dancing first with Balanchine's Ballet Society and then with the emergent New York City Ballet when it opened in October before, once again, frustration or boredom hastened her departure.

Mary Ellen Moylan had returned, after spending the better part of the past two years dancing on Broadway, and with Balanchine's Ballet Society in its very short, intermittent seasons. Moylan provided a textbook demonstration of technical virtues as well as Balanchine style, inculcated in her by the master over several of her twenty-one years. "He loved her line," Wilde recalled. Moylan's legs were hyperextended, which meant that her knee swayed back in the socket, creating a very decorative curve to the supporting leg in arabesque. Unusual at the time, it is privileged in ballet today even though it creates equilibrium issues, shifting weight back toward the ballerina's heels. Mimi Paul, a New York City Ballet star of the 1960s, remembered that the first words Balanchine spoke to her were "Oh, you have legs like Mary Ellen Moylan." Moylan also had beautiful feet, always a prize attribute in ballet. Balanchine, however, was more concerned with strength and articulate accent; through hard work, Moylan was able to give him exactly what he was looking for.

Hyperextended women often have trouble turning, but Moylan's pirouettes and fouettés were secure. She had a beautiful classical *développé*: her leg was turned out, and she extended it with grandeur and finesse. Her classical precision impressed Wilde: if Moylan extended her leg forward in a *tendu*, it explicitly followed the body's central axis, directly in line with her nose.

Wilde thought that Moylan's *Ballet Imperial* was a pinnacle of Balanchine expression. Over the course of its forty-five minutes the ballerina has to do nearly everything possible in the academic syllabus, and the first thing she does is often called her most difficult hurdle. To a Tchaikovsky piano cadenza, she performs a series of turns with her working leg skating flat on the floor, punctuated several times by an abrupt full stop that often turns into a bumpy skid. Not only did Moylan's legs look gorgeous as they whirled around, however, but she also seemed to be stopping only when she chose to, completely, indeed imperially at her own discretion. Momentum, control, beauty: all were espoused in her performance.

Moylan had the cleanness and lack of mannerism Balanchine was pursuing in his attempts to forge an American classical ballet. Dancing Danilova's role in *Danses Concertantes*, Moylan did not have the same effervescence. Moylan was "pure dance," Nora recalled. Unlike Danilova, "she was not expressing herself all over the place onstage." Both White sisters enjoyed watching, learning from, and working alongside both contrasting exponents.

On September 10, the day of the New York premiere of *Cirque de Deux*, Danelian accidentally put his hand through a glass door. Hobi danced his role that night, and Stanley Zampakos took Hobi's role as Wilde's page companion. The ballet was well received and stayed in Ballet Russe's repertory for the next decade. A mishap in one of the early performances puzzled Wilde but proved hilarious for the two leads. In keeping with the circus theme, Boris and Danelian performed a pas de deux on a moving turntable that evoked the center ring. It was Wilde and Hobi's duty to wheel them from place to place on the stage, securing the turntable with a metal dowel with rubber cap. One night they were transporting the turntable when suddenly and inexplicably the rubber piece fell off. "Frank, we lost our rubber!" Wilde whispered. The turntable started to shake with Boris's and Danelian's laughter. Wilde was stumped about what exactly was so funny—"Very innocent I was"—and remained so for some time thereafter.

14

ANNIVERSARY

SEASON

At the Ballet Russe "everybody was guarding their roles," Wilde recalled, defending them against the covetous advances of rival or juniors. Wilde herself joined the ranks of the proactive lobbyists in the fall of 1947, when she lobbied Sergei Denham for the chance to dance the first ballerina role in *Concerto Barocco.* She had been dancing the second lead for two years—opposite Marie-Jeanne, Tallchief, and now, after their departure, with Boris and Moylan. Both women are paired throughout the first and third movements, but only the first lead danced the long supported adagio of the middle Largo movement.

Wilde wrote Denham on October 15, 1947: "You will I am sure remember me speaking to you about my dancing the first part in *Concerto Barocco.* . . . You can imagine how sadly I felt when I learned that someone else was to do it before me. . . . I want you to know that when I signed my contract I didn't ask for anything. But when I spoke to Mr. Franklin he told me I would have all my last year's parts and the number of times I would do *Barocco* depended entirely on what Ruthanna had to do in the new ballets."

Wilde's hunger for the role was such that she apparently was taking some creative license with the truth: "I took over the part in Mexico," she wrote, claiming that it had been one of the biggest successes of her season with Balanchine two years earlier. But *Barocco* was not performed during their Mexico City season. Perhaps Wilde had learned the first role as she rehearsed the second ballerina lead. Certainly by the time she wrote to Denham she knew the longer role inside and out.

"I know that you are a very ambitious girl," Denham wrote back, "and nothing would please me more than to satisfy your ambitions because you are a good dancer and deserve good parts." He pledged to "do everything possible which will not hurt any other member of our organization."

"I of course understand that it is Ruthanna's ballet now," Wilde had written, but Boris's repertory was enormous and certainly relinquishing some performances would not have left her bereft. Doubtless Balanchine, who had just returned from Paris, was consulted and gave his consent. That season Wilde was given the role she coveted. Sonya Tyven now an experienced alternate in Wilde's original role, danced opposite her.

In the spring of 1948, both Nora and Tyven went to Paris together, their first visit to Europe. Later, Tyven's future husband Robert Lindgren, also a member of Ballet Russe, joined them. Tyven went back to work when the new season began; Nora, however, never returned to the company. She loved Paris and found work with Roland Petit's Ballets de Paris, also touring with them to London and to Europe. But a major reason she remained was that Roger Shattuck was there. He went to Paris to devote time to his own writing, also found work as a journalist, and then was hired by the film division of UNESCO. He found inexpensive living space in the back of a church on the rue de Lille on the Left Bank; Nora joined him there when she was not on the road with Petit's company.

FOR THE TENTH ANNIVERSARY of the Ballet Russe de Monte Carlo's debut in 1938, Denham planned to return to the Metropolitan Opera, where they'd made their U.S. debut. It was a grander stage and a more prestigious venue than City Center, but also more expensive to rent. Cincinnati's Julius Fleischman was a principal backer of the company, but Denham was nevertheless perpetually on the hunt for patrons, cultivating celebrities whenever he could. Joy Williams recalled finding herself a guest with him at Mary Pickford's Pickfair in Beverly Hills, where Pickford and husband Buddy Rogers invited them for lunch.

More money must have been forthcoming. Not only did the company open a four-week season September 18 at the Met on Thirty-Ninth Street, but ticket prices were also kept low so as not to alienate the audience they drew at popularly priced City Center uptown on Fifty-Fifth Street. Direct commercial sponsorship made its way to the Met stage in the form of *Quelques Fleurs*, Ruthanna Boris's second ballet for the company. The famous French perfumer Houbigant, which once had supplied perfumes to Marie Antoinette, was promoting its 1912 perfume by that name and agreed to pay for a new ballet using that title. Theoretically, Boris did not have to make a direct allusion to the Houbigant product, but she was careful to work in a perfume motif. Wilde was one of three dancing perfumes presented as seduction tool to a lovelorn Countess by a canny alchemist. Department store windows hawked both perfume and ballet, which critics received with tolerance.

For the Met season, Denham augmented the ranks of the company and also recruited several high-profile guest stars. Opening night introduced the return of Alicia Markova and Mia Slavenska, both of whom had been prominent on the company's original roster. Together with Danilova and Krassovska they starred in Anton Dolin's *Pas de Quatre*, a reconstruction of a piece made in London in the summer of 1845 for four of the greatest ballerinas of the day: Marie Taglioni, Fanny Cerrito, Carlotta Grisi, and Lucille Grahn.

It was choreographed by Jules Perrot, Grisi's husband, who had arranged her solos in *Giselle* at its 1841 premiere. After Cesare Pugni's musical score was rediscovered at the British Museum during the 1930s, first Keith Lester and then Dolin devised speculative reconstruction of what this epochal collaboration might have been like.

An undertone of one-upmanship between the four principals in *Pas de Quatre* is always present, and was certainly more present when the four contemporary impersonators were themselves as renowned as the original quartet. Danilova and Markova were friends and colleagues dating back to the Diaghilev company. Danilova and Slavenska had been fiercely rivalrous during the four years, 1938–42, that they jointly danced with Denham's Ballet Russe. Krassovska was a lovely dancer but younger as well as less high-powered and less high-profile. A certain amount of jockeying went on in rehearsal and even onstage—there it would have blended seamlessly into the choreographed byplay between the four.

For Markova, the most renowned living exponent of the Romantic ballet was dancing the role of Marie Taglioni, perhaps most celebrated of all four of the original quartet. Taglioni is credited with establishing in 1832's *La Sylphide* the template of the Romantic ballerina. Now, without question, Taglioni was the most important of the four in Markova's estimation. "No, no, no!" she exclaimed when Slavenska as Grisi followed Dolin's instruction that she cross in front of her. "Darling, after all," Markova explained to Slavenska, "Taglioni would never go behind people. I must go in front, always."

Pas de Quatre had first been seen in the United States when Dolin staged it for Ballet Theatre in 1941. In the *New York Times*, John Martin complained that the four ballerinas on the 1948 opening had offered "as heavy, farcical, and styleless a presentation as the little piece has had within memory."

As far as Wilde was concerned, however, each ballerina characterized without undue exaggeration. Neither Slavenska nor Danilova was particularly known for Romantic ballet, although both had considerable experience with it. Each was emphatically present onstage, whereas Romanticism pivots on the evocation of something ephemeral. But both simulated as much stylistic accuracy as was needed.

"Miss Glamour Puss," Wilde called Slavenska, entertaining in her mind the possibility of the Yugoslavian ballerina walking onstage and tossing her mink coat to the ground. Slavenska was always a technical virtuoso, while Markova, even at her technical peak, pursued the more illusionistic concealment of effort. Wilde admired Slavenska's arabesque: each segment of her legs had some type of presence, individual length and articulation. Presenting herself assertively in space, holding extended balances when called for, Slavenska gave the spectator ample opportunity to study her admirable structure.

As the Met run continued, Gertrude Tyven alternated with Slavenska as Grisi and Wilde was given the opportunity to dance Krassovska's role of Grahn. Grisi and Grahn were each younger than Cerrito and Taglioni. The evocation of 1845 and the reality of 1948 meshed well. "I didn't have to use too much imagination," Wilde said. "I was definitely the junior member. I was the jumper, buoyant, and I was a ballerina, but they were more of a ballerina."

Wilde was very nervous before a performance in which she again replaced Krassovska but the rest of the opening-night star lineup was intact. After the performance she went out with friends and they celebrated over beers. Walking Wilde home, they were in high spirits as they stood around outside her walk-up on Second Avenue and Fifty-Sixth Street. Suddenly appearing on a low-story balcony in a new apartment building across the street were celebrated elders Dolin, Markova, Danilova, and Franklin. "You go home!" they called down good-naturedly.

AT THIRTY-SEVEN, Markova had lived any number of professional lives since joining the Diaghilev company at age fourteen in 1924. Born Lilian Alicia Marks, she was sole support for her mother and three sisters after business reversals led her father to kill himself. Markova became the first British ballerina to achieve international renown. She had danced every conceivable genre of ballet in every conceivable venue, from opera house to cinema palace. But it was in the Romantic ballet that she reigned supreme in Western ballet. Romantic style's emphasis on concealment of effort had by now somewhat degenerated into diminishment of athletic expenditure. In the process of her becoming ever more quintessentially cloudlike, steps began to be elided or downsized. As guest with Ballet Russe, Markova repeated her legendary performance of Giselle. Wilde was Moyna, handmaiden of the malevolent Myrtha, with whom Giselle faces off in the spectral forest of act 2. Onstage, watching Markova, Wilde was admiring, but also, "I'd be thinking, Come on, you can get that leg up one inch higher!"

By now, Markova's colleagues were not entirely sure how she stayed in shape to dance. She didn't seem to attend any organized class, but for some time was known to have taken private lessons from Vincenzo Celli, whom Wilde recalled being backstage at the Met. In *The Making of Markova*, biographer Tina Sutton seems pleased to have discovered in the ballerina's diaries evidence that she frequently went into the studio to work by herself. Certainly she didn't perform a full warm-up onstage before a performance. As far back as 1941, when she was starring with Ballet Theatre, Markova made do with a warm-up in her dressing room, according to colleague John Taras.

At Ballet Russe's founding in 1938, Markova had been a full member, as she later was with Ballet Theatre—going on every tour, every train and bus ride. But now she provided Wilde's first glimpse of the isolated trajectory of the international guest star. "She was always perfectly pleasant," Wilde recalled, "but I don't think she spent any extra time around. She came in, she did it—that was it." Wilde observed the perquisites of balletic superstardom in the person of a stage manager who knocked on Markova's door and brought her to the stage.

Markova believed that not aiding her partner's lifts with the customary slight spring off the floor made her look more ethereal. It certainly made her feel much heavier to many of her partners than ballerinas whose actual weight was considerably greater. Although their relationship was tempestuous, Dolin seemed completely acclimated to her quirks. He had partnered her since she was a teenager with Diaghilev, and "he was still partnering her fantastically," Wilde recalled. "He just plucked her up. . . . It was smooth and lovely, and she looked as light as a feather."

That season, Léonide Massine, around whom Denham's company had been organized a decade earlier, returned to the company to revive *Seventh Symphony* and *Rouge et Noir*, which the company had premiered in its first seasons. They were two examples of his "symphonic ballets," which began in 1933 with *Les Présages* to arouse controversy. Some in the classical music camp considered heretical his use of "serious" music, never intended for ballet. Massine matched the size and scope of the orchestral design to appropriately weighty themes. To the Beethoven, the gods gave birth to humanity, frolicked in the heavens, and then, disgusted with man's vagaries, finally decreed Armageddon. *Rouge et Noir* was set to Shostakovich's First.

Henri Matisse designed unitards—which remained, in 1938, a daring and novel sheathing of the dancer's body—in four different colors, animating ensembles out of which emerged a persistent theme of oppression. Both works seemed particularly relevant to the Europe of the late 1930s.

Ten years later, in *Seventh Symphony*, Wilde danced a soloist role in the third movement Scherzo, led by Markova and Igor Youskevitch re-creating their original roles amid an interlude unfolding in the empyrean. Wilde was astonished to see the way Markova's way with a jump could still be unsurpassed. Here the senior ballerina performed double *saut de basques*, turning not once but twice consecutively in the air, one leg pulled to her knee in *passé*. Whatever Markova's training methodology, "when she wanted to she really could."

Wilde's later career as artistic administrator and company director could be said to have begun now, at age twenty, with *Rouge et Noir*. Massine asked her to help reconstruct and rehearse the blue ensemble. As she had with *Seventh Symphony*, Wilde learned the choreography watching the silent footage Massine made of most of his works. The choreographer himself did not reliably remember the work. Nor, as it turned out, did original cast members brought back into the rehearsal studio to help. Wilde found herself in the middle of disputes between dancers who remembered what they themselves did and had discounted what was going on simultaneously across the stage. "That's how things often work out," Wilde says today. "Nobody notices or remembers what the other side of the stage is doing." Wilde was younger than any of them but, empowered by Massine, she finally imposed a definitive compromise. "You may both be right, but this is the way we're going to do it!"

"I adored Massine," Wilde recalled. "He was demanding, but not in a nasty way." In rehearsal his movement enchanted, as it had when she and Nora had been onstage at the Met for his *Petrushka* six years earlier. Wilde couldn't forget watching him show Robert Lindren something in *Seventh Symphony*. "It was mesmerizing." Massine's hands truly seemed to be speaking.

Onstage in the ballet, she was a member of the corps in three different and distinctly colored movements, requiring complex layering of multiple tights, as well as lightning-quick changes of slippers lined up in the wings. Wilde "got a big lift working with Massine," Nora said. "She gave me the feeling that he had meant quite a bit to her."

Reviewing the company's four weeks at the Met, Anatole Chujoy declared in *Dance News*, "It has been a long time since Ballet Russe de Monte Carlo has had as thrilling and glamorous a season." Fall 1948 was altogether a high-water mark for ballet in Manhattan. At City Center, the Paris Opera ballet made its New York debut immediately prior to the inaugural season there of New York City Ballet on October 11. Balanchine would have certainly been willing to stay on permanently in Paris; had Lifar not been cleared of collaborationist charges, there might never have been a New York City Ballet. As it was, however, his choreography for Ballet Society so impressed Morton Baum, head of City Center, that he invited Ballet Society to become its resident ballet company. Initially, it performed during 1948–49 in the New York City Opera as well as giving its own ballet programs on Monday and Tuesday nights during the season.

As important as Balanchine was to Wilde, she did not think of joining his new company. Ex–Ballet Russe colleagues Tallchief, Marie-Jeanne, Magallanes, Hobi, Beatrice Tompkins, and Herbert Bliss had joined. But the company's employment was so sparse that when a long layoff loomed n 1949, Balanchine arranged for Tallchief to spend time with Ballet Theatre as guest artist.

The body of the company was School of American Ballet students for whom in 1946 Ballet Society had been their first step onto the professional stage. "No one was really professional in Ballet Society," Pat McBride recalled. "There were just a few. They just took, in a very generous way, the top class. When I began I'm not even sure I was in the top class. I was probably in the intermediate." Much of what Wilde saw seemed amateurish to her.

On the long tour that followed Ballet Russe's month at the Met, Wilde made her debut in the lead role of Agnes de Mille's *Rodeo*, most frequently danced in recent years by Nora as well as Vida Brown, who now had also left the company. During the Met season de Mille herself had danced the Cowgirl, as she had when Ballet Russe gave the first performance in 1942.

Rodeo gave Wilde to chance to excel at both bronco-bucking slapstick and pathos.

Markova and Dolin were again prominent guests when Ballet Russe returned to City Center for a month's season on February 21. By this time, Wilde was growing actively disenchanted with the company, not only because of the onus of touring but also because lack of regular classes for weeks on end made her feel that her technique was not improving.

Joining Nora in Paris beckoned as a possibility. Nora was studying there with Olga Preobrajenska, a former prima ballerina at the Mariinsky in St. Petersburg, and with Nora Kiss, a much younger woman who had danced in Balanchine's Les Ballets 1933. Nora highly recommended both teachers. In addition Paris was home to ex-Imperial ballerinas Mathilde Kschessinskaya and Lubov Egorova, as well as many other distinguished instructors with small schools.

What disturbed Wilde most about her present situation with Ballet Russe was Denham's infatuation with dancer Nina Novak, who had joined during the 1947–48 season. Although Wilde's repertory wasn't directly threatened, Novak's rise brought about a palpable decline in company morale. Novak soon became ubiquitous, dancing lead roles she was suited for and roles for which she was not. Franklin's authority as chief ballet master was undermined. Wilde said that Novak was "strong, but she did not have a good line at all. There was something not very classical about her. Her movement was not refined." Many critics agreed.

Novak's relationship with Denham played out in front of the eyes of the company. When Denham traveled with it, he and Novak shared one of the private parlors at the end of the railroad car. Denham's elegant and gracious wife Valentine, who had previously frequently visited the company on tour, was now abruptly not to be seen.

15

PARIS, 1949

Decisions came easily to Wilde. After a season in Montreal following City Center, Wilde decided that she would leave Ballet Russe and join Nora in Paris. It was April 1949, and she was twenty years old. Wilde traveled third class on the *Île de France*, one of the great old transatlantic liners newly refitted after World War II. The crossing was rough, guide ropes a precaution on every deck. She once saw the wind whip off a passenger's eyeglasses as he stepped out of the dining room into the open air.

Wilde moved into the Hôtel de Lille at 40 rue de Lille on the Left Bank, one block away from the Seine, down the street from Nora and Roger Shattuck. Nora took her to dinner the night she arrived. After a year in Paris, Nora's French was better than Wilde's, but not perfect. "I ordered *beurre coquille* and waited for the scallops to come!" Nora recalled. Both sisters had a good laugh when the dab of butter arrived.

Nora was performing with Roland Petit's Ballets de Paris, a new company formed by the twenty-five-year-old choreographer in 1948. She had toured with them throughout Europe and Great Britain; now the company was settled into a long season at the Théâtre Marigny on the Champs-Élysées. The repertory featured works by Petit staring his future wife Zizi Jeanmaire and Colette Marchand. Both young women had ballet training, but both were the talk of Paris as they threw themselves with alacrity into Petit's raffish, chic, flamboyant creations. "Le legs" Marchand romped, strutted, and cartwheeled her way through Petit's *L'Oeuf à la coque* as a chick being hatched. Jeanmaire was also long-legged but less beautifully proportioned. However, Petit's suggestion that she cut her hair to make her neck look longer resulted in a world-famous bob that she wore for the rest of her life. Also, for the next thirty years she would iconically perform Petit's risqué *Carmen*, which she premiered earlier in 1949.

Making the season even more star-studded was the participation of Margot Fonteyn, who had taken a leave from London's Royal Ballet. She revitalized herself dancing *Les Demoiselles de la Nuit*, latest chapter in the long series of ballets about cats, their particular grace seemingly an irresistible parallel to ballet dancers'. It was created especially by Petit for Fonteyn, who was enjoying a respite from austerity-plagued London.

Ballets de Paris featured works by other choreographers as well. When a substitution was needed in Massine's *Le Beau Danube*, Nora recommended her sister to Petit. Wilde had danced a minor role in the ballet all through Ballet Russe. Now she danced one of the leads: the young girl whose Hussar fiancé dallies with his old flame, the Street Dancer.

Petit and his company were welcoming. It was international: besides Fonteyn, there were a number of other British dancers, and in addition to Nora, ex–Ballet Russe colleague Joy Williams. It was blissful for Wilde, almost immediately after arriving, to be working, being paid, dancing in one of the top theaters in Paris, member of a company with cachet. It was "just a perfect thing to have happen at that moment."

An entire generation of late-Imperial ballerinas had fled to France after the Revolution and were teaching there, mostly in Paris. Balanchine had advised Wilde to study with Lubov Egorova: "Mr. B. always said that she was the most kinetic." George Skibine, premier danseur in both U.S. and European companies, recalled that in 1947 Balanchine wanted to bring Egorova to New York to teach at his school. Perhaps Egorova, almost seventy by then, did not want to be transplanted.

But Nora had been studying with Olga Preobrajenska, and once more Wilde followed her older sister's precedent. Egorova may have been Balanchine's favorite, but Preobrajenska's class "was fast," Wilde's Ballet Russe colleague Vida Brown recalled, "much more like Balanchine." Brown had studied with both ex–Imperial ballerinas immediately before World War II. It was Preobrajenska who had produced Balanchine's "baby ballerinas" Baronova and Toumanova.

They did things differently in Paris. At the Salle Wacker, an old warren of dance studios, men and women shared the same dressing room but took turns going in to change. Wilde took a morning class that was mostly professionals, including a number of dancers from the Opera. They would invite Preobrajenska to their performances and solicit comments the next morning. At age eighty, Preobrajenska was tiny, with a body that was "all pulled together." She wasn't moving around much, although she could still alight on the piano bench or a stool to keep a watchful eye over her class.

When Petit's season closed, Nora left with Roger to travel through Italy and the south of France. Then he went to visit a college friend in Marseilles who was now the U.S. consulate there. Wilde joined her sister for ten days in the town of Sète on the Mediterranean, where a friend of Roger's named Baucion, an artist who was a veteran of the Resistance, had friends with property.

Sète sits on a spit of land that faced out to the Mediterranean and inland from what is called a lake but more closely resembled numerous backwater pools. The house they'd been lent was high in the hills, overlooking the sea. The Whites wandered down a dirt path to the village to shop, and to swim. The owners of the cottage were wine importers who lived in town. They brought the Whites bottles of an Algerian vintage that was unexpectedly potent. Weight-conscious as always, they allowed themselves one glass each at lunch and wondered why they nevertheless felt so sleepy.

They decided to take a tiny train that took them up into the Pyrenees mountains, the high country where wild horses run. Back in Sète, they left for Marseilles, where they stayed briefly with Roger and his friend. Attending a bullfight there, Wilde was as always fascinated, but for Nora her first bullfight was more than enough to satisfy curiosity. All three got on a train, dropping Nora and Roger off at a resort. Wilde stayed on until the town of San Raphael beckoned to her. She found a rooming house outside town, and called her sister to let her know where she was. Soon she and Roger joined Wilde there: in the interim they had decided to get married.

Back in Paris, Wilde found a letter from Sergei Denham, written as Ballet Russe contract renewals approached. She had apparently told the company that she was leaving only for the following season. In any case, this was Denham's interpretation, and sufficient separation for him to express regret. He was "personally . . . very sorry to let you go." Wilde herself never felt that he had greatly appreciated her, but then dancers rarely, if ever, feel sufficiently appreciated. And despite all the solo and principal roles he had given her, he had never promoted her out of the corps. She never went back to the company.

Having just settled into Paris, and living on a meager budget, Wilde did not return to America when Nora and Roger were married August 20 at a country inn near Windsor, Vermont. Elder sister Bet was now renting a nearby farm with a woman, Pinky, whom she'd met in the Red Cross transport; after the war, both divorced their husbands. Pinky's family had some money, and her ex-husband was an eye doctor; she didn't work. Bet, however, managed the stables at a private school in Windsor. They did most of the arranging of Nora's wedding, and Eileen footed the bill. It was a simple outdoor ceremony with only family present. Eileen never particularly liked Pinky, who both drank and expected to be waited on. But she accepted Bet's relationship. Neither Nora nor Roger, however, would have ever dared tell either of their parents that they had been living together in Paris.

Also visiting Paris from New York that summer had been New York City Ballet's Tanaquil Le Clercq, together with Betty Nichols, who had attended School of American Ballet and then danced in Ballet Society as well as on Broadway. They were naturally curious to see the Ballets de Paris. "We thought it was charming," Nichols recalled about *Carmen*. "We were not shocked, but—'Well, that's French!'" Wilde herself wondered just how much French the American dance public was ready for. That was why, footloose as she was, she decided to turn down Petit's invitation to accompany the company when it made its U.S. debut that fall. As it turned out, U.S. critics dismissed the frothy repertory, but the dancers were acclaimed.

For Wilde an ad hoc existence had its charms after years of regimentation and perpetual movement. It crossed her mind that Nora and she had blazed a White family trail into the Old World. She knew of only one other family member to have visited Europe: eldest brother Lester. He'd gone as a member of the all-star Canadian hockey team in the early 1930s. They competed in Central Europe and Scandinavia, where he got "the thrill of his life," dancing with famous skater and, later, movie star Sonya Henie.

All around Wilde's hotel were cafés where she hung out with people her own age. A young writer who lived above her introduced her to art students at the Beaux Arts academy. Their routine seemed casual, unlike what her life had been. "They were not getting to class on time, I don't think," at least early in the morning. With them she didn't feel like an accomplished artist, but rather a junior member of their claque of worldly savants or would-be candidates.

Often she would spend the rest of the day after class with dancer friends from Salle Wacker who lived in nearby Montmartre. Sometimes they'd go out to dinner and she'd be out past the time that buses ran. But walking back to the Left Bank through the Tuileries gardens at night was not a problem.

The Tuileries connects the Louvre, seat of the Bourbon monarchy, to the vast Place de la Concorde, where those rulers met their demise on the guillotine. Wilde was there by day as well. She frequently visited the Louvre or the Jeu de Paume in the garden itself bordering the Place. Named for the tennis courts the building housed when it was built in 1861, it was now home to a fabulous collection of modern art.

At Salle Wacker Wilde also took class with Nora Kiss. She too was a very popular teacher who numbered among her regular students dancers from the Opera. Unlike Preobrajenska, Kiss hadn't been a celebrated performer and, as usually happens in such a case, her class was not imprinted with her own performing personality.

Back at the turn of the twentieth century, Preobrajenska and her colleagues on the Imperial stage had been adopting as many virtuoso tricks as they could from the Italians, who startled audiences with their bravura during frequent guest appearances in Russia.

Preobrajenska's class inevitably ended with fouetté turns. She wanted her students to whip themselves into a whirlwind—"to fouetté forever!" as if the cheering audience were still sitting in front of them. Kiss demanded a more methodical dissection of the step. In her class, fouettés were executed accompanied by a slow waltz. The extended leg's turnout had to be strictly maintained. Keeping the supporting leg longer in plié meant that great control was necessary.

Wilde herself sometimes taught fouettés that way, "and it kills them!" she said in 2009, when she was still an active guest teacher. "Whereas everybody can do fast fouettés."

Most of the time, Wilde was "living on nothing," cooking on a hotplate in her room. But occasional work did come her way. She had no phone, but there were always people coming to Studio Wacker recruiting dancers for short jobs. A woman that choreographed for the Opera was also frequently staging things in surrounding provincial cities, sometimes mixed bills of singers and dancers. Whatever was in the offing, Wilde was always available: "anything to get some money." For several days, she danced in a production number on a movie soundstage. She didn't know much about it and never saw the completed film.

Wilde received an exciting invitation from Nicholas Beriozoff, dancer and choreographer, who had known her in the Marquis de Cuevas's company. He was now chief ballet master with London's Metropolitan Ballet, a small company recently established with his teenage daughter Svetlana as leading ballerina. Svetlana was already known as something very special: Pat McBride recalled her visiting the School of American Ballet. "She came and just did a kind of trial class. She was absolutely ravishing." Watching was Ninette de Valois, director of the Royal Ballet, where Beriosova would later become one of its most celebrated ballerinas.

Beriozoff was Lithuanian, but his daughter was born in the United States and was an American citizen. The Metropolitan was booked for a tour of Holland beginning October 26, and then a London season at the People's Palace in the East End, but Beriosova had to go back to the States. She didn't have a green card, and was required to leave Britain periodically. Therefore the Metropolitan needed a principal dancer. Wilde went to London for a week's rehearsals. There was a lot to learn: the company's repertory was rich and diverse. The company loaned her an apartment. Her first morning there she woke up to find that she couldn't see across her room. Her first panicked reaction: fire! But it was only a window left open, through which fog now permeated her room. Fog occluded the streets as well; she was hard-pressed to find the local Underground station.

In London Wilde studied with Vera Volkova. An émigré from the USSR, Volkova was one of the first students of Agrippina Vaganova, immediately after the Revolution. Vaganova was then teaching privately—some years before becoming the dominant influence in Soviet ballet instruction. Volkova's class seemed modern. Her combinations weren't long and heavy and her preferred style economical. Volkova became and remained one of Wilde's favorite teachers, so much so that she still took class with her after she was no longer performing.

During much of Metropolitan Ballet's tour, they were based in the Hague, taking bus trips to surrounding towns. They played a coliseum that had just hosted the circus—and smelled like it. Then they returned to London for their two-week season, opening November 21. On the modern side, Wilde starred in *Design with Strings*, created in a Balanchinian manner by American John Taras for the company a year earlier. An important part of the repertory were works by Andrée Howard, one of the pioneer choreographers of British ballet; she choreographed Bizet's newly rediscovered *Symphony in C* a year before Balanchine.

Wilde was also White Swan Odette in act 2 of *Swan Lake*. The full ballet was now performed by London's Royal Ballet, but the excerpted lakeside act, containing the famous adagio, was all that most Western companies then performed. Wilde's debut as Swan Queen was strongly colored by memories of Danilova, whose adagio she had studied as she stood posed at the side of the stage in the corps de ballet, sometimes one of the four "little swans" and sometimes one of the four waltzing "big ones."

Danilova created an aura, an atmosphere. "She was never very soft about anything she did," Wilde recalled, "but she filled the time luxuriously. She was rather sensuous without being sexy." When Prince Siegfried enclosed her in his arms, "she was regal and at the same time there was a feeling of warmth."

Wilde liked the Metropolitan very much, but she returned to Paris with money still owed her from Cecilia Blatch, the Metropolitan's British patroness. Wilde soon discovered that the company owed money everywhere. The Metropolitan closed for good at the end of 1949.

But in Paris Wilde received a message from Nora: Balanchine was looking for her. He was going to London to stage *Ballet Imperial*. She was simply to find him in London. A summons from Balanchine was something to be heeded: she came back to London and stayed with a friend, Olwyn Vaughan, whose husband was company photographer for the Metropolitan Ballet. Vaughan owned a restaurant in St. James Place, Le Petit Club Français, which was popular for after-theater dining; the food was good, few London restaurants were open as late, and grocery shopping was still governed by rationing. Wilde enjoyed the artists and performers who flocked to it, as well as its cachet as a former hangout for exiled members of the French Resistance during World War II.

Wilde bought a ticket for *Ballet Imperial*'s April 5 premiere at the Royal Opera House in Covent Garden. She found Balanchine, and they talked in the Crush Bar during the intermission. *Ballet Imperial* had not gone particularly well. As a rule, Wilde found Fonteyn delightful onstage and off: they frequently took class together with Volkova. But it was the first and, as it turned out, the only Balanchine ballet Fonteyn ever danced, and it was a trial by fire. In Wilde's recollection, Fonteyn fell three times on that opening night, once even when she was supported by her frequent partner Michael Somes. Nevertheless, the reception for the dancers and for Balanchine had been rapturous. But Balanchine didn't say anything about the performance. He cut to the chase: he wanted her to join his eighteen-month-old company. It had just finished a very successful five-week season at City Center. It was scheduled to make its London debut at Covent Garden in July.

Wilde was at first reluctant. She told him how much she loved living in Europe. "Yes, I know, I love Europe, too," he said. But he asked her to "come back. See your mother. Rehearse, and then come with us to London." She would sign a contract, but he made it clear that if she wasn't happy, she was free after London to make other plans.

Wilde was flattered that Balanchine seemed to recognize that she was no longer the teenager he'd taken to Mexico five years earlier. He was "offering me a place and an opportunity in his own company, and at the same time giving me the respect to say that well, maybe I wouldn't like it." Translated to the culinary terms that Balanchine himself liked to employ, she would have paraphrased his offer this way: "I'd like you to taste the hors d'oeuvres, and if you don't like it you don't have to eat the whole meal!" Before they returned to their seats, she had accepted.

16

ROYAL

OPERA HOUSE

Paris was a large city that had come to feel to Wilde like a small town. She was sorry to be leaving, but as Balanchine had made clear, after the London engagement she would be free to return if she chose. In New York Wilde would have to find a place to live, but in the meantime she could stay with her sister. Nora and Roger were living on Stanton Street on the Lower East Side. Roger was again working in publishing.

Her first order of business was ballet class. As soon as she was back in New York, she went up to the School of American Ballet at Madison Avenue and Fifty-Ninth Street, which was now home as well to New York City Ballet. At the barre were any number of former Ballet Russe colleagues who, like Wilde, were now joining Balanchine's company. They recognized that their old troupe had become something of a sinking ship. Although it still employed many fine dancers, Ballet Russe was embarked on a steady decline. Over the remaining decade-plus of its existence, it would play New York only rarely.

Wilde found a cold-water flat at 39 First Avenue, just above Houston Street, a studio with separate kitchen. The toilet was down a hall, shared with the other apartment on the floor. She showered at the school or at the theater. Primitive as it was, the price was right, renting for $18 per month.

Her rehearsal salary was $45 a week for a period of up to five weeks, and after that half of her $100 weekly performance salary.

Rehearsals for New York City Ballet's London debut began June 12, in preparation for their July 10 opening at the Royal Opera House in Covent Garden. New York City Ballet had to work around ongoing classes. The company took class there at eleven in the morning and rehearsed until three in the afternoon. Sometimes Balanchine would shoehorn in a short rehearsal after that, but usually the company had a break until six or seven, when rehearsals resumed, sometimes running until ten o'clock.

As their departure for London approached, Balanchine kept asking Wilde to familiarize herself with more and more new roles. He never discussed rank or made promises about repertory, but she was instantly in the front ranks of NYCB at the center of his most emblematic repertory.

"Balanchine loved that I would just *go!*" Wilde said about two jumps in *Serenade* that he had first assigned her when she was in the Ballet Russe corps. In one, she jumped backward in arabesque over two other women sitting on the floor. It was more precarious than it is onstage today, Wilde notes, because the women's skirts used to be spread on the floor around them. Now they clear a space for the dancer to jump. In the second jump she threw one leg behind her, turned midair in arabesque, and was caught midleap by her partner.

Now at NYCB she was going to dance what is called the "Russian ballerina," since she leads the "Russian Dance" movement in Tchaikovsky's *Serenade for Strings*. But the same two jumps she'd done in the Ballet Russe corps would also remain hers.

"As much as the actual jumping was the daring: that was the spirit that Mr. B really loved," Wilde says today. She had to push off fearlessly despite a limited amount of space. Thinking back, she was convinced that her youthful exploits in the old stone quarry in Ottawa were now spurring her forward. "I swear I could do it that way because of that quarry." Once more she told herself, "I know I can do it!" The results astonished Wilde's colleagues as much as her audience.

This was now something of a different *Serenade* than she'd danced in

Ballet Russe, where the women had worn short skirts, skating length, somewhat resembling Greek tunics. Now at NYCB they were in long tulle skirts, echoing their movement in lingering, floating wafts of fabric, encouraging the audience to view the ballet in a direct lineage to the romantic ballet of the 1840s.

The Maria Tallchief who now reigned as NYCB prima ballerina was also a different construction from the dancer Wilde had known at Ballet Russe. During her six months in Paris with Balanchine in 1947, "Mr. B. really dug in on her," Wilde said. Tallchief was transformed by him from the lyric and dramatic dancer she had been into the neoclassical equivalent of the Imperial ballerinas Balanchine had watched as a child.

Tallchief's "whole impetus, her whole concentration became totally different," Wilde observed. Tallchief's feet became more beautiful, more articulate. Her toes stood up straighter in her pointe shoes; Balanchine corrected her habit of knuckling her toes under a bit. Her ankle was no longer slightly retracted; she was up and above, slightly forward, a position of readiness and slightly anticipatory propulsion that he liked. Her arabesque was now quite different than what Nijinska's early training had instilled. Balanchine wanted the hip of the supporting leg more open to the front than the traditional position, but the working leg dead center behind the torso, at more of a right angle than Nijinska's. Tallchief's turnout was more pronounced, her extension higher.

Tallchief was twenty-two when she left for Paris—young enough to make significant changes. On the other hand, even by that point the body is set in certain patterns and habits. "In a way it's a miracle what she did," Wilde said. And as always in this type of concentration, something was lost as well as gained. Tallchief "did lose that wonderful kind of fullness" her movement had had at Ballet Russe. Wilde's opinion was that Tallchief was now "much more angular." Her line was longer but also harder.

Wilde's adjustment to the new company and repertory was made easier by Lew Christensen. Like the Littlefields, the Christensens were an important family of U.S. ballet pioneers. Lew and his two older brothers had studied ballet from childhood but toured in vaudeville before moving into more rarified echelons of dance. Eldest brother Willam took over the San Francisco Ballet in 1938, while Lew and older brother Harold danced with Balanchine in New York.

Since being mustered out of the army after World War II, Christensen had begun to wind down his performing career. He was back and forth between NYCB and the San Francisco Ballet. Christensen had started to choreograph as well as assisting Balanchine. At NYCB he often taught company class and conducted many rehearsals. Balanchine respected him and allowed him some autonomy. Christensen was "very handsome and we all adored him," Wilde recalled. He was courteous, "thoughtful about what was happening to people in the company," someone Wilde could talk to and confide in. He, too, would be going to London together with his wife, Gisella Caccialanza, who until a recent injury had also been essential to Balanchine's successive companies.

ONSTAGE AT THE ROYAL OPERA HOUSE, tensions were high. Along with every member of the company, Wilde was acutely aware of the importance of their London debut in establishing the company internationally. On the first night, the opera house was packed with diplomats, critics, balletomanes, and members of London's different cultural sectors, as well as fellow dancers, including a large delegation from the theater's own resident troupe, the Sadler's Wells Ballet. In the first ballet, *Serenade*, Tallchief slipped and injured her ankle. As if to confirm to Wilde the claims she'd made about ankle resilience three years earlier in Boston, Tallchief insisted on dancing as scheduled the first movement of Balanchine's *Symphony in C*, which was concluding the performance.

Created for the Paris Opera in 1947 and given its U.S. premiere by Ballet Society a year later, Balanchine's *Symphony in C* was and is the quintessential closing ballet, sending audiences home euphoric after three allegro movements, one very romantic and moody adagio, and an extended finale featuring surging wave after wave of dancers. At the London opening, Wilde was dancing the fourth movement, which is short but very difficult. Then she and partner Frank Hobi returned for the long, reprise-ridden finale.

By the time Tallchief finished the first movement, however, the ballerina had realized her folly, and she was offstage for the next week. Melissa Hayden, who had danced the role in New York, replaced her for the duration of *Symphony in C*, which earned the company fourteen curtain calls. The next day, Wilde too was quickly prepared to make her debut in Tallchief's role, dancing her first performance, "thinking, thinking, thinking—what comes next?" The role itself was and would remain exhilarating for her, giving her a limitless trajectory as she was frequently in supported flight, lofted on her partner's arms in one exuberant jump after another.

It was an incident-prone season. One ballerina had been so nervous on the first night that she not only urinated onstage immediately after an entrance, but later in the performance slipped and fell in the same spot. On another occasion, Hayden, who had left Ballet Theatre to join NYCB in 1949, was performing William Dollar's *The Duel*. She kicked her leg behind her with so much force that her standing leg gave way. She fell flat, knocking the wind out of her. A colleague slipped out and dragged off Hayden's unconscious body. In the wings, a knot of dancers did their best to revive her. The curtain came down and went right back up again: Hayden was unstoppable. "She got up and got her breath and did the rest of the ballet." Wilde recalled.

The company's most uncomfortable moment that season probably came with Balanchine's *Pas de Deux Romantique*. Set to Carl Maria von Weber's *Concertino for Clarinet and Orchestra*, Balanchine had created it earlier in the year for Janet Reed, who had arrived in 1949. Reed was one of the most experienced dancers Balanchine was recruiting to fortify the new company. "But what'll I do?" Reed asked Balanchine and Tallchief when they presented an invitation over dinner. "I'm not a Balanchine dancer." At the moment, however, that was beside the point.

With the San Francisco Ballet in 1940, Reed had starred in the first American performance of the full-length *Swan Lake*. With Ballet Theatre during the 1940s she had danced every kind of role and had also been a leading dancer on Broadway. She had a strong technique, but it was in acting and comedy roles that she was most notable. In her first seasons with New York City Ballet, she was given many different opportunities and challenges.

In *Pas de Deux Romantique*, Balanchine incarnated Reed as a full-fledged classical, tiara-wielding ballerina. But London was no more willing than New York had been to accept this "little red-haired ballerina, a sweet little thing," as Wilde called her, amid the trappings of Imperial regalia. "To Laugh or Not to Laugh," John Martin had headlined his *New York Times* review of the City Center premiere four months earlier. Backstage, Reed herself muttered furiously, colleague Walter Georgov recalled, bewildered because the pas de deux was apparently supposed to be played entirely straight. Amid the far more baronial setting of Covent Garden, the apparent incongruity between ballerina and vehicle became that much more jarring, Wilde did not envy Reed the task of maintaining a semblance of serene composure amid titters from the London audience.

Wilde's own moment of greatest trauma in London came on July 18. She had taken advantage of a night off to attend a four o'clock cocktail party given by the Royal Academy of Dance. Guest of honor was Tamara Karsavina, one of RAD's founders, the great star of the Mariinsky and Diaghilev's Ballets Russes. She had moved to London with her British husband after the Revolution. At the party, a NYCB colleague told Wilde that Balanchine was looking for her. As she recalled, she "made the mistake" of leaving immediately to find him at the party.

Balanchine's *Symphonie Concertante* was going to receive its London premiere that night, led by Le Clercq, Hayden, and Todd Bolender. Just that day, however, Le Clercq had an infected corn removed from her foot. The doctor had forbidden her to dance that night. Wilde had never danced either ballerina role in *Symphonie Concertante.* But she was going to replace Le Clercq—no questions asked. Her crash course in *Symphony in C* first movement a week earlier now looked like a picnic. The curtain was due to rise in two hours. Lew Christensen was waiting to rehearse her, Hayden, and Bolender.

The ballet is named for, and performed to, Mozart's *Sinfonia Concertante* for violin and viola. In the opening Allegro, the two ballerinas work in canon, repeating the same steps just as the two solo instruments repeat the same phrase. Wilde's violin followed Hayden's viola personification. Thus it was possible for her to watch with peripheral vision what Hayden did before she had to repeat it moving to the reverse side.

More complicated was the second movement, the Andante, a very long and tangled trio in which Todd Bolender partnered both women. On-stage, both Hayden and Bolender kept up a steady stream of instructions. The third movement, Presto, again features all three leads, but moving more independently. Interspersed with rapid, short appearances by the three leads amid a continually shifting corps of twenty-two women, a miscount could have proved hazardous for Wilde—if she were a moment late getting out of their way she could have been blindsided. By the time the curtain fell, "I was totally numb." The trauma was lifelong; unlike most of her repertory, it proves impossible for Wilde to recapture in her body a sensation of what it felt like to dance that ballet, even though she continued to perform it for three more years, dancing Tallchief's role as well. But as far as the London critics were concerned, both Hayden and Wilde had danced wonderfully.

The nearly century-old opera house provided a different orientation for the performers: like many old monarchial theaters, the first tier of boxes sat almost on the stage itself. Exiting downstage as she was required to do in so many ballets, Wilde was eye-to-eye with her public. Choreography dictated an arabesque facing offstage but then a look back at the audience before exiting. Wilde did her best to look up, so as not to make direct eye contact and break the imaginary fourth wall. Avoiding a possible breach of protocol was also an issue when boxes were occupied by the two Windsor princesses, Elizabeth and Margaret, who were frequently in attendance.

Beyond Wilde's sightline but definitely a presence to be reckoned with were the "galleryites" who occupied the cheapest seats, way up high. They were impassioned ballet devotees. They sent New York City Ballet flowers and notes, and engaged the dancers in conversation at the stage door. Wilde was again staying above her friend's restaurant on St. James Place. Usually she'd walk the mile and a half home, since public transport closed early. No matter how late it was, food was waiting and more than welcome.

OVER THE COURSE of the Covent Garden season, it became clear that Tallchief and Balanchine were separating. For both it had been a union, above all, of mutual artistic convenience and respect. Tallchief sought and was granted an annulment on the perfectly accurate grounds that Balanchine did not want children.

Balanchine's need for a muse and his preoccupation with his favorite-of-the-moment certainly engendered resentment by those not bestowed equal attention. But there was also an awareness in the company that his nearly obsessive preoccupation with the current Galatea sustained his creative enterprise and the company's very existence. His infatuation with one dancer after another "gave him impetus," Ballet Russe's Vida Brown said. She too had by now joined City Ballet and would soon become a rehearsal assistant to him as well. "It was his inspiration, and when he was inspired, it was delightful, because he created masterpieces."

Who the next candidate would be, no one knew. Marian Horosko, who joined NYCB's corps in 1953, recalled that dressing-room talk frequently turned to, "Would you sleep with Mr. B.?" The question "came up all the time." Most of the women said, "Yeah, for a while"—on account of not only ambition, but also the promise of a catapult into the most rarified firmament of inspiration and creativity. "We would say, 'Oh, how wonderful life would be with a genius. It would be an interesting life.' Because the guys we knew were just stage-door Johnnies."

Balanchine would have been the last to discourage such ambitions. "He loved the girls flirting with him," Wilde recalled. But for her, plying coquetries with the boss "wasn't my thing." And for his part, Wilde was never a candidate: "Mr. B. never went after me, never even flirted." She believed herself an unlikely object of his personal adoration. "I wasn't mysterious, which he also liked." Indeed, elusiveness as the key to infatuation meant that availability could only spell a quick waning of interest on his part.

In London, Balanchine was sharing a small house, a converted mews, with Nicholas Magallanes, who was part of the choreographer's inner sanctum. They spent a lot of time with Richard Buckle, a young dance critic for *The Observer* and a great admirer of Balanchine and the company. Balanchine and the others did a lot of entertaining, and a frequent guest was twenty-year-old Tanaquil Le Clercq. Forty-six-year-old Balanchine had known her since she was a girl, and she was a close friend of Magallanes. She had been awarded the School of American Ballet's first scholarship in

1941 and had been a leading member of Ballet Society and NYCB at their inceptions. Le Clercq had made a great success on the opening night of the London season, dancing the Adagio in *Symphony in C.*

Le Clercq and Pat McBride were close friends as teenagers in the 1940s, at which time, McBride recalls, "I don't think she was at all interested in him in that way." Indeed, letters to McBride that Le Clercq wrote from Paris during her trip with Betty Nichols in 1949 cast a rather skeptical and cynical eye on him. "Tanny never had any designs on Mr. B.," Wilde agreed. Moreover, in 1950 she was committed to some type of romantic engagement with young Dutch composer Jurriaan Andriessen, who had just composed a ballet for NYCB. But the master's adoration was difficult to resist and highly infectious. In addition, there were the ambitions of her mother Edith. Le Clercq was swept off her feet—or perhaps "swept into the maelstrom" might be a better description, given the events to come.

PUTTING

NEW YORK CITY BALLET

ON THE MAP

Reviewing the London season, an unsigned editorial in the monthly *Ballet Today* declared that Wilde "seems to typify what we are already beginning to think of as 'a Balanchine dancer.'" As far as the United Kingdom was concerned, this was perhaps the first time such a construction had been imagined, even though dancers had been performing his choreography there since 1925. But his years in America had produced a company and a company style different from anything yet seen in London. Balanchine was presenting classical ballet mediated through the American temperament, brisker and cooler than other national models.

In that day, it was customary for ballet dancers to use their eyes almost as dramatic actors did—they were, after all, almost always performing narrative ballets. Certainly the eyes were always actively coordinated to the rest of the body. Balanchine wanted something different. He told Tallchief that "the eyes take care of themselves," she recalls in her memoirs. "Their expression comes from deep within and reflects everything else that you're doing."

Before extending an invitation, David Webster, general administrator of the Royal Opera House, had expressed his concern about the company's lack of "dressed" ballets, since so many of Balanchine's neoclassical ballets were performed with minimal production values. As Webster had feared, that aroused considerable critical dismay in London, despite the company's attempt to bring as many dressed ballets as it could—some of them, like Balanchine's *Orpheus*, designed by Isamu Noguchi and thus dressed most unusually too.

Making Balanchine ballets intriguing but also difficult to assimilate was their rejection not only of elaborate costuming and set but also of any more overtly theatrical pretext than steps matched to music. There was no plot, no dressing, no explicit message.

Balanchine's dismissal of tradition could rankle. His new *Firebird*, a great hit in New York, had not gone over well in London, where Fokine's 1910 original was much preferred. Balanchine's sensibility was highly personal and could be received as contrarian, even perverse. His lifelong privileging of the woman's role reached an apex during the London season in *Symphonie Concertante*. There was no male presence at all in the first movement. As far as some quarters were concerned, insult was added to injury during the long cadenza at the end of that movement. Here male necessity was seemingly obviated by having the violin personification that Wilde danced usurp male prerogative and partner her sister viola ballerina. Something of the same exchange is to be found in the works of nineteenth-century Danish choreographer August Bournonville, which continued to form the basis of the Royal Danish Ballet. But here Balanchine made it much more prominent. In *Symphonie Concertante* it was greeted, critics noted, with some palpable shudders in the audience.

But a critical consensus prevailed that the company was something emphatically true to itself. The prominent British critic Arnold Haskell, in the 1951 edition of his *Ballet Annual*, wrote that NYCB had done more "for the artistic prestige" of the United States "than a carload of crooners, ten years' run of musicals, a high powered comedian and a million reels of Hollywood celluloid all added together." For Wilde, however, the yardstick of acceptance that almost meant more than any other was the interest and enthusiasm of the gallery.

The season closed August 19. The company had a week's vacation before beginning a three-week tour of the British provinces. Together with colleagues Magallanes, Hobi, and Roy Tobias. Wilde decided that she wanted to get out of the city. Peter Darrell, who had danced with Wilde in the Metropolitan Ballet, was willing to lend his father's car. They planned to drive to Cornwall on the southwestern coast. The first hitch came with a flat tire soon after they left London. Hobi, who did all the driving, fixed the flat. Wilde spotted him from the danger of passing traffic. "Roy and Nicky were over in the pasture picking flowers."

Much of Great Britain is invariably on vacation at that point in August. When the dancers arrived in the town of Penzance, it proved impossible to find a place to stay. Furthermore, Hobi had a minor collision with a bus, and the car had to be left for repairs. Magallanes and Tobias took a tiny plane over to Hugh Town, the largest settlement on the nearby Scilly Islands. They sent word that they were able to secure accommodations of a sort. Hobi and Wilde followed, their plane making not the usual ascent but instead a straight sally off the high cliffs of Land's End. A minister put up the men in his house, while Wilde stayed with an embalmer.

They ate at a local inn, sampling the area's famous clotted cream. They went rowing. They walked through beautiful gardens planted with flowers from balmy climates—thanks to Britain's Gulf Stream, they were doing just fine. Back on the mainland, they spent time at the ruined castle at Tintagel, where fog and drizzle made its misty associations with Arthurian legend all the more convincing.

NYCB's tour took them to Croydon in the southernmost reaches of London, then to Manchester and Liverpool in the far north. On tour Wilde's roommate was Yvonne Mounsey, whom she'd first met in Mexico City five years earlier. Mounsey had joined NYCB a year before Wilde, and she became Wilde's closest friend in the company. Wilde thought that part of their compatibility was due to the varied experience each had acquired before joining. By contrast, the company would be increasingly populated by School of American Ballet graduates who hadn't known any other company. As Mounsey later recalled, prior to NYCB she had already performed "across five continents in theaters, nightclubs, town halls. . . .

I was my own dancer before I was a Balanchine dancer or even a ballet dancer," she claimed. As a child, she had started improvising movement on her family's farm in South Africa.

At NYCB she stood out physically by the pronounced arch of her back and, as Robert Barnett recalled, "bazooms that wouldn't quit." Her physique and the way she presented it made her image onstage "very grand," Wilde said. Mounsey was one of the tallest ballerinas in the company, and Amazonian by virtue of more than physical attributes. She often exuded an attitude of superiority. Her colleagues "always kidded her about being 'the South African queen,'" Wilde recalled. On their tour of the provinces, Mounsey was in "seventh heaven" when they returned to their digs after performances to find that their landladies had a true English tea waiting for them in their room.

"What we want to do at the New York City Ballet," Balanchine had announced, "is to create great ballets, and I don't care who creates them." But for him, NYCB was a showcase for his own work and above all his own new work. The company's repertory did already include ballets by Lew Christensen, William Dollar, and Todd Bolender. All were to some degree aesthetic disciples of Balanchine.

Cofounder Lincoln Kirstein's vision of a ballet company was predicated on diversity. As he wrote in 1940, "A single choreographer, however talented, is not enough, even for a small company." As early as 1936 his path and Balanchine's had somewhat diverged when Kirstein formed his Ballet Caravan, an attempt to create a new repertory based on American subjects. Kirstein commissioned young American choreographers; Balanchine was not involved.

Now it was in part the influence of Kirstein that made NYCB a haven for important choreographers whose work was markedly different from Balanchine's. Jerome Robbins had danced at Ballet Theatre at its inception in 1940. In 1944 he made his first ballet for them, *Fancy Free*, a humorous vignette about three sailors on shore leave. In 1949, several ballets and Broadway shows later, Robbins was so impressed by Balanchine's *Symphony in C* that he asked to join NYCB, where he both danced and choreographed. Also on NYCB's choreographic roster was the Royal Ballet's Frederick

Ashton. In 1950 he created *Illuminations*, his first ballet for NYCB. Set to Benjamin Britten's eponymous setting of Arthur Rimbaud's symbolic poetry, Ashton's ballet evoked Rimbaud and his imagery.

On November 21, 1950, the company opened a three-week season at City Center. Balanchine's approach was not really curatorial; he had little interest in preserving most of his older work. But in the first years of the company he did seem intent on subsuming earlier phases of his career. On November 28, Wilde danced a virtuoso solo in the company premiere of *Le Baiser de la Fée*, originally choreographed for Balanchine's all-Stravinsky program at the Metropolitan Opera in 1937. Wilde knew the work well from Ballet Russe, where Balanchine had revived it in 1946. There Wilde had danced the role of a sinister Shade. Both at Ballet Russe and again at City Ballet the ballet gave Tallchief one of her greatest roles. She was the Fairy who kisses an infant and thus sways his destiny: as a young man, he abandons village, family, and fiancée and joins her in metaphysical isolation. The ballet could be interpreted as a parable of the artist's remove from society, a favorite theme of Balanchine's.

The following February, Balanchine revived his *Card Game*, also created for the 1937 Stravinsky evening. In it Wilde was Queen of Diamonds. At NYCB, both ballets underwent multiple revisions by Balanchine, who could not, however, finally finesse them to either his or the critics' satisfaction.

During these years, Balanchine was also an intermittent presence onstage in performance. During the fall 1950 season he and Vida Brown were one of four couples in a piece he made to the Mazurka from Glinka's *A Life for the Czar*, a staple of the Russian operatic repertory. Watching from the wings, Wilde didn't think Balanchine was still in the shape needed to take on what was a demanding part even if it were not strictly balletic. Balanchine was more often and more happily to be seen in the mime role of the Father in his *Prodigal Son*. Originally created for Diaghilev's final season in 1929, Balanchine had revived it in 1950. With sets and costumes by Georges Rouault, its return to London after twenty years had been warmly received. When she could, Wilde made a point of watching Balanchine in the final scene, when he welcomed home the contrite Prodigal. The Prodigal crawls to his father, a forgiving but magisterial force; the acceptance emanating from Balanchine's erect figure touched her even watching at close range from the wings.

In the fall of 1950, NYCB welcomed Antony Tudor, a celebrated but quite improbable addition. Tudor had started ballet late and choreographed a number of works for the tiny Mercury theater in London before leaving Britain to join Ballet Theatre for its initial season. His career had been almost exclusively connected with that company, although in 1941 he had created *Time Table* for Balanchine's American Ballet Caravan. He revived it for NYCB in 1949, but becoming a full member of NYCB was a dramatic step. With him came Hugh Laing, Tudor's lover and as much of a muse to Tudor as Balanchine's succession of inspiring ballerinas was to him. And with Laing came his much younger wife, Diana Adams.

Although Wilde had witnessed any number of novel professional and personal arrangements, this particular pas de trois was something new in her experience and struck her at the time as "really weird." Laing and Adams's personal relationship seemed encompassed within a joint custodianship by the two men. "Hugh and Tudor took care of Diana," providing intellectual mentorship and fostering her career in NYCB, not simply in Tudor's own work. They wanted her to do as much as she could.

Balanchine, who had already worked with Adams during some time at Ballet Theatre in the 1940s, needed no encouragement. Indeed, he had visited Adams's and Laing's apartment to extend an invitation. As Wilde described it, twenty-four-year-old Adams had "everything working for her." Very tall and long-limbed, Adams and Le Clercq incarnated the physical prototype that would eventually symbolize New York City Ballet. Adams's line was always beautiful, and she had a technique to match. "It wasn't virtuosity-in-your-face technique. But every step was pure," Wilde said. However, she believed that Balanchine's interest was all the more intensely stoked due to her elusiveness. Adams's personal and professional allegiances made her "not quite available" to him. Over the next decade, Adams would be crucial to Balanchine as well as a perpetual source of frustration. Making the whole of Adams more than the sum of her splendid parts would not always prove a fruitful undertaking for either.

Almost forty years old, and never an outstanding technician, Laing would be assigned at NYCB every possible dance-acting role that could suit his intensity and beauty. Wilde's memories were always partial to the roles' original interpreters, but Laing gave his own interpretation to all the roles he inherited.

A few months after Tudor, Laing, and Adams joined NYCB, they were followed by ballerina Nora Kaye. Kaye had been just as closely identified with Ballet Theatre, and nearly as important to Tudor's work as Laing. But perhaps just as instrumental to her leaving Ballet Theatre was Jerome Robbins, with whom Kaye had an intense professional and personal association. News that she was joining NYCB "created a sensation in dance circles," *Dance News* reported.

Kirstein "liked Tudor a lot," Adams recalled decades later, "and thought it was going to be wonderful to have him." Tudor had started dance late. Unlike Balanchine, for Tudor choreographic creation was a halting and strenuous process. There were Tudor ballets that Balanchine openly admired. Nevertheless, he was apt to put him down. Adams recalled Balanchine's saying that Tudor should have been "a nuclear scientist. . . . He felt Tudor's mind was too analytical for dancing."

"Mr. B. welcomed him in but I don't remember them particularly standing and talking," Wilde said about Tudor. But Balanchine didn't seem competitive; she speculated that he could very well have imagined that programming Tudor would only show his own ballets off to better advantage.

"A PLACE OF DELIGHT," Wilde described the ballroom in which Balanchine set *La Valse* in February 1951. Every guest was a full participant sampling and seeking the fulfillment of eager anticipation. "Everything is beautiful and we all feel beautiful," was Wilde's sensation as she came onstage, but at the same time the pace was too anxious to allow for pleasure. Over the course of the ballet, gaiety shadowed by driven breathlessness turns to hysteria and cataclysm.

Balanchine joined the seven waltzes of Ravel's *Valses Nobles et Sentimentales* with his implosion of the waltz, *La Valse*. Wilde and Frank Hobi danced to *Nobles'* third waltz, a frisky gamboling filled with jumps and beats. Balanchine wanted them to perform it with bacchic abandon. Wilde recalled "a wonderful step" that had something of the flavor of an upside-down tango swoon. Balanchine wanted her to throw herself into Hobi's arms with fervor: "I want the back of her head on the floor," he told Hobi. Wilde and Hobi seemed to be dancing in "a coruscant dream," Claudia Cassidy reported when NYCB showed *La Valse* to Chicago two months after the premiere.

Le Clercq and Magallanes danced the culminating Seventh Waltz, a moody duet full of advances, retreats, enervated melancholy. Innocence and foreboding are fulfilled in *La Valse* proper by the appearance of Death, who extends to Le Clercq's Girl in White his invitation to a fatal waltz.

Wilde recalled how expressive Balanchine was demonstrating Death's role, to be performed by Francisco Moncion. Balanchine presented Le Clercq funereal blandishments—gloves, necklace, hand mirror—with a peremptory matter-of-factness. There was no question of resisting: Death's triumph was predestined.

When Death appeared, all the dancers save Le Clercq fell into a trance-like stasis at the sides of the stage, their gaze averted. Nevertheless, they exercised their peripheral vision liberally. Moncion's performance was so powerful that direct sightlines were unnecessary: "When Frank came on, you felt it in your solar plexus," Wilde recalled. For *La Valse*, Le Clercq wore a special makeup that made her paler than the other women. Moncion, too, liked to experiment with makeup. "Sometimes it was very subtle," Robert Barnett said, but in *La Valse*, "he walked in at the back of the stage, and you just wanted to shrink away." Vanquished by Death, the ball's feverish recklessness turns to systemic derangement. Wilde and her colleagues whirled in big and small circles; she was turned and lifted frenetically by Hobi.

"We are dancing on the edge of a volcano," Ravel had said when he composed the music immediately after World War I. The ballet could seem a cautionary tale, perhaps inspired by the world conflagrations through which Balanchine had lived—by the time the guests rise from their slumber, it is too late. NYCB's dancers apparently wanted more of Balanchine's macabre invention, his comment on human folly, venality, and blindness. Looking back to Diaghilev, "we kept asking him to do *Le Bal*," Wilde said. They had seen pictures of the 1929 ballet with sets and costumes by de Chirico. It was also an eerie ball, prominent predecessor in the lineage of *La Valse*. But for Balanchine, as always, his current statement made resurrection of earlier chapters irrelevant. "No, no, no," Balanchine insisted, "that's in *La Valse*. I used it."

18

EAST SIDE,

WEST SIDE

Now twenty-two years old, Wilde quickly struck up friendships with in-
tellectuals in and around her Lower East Side apartment building. Dan
Wolf's apartment was down the hall from hers, and between them they
shared a single common toilet. Wolf was considerably older than she, a
World War II veteran studying at Columbia on the GI Bill and doing some
writing. Together with Norman Mailer and John Wilcock, he founded the
Village Voice in 1955. Soon Mailer moved to the building next door to theirs,
which shared a common roof. In his late twenties, Mailer had become a
celebrity after the publication of *The Naked and the Dead* in 1948. Wilde's
brother-in-law, Roger Shattuck, was a friend of his, and she got to know
him at rooftop parties. Then and forever, he was himself, loud-mouthed and
contentious, determined to hog the spotlight. She was friendly with him
but considered him "a pain in the ass." Wolf manifested a gentler quality
of polemical engagement that was more to her liking. At cocktail parties
around the city, political discussions swirled around Wilde and her friends
as they collected money for refugees from Franco's Spain.

Wilde's new literary friends were different from the people she worked
with, since few NYCB members seemed to take much interest in politics.
Yet a progressive spirit permeated Wilde's workplace. It was important to

Balanchine that New York City Ballet prices be accessible, which was possible because of the sponsorship of City Center governance. Indeed, when City Center had been established in 1943 by Mayor Fiorello La Guardia in a former Masonic temple on West Fifty-Fifth Street, its explicit mandate was first-rate performing arts at popular pricing. The postwar boom in innovation in all walks of American life was reflected in the artistic innovation onstage at City Center and in a new, more egalitarian audience for ballet attracted—at least in part—by the low prices.

From the stage Wilde sensed that energy. The orchestra pit was small and the balcony far forward, close to the stage. "You could almost make out faces," she recalled. "You really felt very close to the audience," and its youth and diversity "was fantastic," Wilde said. "All the students and artists could afford to come—and they didn't come only once a season. Unfortunately they don't have a chance to do that today." That type of government support—whether municipal, state, or federal—has now evaporated.

For Wilde, there were periods when Balanchine's company class was very interesting, and she went religiously. It was less interesting when, day after day, he would pursue the same point, often in a concerted attempt to break down a particular dancer's resistance to doing something the way he wanted it done.

It was a given, however, that much of Balanchine's class would be personalized to the needs of the muse of the moment. As Vida Brown recalled, "Everybody would listen, and you always tried to take whatever he said for yourself, too." At this time, Balanchine was spending a lot of concentration on strengthening Le Clercq, who was willowy, delicate, and extremely flexible. She had a high kick, but Balanchine wanted her to be able to maintain and prolong a high extension in adagio. To that end, what he gave her to do in class was "murder on the rest of us," Wilde recalled. Wilde had the necessary musculature to raise her leg high in *développé*, but muscular weight would submit to the force of gravity. "My leg was getting lower and lower and lower" as she prolonged her extension. "It did not work for me."

Class might be an hour preceding a long day of rehearsals or as long as three hours if they were on a performing layoff. Most enjoyable were the special small classes Balanchine would sometimes teach, mainly for the principal dancers. These were bonus classes outside normal working hours when the company was on a layoff. "I'm going to do class, so come," he told Wilde often. Sometimes he provided his own piano accompaniment.

Balanchine's classical training and technique was still in evidence. Wilde never forgot seeing him execute a double air turn in the studio. He was explaining to one of the company men the Russian way of executing the turn: pulling one's body together and taking off in one piece. Not a moment was to be wasted—as Wilde says, "You can't go up and then decide to turn; you're turning as you leave." Impulsively, Balanchine launched into one of his own. "It was very good," Wilde said, recounting his rapidity with a sharp "*boom-boom!*"

Frequently Balanchine's class would concentrate on one element of technique to the point where it became a specialized seminar, and that could be very stimulating for Wilde. At one point he was working extensively on their arms: "After giving us a fast barre, he'd get us in the center and have us glued in fifth position. We'd work on *port de bras* for thirty minutes."

Where Antony Tudor and his dancers were concerned, "the only one that Mr. B. was interested in was Diana," Wilde said. Nora Kaye's company debut in February 1951 was a trial by fire. Balanchine cast her in the first movement of *Symphony in C*, which was unlike anything she had previously danced. She was distinctly uncomfortable. Wilde believed that the role's frequent short entrées and exits made Kaye "feel like a windup doll." Her stamina flagged; it wasn't a question of technique—"Nora was as strong as a horse," recalled a NYCB principal dancer—but here, strained by Balanchine's syntax, she "looked rather like a workhorse," he said.

Kaye's "failure made us all cringe, wince, and feel for her plight," writes company member Barbara Bocher in her memoir *The Cage*. Nevertheless, as Bocher writes, Kaye was "not one to take a failure lying down," and she "pushed herself in class and rehearsal to acquire the speed and attack needed to do justice to any of Mr. B.'s work."

Wilde, who danced Kaye's debut part frequently, judged Kaye's optimum rendition acceptable. "She pulled everything off. She certainly gave a performance, and she wasn't falling all over herself." Dramatic roles by Robbins and Tudor were to follow and allow Kaye to make an indelible imprint on these years at NYCB. But even in the least advantageous setting, she was, as Wilde recalled, "a totally fine artist—a force out there."

After making its Chicago debut in April 1951, NYCB reopened in its home theater for a monthlong season in June, Wilde's third in New York since joining a year earlier. She was reunited with Ballet Russe mentor Ruthanna Boris when Lincoln Kirstein recruited her to create a new ballet for NYCB.

Boris stumbled on costumes created in 1947 for Lew Christensen's *Blackface* for Ballet Society, a portrayal of race relations in the antebellum South. That prompted her decision to choreograph an homage to minstrel shows of the same period. Kirstein recommended the music of Louis Gottschalk, whose reputation was in eclipse in the United States. To Boris's surprise, Balanchine was familiar with the composer, since his music had retained its popularity in Russia.

The more odious habits of minstrel performance practice were omitted—for example, there was no blackface. And some of the conventions were turned inside out: the gag-parrying Endmen, for example, were danced *en travesti* by tall Le Clercq and short Beatrice Tompkins. Part 1 was a procession of different cakewalks, in which Wilde led the "Freebie." In part 2 was a sequence of minstrel acts where she danced a "Wild Pony" episode. Intellectually rigorous as always, Boris shared her research with the dancers. The Romantic ballet that was the rage of Paris during the 1940s had made it to America, where its wraithly ballerinas were also the butt of jokes on the minstrel stage. Boris accordingly created for Janet Reed and Herbert Bliss an episode of "Hortense, Queen of the Swamp Lilies," attended by "Her Lover, the Young Poet Harolde."

Cakewalk's humor, its period style and historical homage, were all to Wilde's liking, but rehearsals were "very difficult," she recalled. Boris was "not pleased at all." She was under a lot of pressure, since Balanchine was not entirely enthusiastic about her presence there. He had originally asked her to dance with the young company, and she demurred, having already signed another contract with Ballet Russe and not wanting to heed his suggestion that she break it. Once she was free, however, she presented herself to Balanchine, only to be told that her performing services were no longer needed.

During *Cakewalk*'s rehearsals, "Ruthanna drove me crazy," Wilde recalled. "I ran around that big studio on Madison Avenue a thousand and one times." Balletic runs were something that she thought she did well and something that she loved to do. But a turn and run offstage kept falling short of what Boris wanted. Boris admonished that her chest wasn't far enough forward— she needed to feel the air resisting her. But to this day Wilde is not entirely sure what it was Boris was looking for. "I think she finally got it, but I don't know what I did." At the June 12 premiere, Wilde "pranced and bounced and sped with awesome abandon and to great effect," Walter Terry opined in the *Herald-Tribune*. "As a company, New York City Ballet needs ballets like *Cakewalk*," Doris Hering wrote in *Dance Magazine*. "For it requires them to drop their elegance and restraint and romp like vaudevilleans."

That June Wilde made her debut in Balanchine's setting of the pas de trois from Petipa's nineteenth-century *Paquita*, something of an exercise in autobiography, since he had performed this very same piece as a student in Russia. Newspaper reviews described the numerous bouquets that Wilde had received. And whom exactly were they from? "I had lots of boyfriends that were interested in what I was doing!" Among them was a very proper investment counselor named Bob Weiss, who frequently took her to the theater.

His work, however, didn't interest her at all. On her mother's advice, she had bought an annuity as soon as she was earning money regularly, but that's as far as her thoughts tended toward strategies of financial planning. Hubert Saal was an editor at *Town and Country* and an acquaintance of Balanchine's. Wilde was sent bushels of roses by Philip Leland, a California native who was studying piano at Julliard.

They were intrigued and at times mystified by the exotic profession she plied. "Oh, my God, you have to take another class?" Saal would say when she'd insist on leaving a party early so she could get up early the next morning.

A more serious relationship developed with a young man named Gordon New, who worked at the Canadian consulate. He was dark and handsome. Having been previously posted to China, he had interesting stories to tell. "He wasn't a balletomane, but he was interested. He was very nice, very thoughtful. We had fun."

Wilde was to have a prominent role in the new *Swan Lake* that Balanchine was choreographing in the fall of 1951. He had been staging versions of the first lakeside scene, second of the original production's four acts, for more than twenty years, and now, more than ever before, he was going to do it his way.

In the initial rehearsals, Mounsey and she were "horrified" at what Balanchine was intending. Both had long exposure to the more or less standard text of act 2 as performed by Ballet Russe. "Standard" has to be a relative term, since the Russian Imperial Ballet productions allowed ranking ballerinas the discretion to change choreography at will, resulting in numerous alternate versions. Nevertheless, Wilde and Mounsey had come to view Ballet Russe's version as canonical.

What they found most objectionable was Balanchine's choreography for the swan ensemble. It was "very flat," Wilde said—flat as in one-dimensional. For Balanchine often made classical ballet less nuanced but also less esoteric by orienting the dancer closer to the public, eliminating the oblique depth of field established by opposition of head, neck, and shoulders that is *épaulement.*

"How can he do this?" Wilde and Mounsey asked each other. But as the days went by, they began to look at the production through the new perspective he was supplying. They saw, too, that the corps was going to be less staid, less static than in the traditional versions. And both wound up very happy with the roles Balanchine created for them.

Mounsey led a dance for nine women that was "big and grand and showed off her long legs," Wilde recalled. She herself led a trio to what is traditionally the Waltz of the Big Swans. Balanchine gave her all kinds of jumps, but above all the slicing *sissonne,* including one repeating sequence with changing arms. Two lieutenant swan maidens performed in counterpoint around her. In the finale, she came flying down a center corridor, finishing with a jump that brought her down to the ground in a kneel.

Both Mounsey and Wilde reappeared to participate in the act's concluding coda, prior to Swan Queen Maria Tallchief's reversion to avian form and her wrenching separation from André Eglevsky's Prince. When *Swan Lake* premiered on November 20, Wilde "created a sensation," Miles Kastendieck reported in the *New York Journal-American.*

"I wasn't measuring myself against other people," Wilde says today. "I don't see how one could ever enjoy a role if you did that." But dancers are often terribly aware of what someone else brings to a role and impeded by their own negative comparisons. The great gift of not volunteering invidious comparisons stood Wilde in good stead when Balanchine began alternating Wilde in some of Le Clercq's repertory.

One of the most popular ballets in NYCB's repertory was Balanchine's 1949 *Bourrée Fantasque*, performed to Emmanuel Chabrier's music. It sounded French; it looked French: the men were costumed in berets, while the women wore frothy headpieces and veils. Wilde most frequently led the third movement, a gala affair of big jumps and cartwheel lifts, first danced by Janet Reed. But Balanchine also cast her in the comic first movement, created for Le Clercq and Robbins. Le Clercq's rambunctious sabotage of her shorter partner was projected with a certain feyness, so that, as Wilde observed, "she could get away with the jokes and it was never harsh or too vulgar." A lot of the horseplay exploited the comic potential of Le Clercq's very long and flexible legs, but "I was so different physically, I just had to do my kind of fun things."

"Tanny was very sort of sophisticated and nonchalant about it," said Robert Barnett, who partnered them both, "out of the corner of her eye. Patty played it a little more cute, which was more her, and she was smart to do that." Le Clercq was "very 'Madame,'" Wilde laughed. "That was not my personality."

"I can ask her to do anything," Balanchine would later tell Violette Verdy about his choreography for Wilde. For her, choreographic creation with him was "always like a game." He'd try something new and unusual and say, "Try it but I can change it." No, she'd insist, "don't change it; I can do it!"

Early in 1952, Balanchine choreographed *Caracole* to one of his favorite pieces of music, Mozart's *Divertimento No. 15*. The ballet featured an all-star cast: Wilde alongside Adams, Hayden, Le Clercq, and Tallchief, joined by Robbins, Eglevsky, Magallanes, and a small corps of women.

During Mozart's "Theme and Variations" Andante, each ballerina had her own solo. Wilde's included *gargouillades*, a spectacular step that isn't often performed but eventually became associated with her. The *gargouillade* is a jump in which each leg circles in opposite directions. Although it is part of the academic lexicon, "we never did it in class," Wilde recalled, and she thinks Balanchine may even have had to explain it to her. Certainly she spent practice time on her own to master the intricate and difficult step.

When *Caracole* premiered on February 19, 1952, it received ecstatic critical notices. Martin in the *Times* appreciated the "rhythmic invention" in Wilde's variation," declaring hers and Tallchief's "the most stunning" of the solos. "Both are dancers of incomparable bravura."

Balanchine and Kirstein were categorically opposed to lengthy domestic tours of one-night stands that had occupied so much of Wilde's performing weeks with Ballet Russe. NYCB's seasons in New York, no matter how long, were less exhausting for her than Ballet Russe road tours. But though City Ballet did far less touring, her repertory was larger and the roles she danced were more important. During the company's City Center seasons, Wilde became accustomed to performing two or even three ballets at every performance. By the time Sunday's two performances were done, she and colleagues were both bleary with exhaustion and so keyed up that they weren't yet ready to go home. So frequently on Sunday nights Wilde and a group of dancers would troop down to the second-run movie theaters of West Forty-Second Street to take in midnight shows of interesting foreign films.

19

GRAND TOUR,

1952

Magazine features on the emerging New York City Ballet grew out of a media landscape totally unlike today's relentless pursuit of the lowest common denominator. America in the 1950s was an aspirational society. Ballet, like all forms of conservatory culture, was viewed by the media as a rarefied art form that symbolized not marginal elitism but rather the very top of the cultural tree.

Media support undoubtedly was motivated in part by the United States government's realization that ballet was an artistic export that could burnish the country's image overseas and perhaps even win the war of cultural diplomacy launched by the Soviets in the immediate postwar years. NYCB was certainly useful in proving that capitalism could produce a manifestation of artistic excellence just as potent as those of the state-funded companies of Europe and, most provocatively, the Soviet Union.

Just as NYCB was launched on its first tour of Europe in May 1952, *Life* magazine asserted: "This season, it suddenly became clear that the U.S. has the best-balanced and most theatrically satisfying ballet company now performing. Though only four years old, the New York City Ballet has earned a place with the world's oldest established companies."

NYCB was going to make three separate Paris appearances on this tour, and one of them would be part of an enormous festival, "Masterpieces of the Twentieth Century," organized by the Congress for Cultural Freedom. Founded in 1950 and covertly funded by the CIA, the Congress was directed by Balanchine's friend Nicholas Nabokov, a composer. Nabokov had created ballet scores for Diaghilev but had now abandoned his musical career. Like Balanchine himself, Nabokov, a cousin of the writer Vladimir Nabokov, was fiercely anti-Communist.

The dancers' desire to see Europe meant that they were willing to subsidize themselves if need be. Wilde recalled that she and the company took a pay cut for the tour, bolstered by a small per diem that was the union's condition for agreeing. The dancers wound up losing money on this and subsequent tours, however, since they had to pay for accommodations entirely on their own. On their first night in a European capital the dancers customarily stayed in the hotel booked by the company, which was often expensive. The next day, an exodus of dancers ensued, fanning out to find something cheaper.

Principal dancer André Eglevsky, who was married, with children, originally said that he couldn't afford to go. Eglevsky was one of the very few male dancers who had an international name and a virtuoso technique. NYCB needed him, and money was found to augment his salary.

The European opera houses provided the dancers with a vastly different performing experience. The old houses had enormous stages, at least twice as wide and deep as the one at City Center, where backdrops fluttered if someone tried to cross behind it. In Europe, "you really felt you could get out there and breathe!" Wilde said. It also meant a great deal more ground to cover and thus could be much more tiring.

The ancient wood stages were rough and hazardous. Old boards were slippery, splinters were rampant, and holes cut into the floor for scenery dowels were wider than the tip of a pointe shoe. Trap doors wiggled; crevices between door and trap yawned. At City Center, by contrast, a heavy-gauge "battleship" linoleum dance floor was put down to provide resilient spring, as well as grip to hinder slips. They started taking their dance floor on tour with them, then applying it over the old wooden stages.

At City Center, the dressing rooms were small and communal, and backstage was cramped. Wilde didn't recall a lot of entertaining backstage after the performance. The European opera houses by contrast were filled with greenrooms and reception rooms, most lavish of all the Foyer de la Danse behind the stage of the Paris Opera, once the hunting ground of wealthy roués looking for mistresses.

NYCB's five-month tour opened in Barcelona April 15 at the Gran Teatre del Liceu. Tradition dictated that the curtain didn't rise until 10 p.m., and the performance included a forty-five-minute dinner break for the audience, so they left the theater only at 2 a.m. But class was still held at 10 a.m., in a grim dark basement under the stage. The dancers were, however, given a siesta in the afternoon.

It was here that Wilde met her future husband, George Bardyguine. He was working for impresario Leon Leonidoff, who was producing the tour, as liaison to the stage crew. Bardyguine's mother, Maria Nevelska, had been a soloist with the Bolshoi in Moscow; his father was a professor of religious history. He had grown up with ballet. After his parents emigrated first to Berlin, and then to the South of France, his mother not only taught but directed a small touring company.

Bardyguine was eight years older than she; before the war he had run a shoe factory, which was a casualty of the German occupation. After hostilities ended, he worked first helping his mother with her tours, then for the Marquis de Cuevas, Wilde's first boss, whose company was also managed by Leonidoff.

With NYCB, Bardyguine ensured that scenery was hung as it should be, that lighting plots were fulfilled, working with the stage manager as well as lighting designers Nananne Porcher and Jean Rosenthal, who often accompanied the company on tour. He arranged transportation for sets and oversaw customs inspections. When NYCB reached Italy in May, Bardyguine hired department heads for lighting, sets and props who traveled with the company until they visited Great Britain in July.

In Barcelona, Bardyguine left a party with Wilde and Mounsey, hailing a cab to their pensione. The next day Wilde received a big bouquet of roses. "I looked at the card and said, 'Who's Brandywine?'"

Madame Nevelska, as Wilde invariably called her, had been principal dancer Eglevsky's first teacher and she and her husband had recently emigrated to the United States. Eglevsky contributed funds to help her begin teaching in a studio at Carnegie Hall. Bardyguine and Eglevsky were "big pals, always together, and with the girls," Wilde recalled. Eglevsky was a father, happily married to Leda Anchutina, a virtuoso in Balanchine's American Ballet, but he was perpetually libidinous, and Anchutina had not joined him on this tour.

"I thought, I'm not getting mixed up," Wilde recalled; "I've got other things to do." Her sentiments remained with Gordon New in New York; as far as she was concerned, "I was not available." Little did she dream that by the end of the following year she and Bardyguine would be married.

Writing to pianist friends Arthur Gold and Robert Fizdale in New York, Le Clercq complained that applause had been reserved all through the Barcelona run, despite praise in the press. The last night of the three-week season, however, was a different story. The performance closed, as so often at NYCB, with *Symphony in C*. "They threw bunches of flowers at us," Le Clercq recounted, and laurel leaves came raining down as well. All the company women were presented with lace mantillas, and the men given cuff links. To top it all off, pigeons were released. A standing ovation lasted for five minutes—"so we all feel a little more kindly towards Barcelona."

Flying to Paris from Barcelona, Wilde and Mounsey showed off their new straw hats, which their colleagues named *platillos volantes*—flying saucers. They boarded a bus from the airport into one of the major train stations in the city, where waiting for Wilde was sister Nora, her husband, and six-month-old daughter Tari. They had spent the past year in Paris, made possible by Shattuck's being named a Junior Fellow of the Society of Fellows at Harvard. He was working on his first book. Wilde had seen them off on their Atlantic crossing from Manhattan's West Side piers; she would give them similar send-offs in years to come, as Shattuck's writing and teaching took him to residencies around the world.

NYCB's dancers felt that Balanchine was particularly nervous before any Paris appearance of the company. Paris was where Diaghilev had collected what he considered his most discerning aesthetic arbiters. With the approach of any Paris season, Balanchine would become more than normally picky about details he might not bother with anywhere else.

Organizing this European tour as well as subsequent visits over the following decade, impresario Leonidoff customarily opened them at the most hallowed and prestigious theater in each city. Sometimes after that they'd move to a slightly less deluxe venue. It was a question of cost, but also of the ongoing performance of the great state-run opera houses.

Certainly it meant a great deal to Balanchine that they be showcased at the Opera, if only for one night. They opened there May 10 under the auspices of a "Masterpieces of the Twentieth Century" series. *Swan Lake* was danced with its opening-night cast of the previous fall. Wilde's pas de trois "used to bring down the house, which I'm sure was just what he intended and expected." In Paris her success could also have been boosted by the fact that in the audience were dancers from the Opera with whom she'd taken class, as well as her teachers Nora Kiss and Olga Preobrajenska. Wilde got word that Tallchief had insinuated that Wilde had milked the Parisians' applause. But Balanchine didn't say anything to her, "so I didn't pay any attention."

The next night they moved to the Théâtre des Champs-Élysées. Immediately after it opened in 1913, forty years earlier, it had been the scene of Nijinsky's riotous *Sacre du Printemps* premiere. It was a lovely theater, a popular and well-respected venue.

Jerome Robbins joined them in Paris from Israel, to which he had been sent by the American Fund for Israel Institutions to sample, assess, and stimulate the local dance scene. His ballets were naturally included on NYCB's tour repertory, and he was himself prominent onstage as well. He was a frequent partner for Wilde in the role he had created in *Bourrée Fantasque*, impressing her with his ability to make visible a fully inscribed comic character via a twist of the shoulders, an angle of the head, a glance. His dramatic gifts were equally eloquent. One night at the Champs-Élysées, *Prodigal Son* was in progress as Wilde made her way to the stage. A knot of people was so unusually compacted that she couldn't get near the wings. She discovered that the usually blasé stagehands were mesmerized by Robbins as the Prodigal making his halting crawl home to the arms of his forgiving father.

Scheduled frequently on this tour was Balanchine's 1946 *Divertimento*, a chamber ballet, a little gem different from anything else in the NYCB repertory. Performed to a bluesy contemporary score by Alexei Haieff, the cast contained four soloist couples as well as two lead dancers. Balanchine had created it for Ballet Society in 1947, when it was headed by Mary Ellen Moylan, and then, at NYCB, by Tallchief, partnered by Moncion.

Divertimento was typically Balanchine in its evocation of existential isolation, here portrayed humorously. When the curtain rose, the four supporting couples were onstage, but the lead man was alone. The man keeps bowing to his as-yet-invisible partner. The ballerina arrives late and leaves early—at the very end of the ballet sashaying to the wings, then leaping off while he raises a yearning arm toward her.

The small cast was frequently star-studded, Balanchine often casting principal dancers in the soloist roles. "We all loved dancing it," Wilde recalled. Everyone felt visible. And when they were not dancing themselves, there was a lot to see: the principal ballerina had an interesting solo, slowly evolving into different shapes, somewhat reminiscent of Markova's solo in Massine's *Rouge et Noir.*

Divertimento was always programmed near the beginning of the program; once the curtain fell, the dancers were rushing to get ready for what was coming later. There'd be a little bit of swearing, perhaps, if something had gone drastically amiss, but there was never any time to linger.

On May 18 they opened in Florence at the Teatro Comunale as part of the Maggio Musicale summer festival, one of Europe's most important. On the bank of the Arno, the Comunale had been rebuilt after extensive bombing during World War II. It had a splendid rooftop rehearsal studio with sweeping views of the city. The stage was odd: wide and not that deep. "You run miles to get on the stage."

Their performances in Florence were spaced two days apart, and Wilde and Vida Brown took advantage of a lull to visit Venice. "We had to get there and get out," Brown recalled, but "we wanted to see as much as we could: we both walked fast!"

After two weeks in Florence, they spent a week in Lausanne and then Zurich. Living in Lausanne was Betty Nichols, an alum of SAB and Ballet Society who had traded her career for matrimony. "I was overwhelmed, absolutely," Nichols recalled, "in complete amazement to see their development."

They returned to Paris where they settled back into the Champs-Élysées, now for a two-and-a-half-week run independent from "Masterpieces of the Twentieth Century." They were well entertained by the American ambassador. Not a smoker, Wilde was urged to "take a cigarette, take a cigarette," by colleagues at consulate parties given for the company—they were considerably more expensive than what the dancers could afford.

They spent a week in The Hague before opening in early July a six-week repeat season at Covent Garden. Its stage proved just as treacherous as it had two years earlier.

At the conclusion of the Russian dance in *Serenade*, the entire cast travels by way of hops in arabesque to the sides of the stage and reverses course, pivoting back to the center. Balanchine would urge the dancers to travel so far that they edged into the wings, his choreography engulfing, subsuming the stage, making it almost seem to contract and expand in response to the dancers' appropriation.

But it was just when the dancers were making this happen on the enormous stage of Covent Garden that a slippery spot at the front of the stage proved subversive. "The whole front line went down," Barbara Walczak recalled. "At least four of us." Waltz ballerina Diana Adams was farthest downstage. Flat on her back, her feet dangling over the footlights, she raised herself on one elbow and let out a "Jesus Christ!" Adams recovered just in time to run over to stage right and dive once more to the ground, this time as part of the choreography.

Ruthanna Boris's evocation of American vernacular in *Cakewalk* made it the hit of the Covent Garden season, much to the dismay of Balanchine and Kirstein, whose ambitions for the company rested above all on its acceptance into the top rank of classicism. In addition to *Cakewalk*, works by Robbins and Tudor were performed. But just as two years before, there was a mixed response to the preponderance of plotless Balanchine ballets.

Yet Wilde and her ballerina colleagues were acclaimed. A. V. Coton, dance critic of the *Evening Standard*, was also London correspondent of *Dance News*, to which he forwarded a bulletin describing "the sensuous splendor of watching so much exuberant, masterly and revealing dancing—Tallchief, Adams, Hayden, Mounsey, Wilde, and Le Clercq were a constant delight during the season."

Surprisingly, Balanchine's reworked *Swan Lake* was well received by the tradition-conscious British critics. In *Ballet Today*, Caryl Brahms wrote: "To Ivanov's tired old swans, Balanchine has brought a new urgency. In particular I found the pas de trois, with Wilde in startled flight from the smooth waters of the lake, and the final flurry of disturbed doom-driven swans, dramatic and exciting."

A craze for Vespa motor scooters had broken out in NYCB. During the Covent Garden season, Frank Hobi regularly gave Wilde a ride back to the apartment she and Mounsey were renting near the British Museum. "My ambition is to learn to drive the Vespa *very* well," Le Clercq wrote to her friends in New York. Balanchine not only bought a Vespa but also entertained the idea of obtaining a franchise to sell them back in the States. Hobi was going to go into partnership with him. "You see," Balanchine wrote to impresario Leonidoff in September, "I must find a way to make some money because as you know, what I get from the ballet company does not cover my expenses and I don't want to do Broadway shows in order to live."

Nothing came of the idea, but Balanchine insisted that "although we may be considered artistic, we are also good businessmen." This was wishful thinking on Balanchine's part, but the need to make a pretense of business acumen was certainly something acquired since his emigration to the United States. His need for funds, however, was genuine. Edward Bigelow, a NYCB dancer but most of all indispensable factotum to Balanchine, had an abiding interest in get-rich-quick schemes.

From London they went north to the Edinburgh Festival, where they were in residence August 25–30. Then they flew to Berlin for their last stop. Their plane was a troop conveyance that lacked a proper floor. As a trouper and traveler, Nora Kaye was "no problem ever," Wilde said. "Fun. A good pro: 'All right, what are we doing now?'" But she did hate to fly. Kaye took one look at the bare-bones aircraft and decided, "I'm not going. . . . No, no, no. . . . I'll see you there." And when they opened at the Schiller Theater September 3, Kaye was in her proper place onstage.

IN THE

DRESSING ROOM

At New York City Ballet Wilde almost always shared a dressing room—at City Center, on tour in the United States and in Europe. On occasions abroad she had a room to herself, but that was indeed a rare luxury. A delicate balance between competing demands, and a tolerance for accommodation made for good dressing-room relationships. Nevertheless, it was easy to get rubbed the wrong way, as Wilde explained: "Somebody's noisy and you want to be quiet. Somebody always has the radio on. . . . You want to have your own kind of concentration, but you're not alone and can't expect to have your preferences catered to."

Wilde frequently dressed with Tanaquil Le Clercq, whose antic irony made her a vital partner in "girl fun—jokes and crazy silliness." She was just as good at serious talk. What was Le Clercq reading?—Wilde always made it a point to inquire. Within the company, "more people than didn't felt that they should be literate and educated," but Le Clercq was "more intellectual than any of us and probably just plain smarter as well." Le Clercq wanted to dance but also wanted to be free to explore many interests. But the one thing she did not have was freedom: "Everybody was stage managing Tanny," Wilde recalled. Among those supplying cues was, first and foremost, Balanchine himself, but also her mother Edith and various allies, as well as Jerome Robbins. Le Clercq was as much muse to him as she was to Balanchine. There had been some romantic connection between them before she married Balanchine in December 1952.

Le Clercq and Diana Adams were the closest of friends, despite or perhaps because of the fact that their familial relations were quite dissimilar, if both vexing. Wilde never remembered Adams's parents' being present; she didn't seem particularly close to her mother, father, stepmother, or sister; she "seemed to be surrounded by problematic relationships."

Wilde experienced the not uncommon syndrome of having to battle more stage fright as her performing experience as well as repertory responsibility grew. "My sister Nora was always a nervous wreck before performances," she would tell a reporter in 1956. "I didn't used to get nervous in those early years. I could always say, 'This is ridiculous!' But I can't talk myself into it anymore."

And a colleague's nerves could be contagious. Le Clercq was nervous before a performance, but Adams's nerves were more severe and more unsettling for Wilde when they dressed together. Adams "was a strange girl," Wilde recalled. As many Tudor roles as Adams danced, one role Wilde could never imagine Adams doing was Hagar in Tudor's *Pillar of Fire*. That required too much raw emotional revelation. Adams "couldn't allow that kind of thing. She was too much, pushing everything away from her: people and the public."

For Wilde it was easier to dress with someone whose physical type and company repertory were as different from hers as Adams's and Le Clercq's. Whereas Melissa Hayden was about the same height as Wilde, she was, also like Wilde, compactly built and very strong in allegro. They shared many roles. "Millie and I respected each other completely," Wilde recalled, "but we were competing all the time," which made it trying as well as congenial to dress with her. Hayden "screamed louder than any of us: 'Oh, Mr. B., that's not fair! I should be doing that.'" Balanchine himself "would do anything to avoid a screamer," Wilde said, which meant that Hayden could sometimes get just what she wanted, and sometimes at Wilde's expense.

Hayden "was always wanting to do the first performance," Wilde said. "I wanted to do them, too, but I thought, That's the way it's scheduled. If that's the way they want it, okay.

"Millie was a good person," Wilde said. "She wasn't doing it in a nasty way—she was just getting what she wanted." But she also had the sense that Balanchine was fostering competition, "always pitting Millie and me against each other."

Despite the inevitability of friction, the ballerinas had to work in the closest cooperation onstage and off. They did their own hair and makeup and frequently assisted each other, for instance as Balanchine's Firebird, which required some body makeup and glitter applied to the arms and hands. The company had only a small wardrobe staff. Their costumes were brought to their dressing rooms and a wardrobe mistress waited in the corridor to hook up the back of their tutus. But searching for an extra pin to secure a chignon or headpiece was something they did on their own, making quick changes in the wings especially nerve-racking. If Wilde was free she might look in on the dressing room of a colleague dancing back-to-back ballets, changing headdress, tutu, tights during the intermission: "Anything I can do?" An accoutrement might have malfunctioned, a ribbon might have needed mending, but almost invariably came the request "Light me a cigarette."

They solicited each other's advice: something felt terrible; what did it look like? Was that a good line for an individual body? Balanchine so rarely had comments to make after a performance that the reactions of colleagues was all the more appreciated. As great as was their respect for him, reverence was not the watchword of dressing-room exchange. His decisions about repertory and casting were frequently inscrutable and seemingly arbitrary. The dancers were baffled when his frequent programming of *Divertimento* during the 1952 tour to Europe spelled the ballet's demise. When the company returned to New York, Balanchine dropped the ballet from NYCB's repertory, despite many pleas from the dancers that it be revived. As so often, his decision was not subject to appeal.

Wilde recalled buttonholing him any number of times about an issue that she had, only to receive in response a sniff and a "We'll see." For her,

Eileen Lucy Simpson.
Courtesy of Patricia Wilde.

John Herbert White.
Courtesy of Patricia Wilde.

Wilde (left) and siblings Elizabeth,
Lester, Herbert, and Nora,
outside "the cabin." Courtesy
of Patricia Wilde.

Wilde in Nijinska's *Pictures at
an Exhibition* with Marquis de
Cuevas's Ballet International, 1944.
Photo by Fred Fehl. Courtesy of
Patricia Wilde.

ABOVE
Nora White in *Danses Concertantes*.
Photo by Maurice Seymour.

LEFT
Rehearsal break, Hollywood Bowl,
1947. Courtesy of Patricia Wilde.

Wilde (center) in Valerie Bettis's
Virginia Sampler. Photo by Fred
Fehl. Courtesy of Patricia Wilde.

John Taras's *Design with Strings*
with the Metropolitan Ballet.
Photo by Duncan Melvin. Courtesy
of Patricia Wilde.

TOP

August 16, 1950: backstage at
Covent Garden with Yvonne
Mounsey and critics Mary Clarke
and P. W. Manchester, during New
York City Ballet's London debut
season. Courtesy of Patricia Wilde.

BOTTOM

With Nora Kaye in Robbins's *Age
of Anxiety*. Photo by Maria Austria
and Henk Jonker. © Particam
Pictures, Amsterdam. Courtesy
of Patricia Wilde.

With Frank Hobi
in *La Valse*. Photo by
Maurice Seymour.

Caracole. Courtesy of
Patricia Wilde.

TOP

New York City Ballet arrives in
Paris, May 1952: Balanchine flanked
by Hayden, Kaye, Le Clercq, Reed,
Adams, Wilde, Tallchief, and
Tompkins. Courtesy of the author.

BOTTOM

New York City Ballet in Berlin,
September 1952. Courtesy
of Patricia Wilde.

Backstage at City Center, dressed for Dewdrop in *The Nutcracker*, 1954. Photo by Saul Goodman. Courtesy of Patricia Wilde.

With *Square Dance* partner Nicholas Magallanes and caller Elisha Keeler. Photo by Philip Bloom. Courtesy Mollie Keeler James.

Gounod Symphony with
Jonathan Watts. Courtesy
of Jonathan Watts.

TOP

New York City Ballet in Moscow,
briefed on Cuban Missile Crisis.
Courtesy of Patricia Wilde.

BOTTOM

With Balanchine in New York
State Theater studio, 1964. Photo
by Martha Swope, © Copyright The
New York Public Library.

Signing autographs, early 1960s.
Rothschild Photo, Los Angeles.
Courtesy of Patricia Wilde.

RIGHT
Wilde with family, Geneva,
1969. Courtesy
of Patricia Wilde.

BELOW
Rehearsing with Natalia
Makarova at American Ballet
Theatre, 1971. Photo by
Herbert Migdoll.

On vacation in Europe
with family, 1983. Courtesy
of Patricia Wilde.

With Anya and Youri
Bardyguine after gala
celebrating Wilde's tenth
anniversary at Pittsburgh
Ballet Theatre. Courtesy
of Patricia Wilde.

it was like petitioning a void, and "God knows I got awfully angry with him many times." Le Clercq's marriage didn't prevent no-holds-barred palaver between her and sister ballerinas, including the not infrequent commiseration "What the hell does he think he's doing?"

While NYCB was performing in Edinburgh in August 1952, Balanchine, together with most of his company, had gone to see Her Majesty's High-landers perform outdoors—a spectacular occasion, lit by torches. Wilde believed that it was seeing them dance that put a bee into his bonnet that became manifest when the company reconvened for rehearsals in New York.

He began working on a new ballet, *Scotch Symphony*, performed to several movements from Mendelssohn's Symphony No. 3, informally given that national identification. Balanchine's new ballet would be a tribute, a distillation of Filippo Taglioni's 1832 *La Sylphide*. Depicting a Scottish laird seduced by an evanescent sylph, the ballet's premiere in Paris is considered a landmark in the introduction of the Romantic ballet aesthetic. (More recent, and closer to home, was William Dollar's *Highland Fling* for Ballet Society in 1947.)

Balanchine had always been insistent that the dancer's tread on the ground convey the illusion of weightlessness. He demanded landings from jumps "where you keep it going into the floor with absolutely no noise," Wilde recalled. "He always wanted us wearing old pointe shoes; he never wanted a sound when we landed, when we ran."

Perhaps he felt that he could get the quietest landing possible by having the dancers hardly put their heels down on the ground at all, in the manner of Highland dancing. Its dancers are consistently on half-toe, which facil-itates the particular speed of their flurried feet-crossings. Wilde believed that's what had inspired Balanchine to ask her to do what he now asked her to do in class.

It wasn't unusual for Balanchine to ask Wilde to demonstrate batterie in class. Now he wanted her during center exercises in class to sink into a grand plié, then rise into *entrechats six* and back into the ground without putting her heels down. It was "killing," not to have the cushioning relief as well as the springing impetus of a traditional plié with heels pressed into the floor. Nora White said, "When she told me about that I thought, it's a wonder she ever danced after that." Wilde herself resented being used as a guinea pig in this way.

Having demonstrated that it could be done, Wilde and her colleagues were asked to apply the principal wherever they could. And this was how, Balanchine informed Wilde, he wanted her to perform the solo he was making for her in the new ballet.

Corps member Una Kai, who later during the 1950s became a rehearsal director for Balanchine, remembered it slightly differently. She had taken his classes at School of American Ballet beginning in 1947, when she recalled him already admonishing his students not to let their heels descend all the way into the ground. According to Balanchine, it had been an emphasis even in Russia. He told Kai and her classmates that as a student in St. Petersburg his shoes were inspected after class, and if the heels were darkened by contact with the ground he would be punished: a favorite food would be withheld from him at dinner. Perhaps Balanchine in 1952 was mapping out a new horizon, as he did frequently, on the theory that aspiring to the impossible permits a readier achievement of the just-out-of-reach.

Marie-Jeanne, now briefly returned to Balanchine's orbit, also recalled decades later that it was at this time that Balanchine decided "you can't put your heels down in landing. What he was trying to avoid was landing heavily—*boom*!" He told her that he was trying to get the dancers to approximate the famously supple landings of André Eglevsky.

Wilde agreed that Balanchine particularly admired Eglevsky's "lushness." She recalled Balanchine telling a story of Eglevsky being asked to perform a big jump and doing so without disturbing the change he was carrying in a pocket in his rehearsal trousers—so soft was his landing. Eglevsky had very strong feet, each part of which he was able to utilize, aided by his Achilles tendon and thighs, so that, as Wilde saw again and again, he "just melted into the stage."

Although Wilde herself understood that no dancer should, particularly in Balanchine's work, sit too long or heavily in a plié, both she and her colleagues were now in "agony." Their emulation of the Scottish dancers raised the likelihood of comparable injuries, "terrible calf cramps and shin splints," to which the Scottish are prone.

In *Scotch Symphony*, Tallchief was the Sylph disturbing the peace of Highland brave André Eglevsky. As Balanchine preferred to do, however, linear and explicit narrative was scanted. Wilde led the first movement, prior to the appearance of the rapturously spellbound hero and mysterious, elusive heroine. Sometimes alone, sometimes in tandem with Michael Maule and Frank Hobi—all dressed in tartans—sometimes threading through a corps of men and women, what she danced was an extremely complicated and dense blend of ballet pyrotechnics and Scottish flavor to the upper body and arms. It was charming and scintillating and extremely taxing. Barbara Walczak, who followed her into the role a year later, recalled, "It was one of those roles that to get through it once, you already had second wind and you thought you would die. All of Pat Wilde's roles were like that."

Wilde made it seem effortless. Reviewing the November 11 premiere, P. W. Manchester in *Dance News* described her evocation of a "sonsy Scotch lassie" extolling the way she "spurs the ground with her steely points or flies above it as though the laws of gravity have ceased to apply as far as she is concerned."

It was an oddity of this work that Balanchine did not follow his usual practice and bring all the leads back for the final movement. Here it was led by Tallchief, Eglevsky, and corps—no Wilde. As she ran off at the end of the first movement, her path intercepted Eglevsky's as he made his initial entrance. Unseen by the audience, she greeted him with a smile that said, "It's all yours now!"

Wilde's pas de trois was deemed appropriate party fare for a November 28 dinner dance given in the company's honor by Ballet Associates, a fund-raising organization. Wilde, Hobi, and Maule performed on the small stage of the Waldorf-Astoria ballroom before six hundred guests, including Edith Sitwell.

Onstage, Wilde duly observed to the best of her ability Balanchine's injunction that she stay perpetually up on her pointes—but only so far as physical survival allowed. It took a while for her as well as the company to learn how to accommodate what he wanted. There was a point when Wilde, Tallchief, and many others in the company were suffering painful tendonitis, which Wilde attributes to their striving too literally for what he'd ask her to demonstrate at the barre.

Having established a precept, Balanchine now maintained it as a guiding philosophy but relaxed his absolutism, certainly where Wilde was concerned. NYCB's dancers would become famous for their fleetness, their abjuration of anything that could inhibit skimming speed and instantaneous changes of direction.

21

BY THE SEAT OF

HER TUTU

Nora White recalls Balanchine during his Ballet Russe years rehearsing the company in *Serenade* at the Hollywood Bowl, making adjustments to accommodate the enormous semicircular stage and the lack of concealed wing space. One thing that was not going to change, however, despite the size of the stage, was the tempo. The ensemble was going to have to cover a greater amount of space in the allotted amount of time. In a situation like this, was there no possibility of slowing down the music? "Oh, heavens no," Wilde said, speaking from the benefit of her many years in *Serenade* with both Ballet Russe and New York City Ballet. Recalling that particular rehearsal in Los Angeles, in fact, Nora said that in fact he might have been speeding it up, making it more challenging for the dancers and creating that much more excitement for the audience. Certainly it was a prod for the performers: "You get the kick in the pants and off you go!" is how Wilde puts it today.

The kick in the pants was something Wilde quickly acclimated to as she moved from Ballet Russe into NYCB; now that he had his own company, Balanchine was making that kind of goad toward the impossible a governing aesthetic value as well as philosophy of performance.

Barbara Walczak recalled that Balanchine "had a way of demanding, of asking you to do a little bit more than you thought you could, of keeping you on edge, keeping that carrot in front of you. And that's what the audience felt. When these dancers got onstage, they were dancing to the edge of their ability. They were going over the precipice."

Embedded in the technique itself were moments of possible peril over which the dancer's triumph enhanced the gratification of the spectator. *Allegro Brillante*, created for Tallchief in 1956, was soon danced by both Wilde and Hayden as well—all three performances became renowned. To a piano cadenza in Tchaikovsky's unfinished Piano Concerto No. 3, the ballerina had to sink down to the floor in a very low and broad fourth position, rise to her full height on pointe, perform two pirouettes, and then sink to the ground again. Balanchine was adamant that the ballerina be as low, as high, and as low again as she could. In performance it was a scary moment for Wilde, if she was tired, but she had no doubt that if she didn't overcome her fear she wasn't going to get to do the role.

Looking back, Wilde recognizes that Balanchine frequently engineered performances so that they were pervaded by an injection of uncertainty. Partly it was a matter of enhancing his own enjoyment by ensuring a constant quotient of unpredictability: "It gave him a little extra excitement, watching the performance."

A NYCB colleague declared that Balanchine did more than utilize, indeed rather took advantage of, Wilde's "incredible facility" for learning choreography quickly. "He loved just throwing me on," Wilde said, but eleventh-hour substitutions were something she wasn't happy with. Going onstage without sufficient rehearsal time happened frequently and was never a pleasure.

In 1952 she was scheduled to debut in the Sanguinic variation of *The Four Temperaments*, created by Mary Ellen Moylan with Ballet Society in 1946 and danced at NYCB by Tallchief and Hayden. Balanchine had commissioned the score from Paul Hindemith, who titled the movements after the four humors that ancient and medieval medicine believed determined the working of the human body and mind. In Sanguinic, the lead woman and man, together with a small corps of women, were appropriately playful, resolute, proactive.

She was going to be partnered by Magallanes, but as the performance approached, no rehearsals had been scheduled. Magallanes had danced Sanguinic many times, and Wilde certainly knew all her steps. Furthermore, Magallanes was an inspiring partner. He "just had the magic touch," Wilde said. "He didn't have to dig his hands into you to give you an impetus that you could still feel." But working out the partnering kinks was still something that needed to happen. Finally, Balanchine sent word that he would rehearse with them onstage at City Center on the evening of the performance. Both dancers waited with a pianist, but Balanchine never showed up.

"You'll just have to refuse to do it," Magallanes told her. "This is impossible. He can't do this to you."

A half hour before the 8:30 curtain, Balanchine turned up. He'd been waylaid with friends at the Russian Tea Room around the corner on Fifty-Seventh Street. Wilde tried to bow out. "Mr. B., I can't do it." He assured her that she could. "It's going to be a disaster," she whimpered. "The music . . . I'm not sure I'll be on the music."

"You do it like it's a rehearsal tonight. It doesn't matter. You'll be fine. Nobody will know except me whether you're right or wrong. You'll be all right." As it turned out, nothing went drastically wrong in the performance, but it wasn't one she enjoyed. "You see?" he told her afterward. "You could do it."

"He was right in a way," she said, "that nobody knew or cared" if she missed a step or wasn't perfectly in time with the music. The ballets and the company were still too new for the audience to have a microscopic knowledge of how things were supposed to be.

Certainly a certain amount of pinch-hitting was inevitable, given the company's small size. Wilde had to be ready to step in at a moment's notice—sometimes midperformance. During a *Serenade* at City Center in 1952, Janet Reed was dancing the Waltz ballerina and Wilde the Dark Angel, or what roughly conformed to what we think of those roles today. Balanchine had a propensity for redistributing this ballet's choreography according to how many leads he wanted to showcase, from three to five.

Soon after the performance began, Reed experienced what she thought was a leg cramp. Actually she had torn her Achilles tendon, a much more serious injury. In the wings she massaged her calf, asking Wilde to perform one quick pass across the stage after another. "No, I can't do the next one. Pat, can you do the next one?"

Wilde and sister ballerinas wanted to be as prepared as they could. They craved as much rehearsal with Balanchine as possible, as much information and specificity as he could give. Sometimes he was happy to return even to a very familiar passage in the quest for maximum brilliance. When something worked well, he wanted to make it work even better. "He loved the way I flew through the air," Wilde said—with drive, purpose, abandon: "I'm coming!" But the more Balanchine approved, the more possibilities he inevitably saw for enhancement. Wilde recalled Balanchine rehearsing her onstage at City Center in her jumps from the Élégie in *Serenade*. He worked out the timing to make it as gasp-provoking in performance as possible. In rehearsal she was cued not by a musical note but by his command. When his "Now!" shot out like a starting gun's blast, she took off to the back of the stage, reversing her flight path as she vaulted into her partner's arms. Balanchine preferred her to start as far downstage as possible to give her time to get as much speed as she could into her run, as much height as well as reach into her jump into the upstage partner's arms. As much as Balanchine's prompting, the customary presence of Magallanes waiting upstage liberated Wilde from inhibition: "As long as Nicky was there, I was OK!"

As spectator, Balanchine could enjoy the experience of Wilde unleashed as much as those in the audience. "Oh, my God, look at that!" he said to NYCB's Allegra Kent one night as they both stood in the wings watching her.

Balanchine was stimulating and insistent, but recalling rehearsals with him, "'considerate' is the word that keeps coming back to me," Wilde said. He took for granted that the dancers would be working as hard as they could, but at a certain point he might say, "Oh, that's enough. That was good." It had progressed as far as it was going to in that particular rehearsal.

Nothing was static in Balanchine's technique. "He changed his mind a lot," deputy Una Kai said. For years he said he wanted big jumps performed "as though you are jumping over something," Kai recalled. "Not flying flat through the air but up and over." But when Violette Verdy later joined NYCB in 1958, she jumped with her legs open in an 180-degree split in the air, and Balanchine loved it. After Verdy, he decided that the split jeté was acceptable. "He didn't encourage it, but he didn't object."

He was also wont to tinker with the shapes of the ballets themselves. Throughout the 1950s, he was expanding repertory staples *Serenade* and *Symphony in C* by adding musical repeats in the original scores and creating choreography to suit. Wilde recalled frequent experimenting in *Symphony in C*. At one point the first and fourth movements were performed with an identical finale. A wild caprice of Balanchine's was asking the dancers to perform the first movement twice consecutively—in its entirety. Dancing the lead, Wilde recalled finishing exited downstage just as the corps women were entering at the back of the stage, cycling though to the first bars one more time. By the time they finished doing it all once again and the second movement finally took the stage, "our legs were falling off." In the wings they bent over, pounding the floor, and Balanchine quickly retired this particular experiment.

He had a different vision of ensemble work than the classical aesthetic, where the corps ideally melds into a single, synchronized expression. By contrast, as Wilde said, "Mr. B. wasn't big on everybody being together," and on occasion the corps was "really messy." In subsequent years, somewhat anarchic corps work was a hallmark of NYCB. In the 1950s, his small rehearsal staff was trying to structure it along more conventional lines, but making that happen was another story. Part of the reason was lack of time. A lot of standard repertory suffered because of the priority given to new works. But sometimes Balanchine seemed to actively sabotage the concerted unanimous ensemble.

Wilde recalled a particular rehearsal of *Serenade* where ballet mistress Vida Brown had figured out a way where all the women could coalesce on time and then peel away canonically in a configuration that recalled a moment in act 2 of *Giselle*. Balanchine arrived. "No, no, no, no, no!" He wanted things organized "so that they couldn't get there—but they got there!" It was to be haphazard, miraculous, and thrill-provoking.

22

THE POODLE

Given that he was still courting Wilde, Hubert Saal was perhaps not totally disinterested; nevertheless, his admiration was undoubtedly genuine. He wrote in *Town and Country* in October 1952 that Wilde and Le Clercq most epitomized the Balanchine dancer. "Miss Wilde has the fundamental force. She embodies the vigor, the dynamic motion of the whole company. In *Swan Lake*, as in *Cakewalk*, *Pas de Trois*, and *Serenade*, she displays an incredible technique and a passionate feeling for her roles that evoke a vision of the abandoned bacchante."

Wilde's repertory was chock-full of technical and pure dance showcases, but she found herself craving dramatic roles that could release her imagination. At NYCB, Tudor in 1951 had made her understudy to Tanaquil Le Clercq as The Woman in His Past in *Lilac Garden*, a tear-wringing depiction of a garden party where the future husband and wife make wrenching farewells to his mistress and the true love of her life, respectively, before proceeding to their loveless marriage. But when it came to performance, it was Mounsey, not Wilde, who eventually alternated with Le Clercq. Perhaps height was an issue: Mounsey was taller, closer to Le Clercq's height.

William Dollar's *The Duel*, however, gave Wilde a most dramatic opportunity and a rather transgressive identity when she danced it for the first time in December 1952. Wilde was Clorinda, a pagan warrior facing off against Christian knight Tancred during the Crusades, neither knowing that the other is actually his or her beloved until Tancred fatally wounds her.

Clorinda was a taxing role—she danced a solo of big jumps—but in performance technical perfection was not the primary goal. At least as important to Wilde was sustaining belief in what she was enacting, entering into the thoughts, emotions, physical and psychological identity of someone else. For her it was like reliving her childhood on her mother's estate, when she would spin little stories in her mind.

Created for Roland Petit's Ballets de Paris in 1949, *The Duel* had entered NYCB's repertory the following year. To date it had been the exclusive property there of Melissa Hayden. Reviewing a subsequent performance by Wilde in May 1953, Walter Terry in the *Herald-Tribune* wrote that in her debut the previous winter "the stylistic and dramatic areas tended to escape her," and she had been "no match" for Hayden. By the following May, however, Terry was commending her for decided improvement. Martin in the *Times*, reviewing her May performance, wrote that Wilde was 'not the fire-eating warrior-maiden that Miss Hayden was, but her qualities of youth and fragile valor carry with them enormous poignancy." Wilde's "fresh colors" had produced in lover/combatant Moncion a "fresh reaction" as well. "There can be no doubt that the little work has taken a new lease on life."

That December 1952, Wilde also danced one of the leads in Ruthanna Boris's new ballet *Kaleidoscope*, to brassy, rather circus-inspired music by the contemporary composer Dmitry Kabalevsky. It was a mélange of incidents, some of them offbeat, among them a strange tango Wilde performed with Frank Hobi. The critics were intrigued but not fully sold on the ballet, and it didn't last long in NYCB's repertory. But it showed again that Boris had a unique view of Wilde's onstage possibilities.

New York City Ballet's winter 1952–53 season wound up being extended six weeks, running all told for more than two and a half months. Writing in *Cue* magazine in its January 10, 1953, issue, Emory Lewis declared that Wilde had during the ongoing season "jumped from soloist calibre to ballerina status."

By now, she had moved from First Avenue to an apartment on Thirty-Fifth Street between Fifth and Madison Avenues. It too was small, but a definite improvement—it did have hot water. Shopping for groceries was a bit of a chore, however, since food stores were few and far between in the blocks around her. The nearest place she liked patronizing was Macy's, but sometimes she'd trek over to the small shops on Ninth Avenue.

After closing in New York on January 25, NYCB performed short debut seasons in February in Baltimore and Washington, DC. But despite the expanded workweeks, the dancers still needed as much employment as possible. Applying for unemployment insurance was anything but pleasant, with the women invariably asked why they weren't looking for some other type of physical work—say, scrubbing floors or waiting on tables? They would explain that daily class was a necessity even when they weren't rehearsing or performing. Eventually NYCB worked out an arrangement with the labor bureau whereby the company would automatically receive unemployment during layoffs.

Wilde eagerly accepted André Eglevsky's suggestion that, together with Melissa Hayden, they should form a small touring company. It began early in 1953 as an all-star "Ballet Sextet" that toured the South for two months. Wilde, Hayden, and Eglevsky were joined by Nora Kaye, Diana Adams, and Hugh Laing. There was standard repertory to perform, and in addition Wilde was Eros in a new ballet, *The Golden Apple*, choreographed by the Metropolitan Opera's Zachary Solov.

Over the next decade the core trio would appear under the aegis of many concert series around the country as well as at the 1958 World's Fair in Brussels. Typically they traveled with a pianist and around four additional dancers. The program wouldn't be all-ballet; they included a Spanish dancer at one point. Balanchine agreed to create a new trio especially for them, on condition that his name wasn't used. Eglevsky was credited instead, as he had been with the *Sentimental Colloquy* that Balanchine created for the Marquis de Cuevas's company in 1944.

Wilde and Hayden left most of the administering to Eglevsky. He was both highly organized and finicky about stage deportment. Hayden had taken to stuffing her bodice with tissue to augment her bust line. During one performance of their little group, Hayden's Kleenex fell out. "Anything like that drove André up the wall," Wilde recalled.

During 1952–53, Wilde, Hayden, and Eglevsky were also semiregular guests on Kate Smith's weekly television show, performing a wide variety of material encompassing nineteenth-century classics. In May 1953, for example, they offered excerpts from *The Sleeping Beauty* arranged by Eglevsky. Hayden was Aurora and Wilde the Lilac Fairy.

On May 6, NYCB opened a five-week season at City Center. Opposite Adams and Le Clercq Wilde made her debut in Hayden's role in Balanchine's *Valse Fantaisie*. Named after its Glinka score, it had premiered the previous December. It was windswept and buoyant, as the three women, each costumed à la Russe by Barbara Karinska, shared one male partner. Wilde enjoyed the way each ballerina would "do our little thing, and then we'd come back together." It was tiring even though it wasn't very long and wasn't "showy technique," she recalled. Indeed, the ballet was described by Martin in the *Times* as "a kind of perpetuum mobile," in which Wilde, Adams, and Le Clercq were dancing "like dreams."

The season was also something of a mini–Lew Christensen festival, in which two more of his ballets were added to the repertory. *Filling Station* had been created for Kirstein's Ballet Caravan back in 1938 and could alone have justified Kirstein's premise that ballet could enliven and be enlivened by American genre settings. *Con Amore*, another Christensen comedy, had premiered earlier in 1953 at the San Francisco Ballet, where he was spending more and more time. *Con Amore* was a mad mélange blending nineteenth-century pastiche and modern-day adulterous entanglement, all performed to Rossini. Both stories come to a simultaneous boil. It was San Francisco's Sally Bailey who danced the Captain of the Amazons, who were redolent of Giselle's Wilis, at the NYCB premiere. Soon thereafter she returned to the West Coast, and both Wilde and Mounsey alternately took her place as leader of the tribe.

NYCB closed its New York spring season on June 14. On July 2 in Red Rocks, Colorado, they opened a two-night preface to a monthlong debut visit to the West Coast. The open-air amphitheater was not well equipped: there were no wings and no crossover behind the scenery, forcing the dancers to run down a corridor beneath the stage if they needed to reappear on the opposite side. Oxygen tanks placed at the side of the stage were there to compensate for the high altitude, but equally debilitating was the wind. "If you tried to breathe, it went past your mouth," Wilde recalled. The dancers found themselves gulping for air as the topiary forming makeshift wings was blown to the ground. The audience, however, didn't mind a bit. In the *Denver Post*, Alex Murphree described their opening as "an occasion for rejoicing under the stars."

Also open to the elements, but a kinder place to perform, was Los Angeles's Greek Theater in Griffith Park, where the company's two-week debut season attracted an eager following. Mildred Norton in the *Los Angeles Daily News* described "a large turnout of balletomanes who seem to have taken up permanent residence in the amphitheatre for the duration of the troupe's stay."

Traveling with the company, teaching class, William Dollar made an uncharacteristically acerbic remark that still amused Wilde fifty years later. Dollar was teaching at the studio underneath the stage of the Greek. Early in the class, he registered his displeasure with Yvonne Mounsey's exertions at the barre: "Yvonne, you look like an old Kelvinator"—the then-ubiquitous clunky and squat brand of refrigerator.

Balanchine's frequent decision to put as many ballerinas as possible into *Serenade* paid dividends. Viola Hegyi Swisher in the *Los Angeles Mirror* extolled the myriad contrasting styles of "joyous little Janet Reed, crystalline Tanaquil Le Clercq, serenely feminine Diana Adams, Patricia Wilde, a beautiful dancer of great tensile strength, and lissome Yvonne Mounsey."

Their four-week stay was the first of many visits to the Greek. Wilde usually stayed with a friend, Sally Forrest, who was publicist for the theater. She lived in the San Fernando Valley and opened her home and pool to the dancers for downtime on their days off. NYCB's Jonathan Watts fondly recalled "swimming, wonderful meals, lots to drink," at Forrest's open houses. Often staying there with Wilde was company manager Betty Cage, who practiced tai chi, which was then novel in America.

After Los Angeles they moved indoors for two weeks in San Francisco at the War Memorial Opera House, well known to Wilde from her Ballet Russe years. They closed their tour August 14, and then, back in New York immediately started preparing for a three-month tour of Europe that would begin in Milan at the La Scala opera house on September 8. Balanchine had worked there earlier in the year, staging works with Le Clercq as guest artist. All told, on this tour they would perform in nine Italian cities before concluding with stops in Germany and finally Brussels.

After a week at La Scala, they had a short season in Venice, before returning to Milan for a second Scala season. Opera house *intendant* Antonio Ghiringhelli did not, however, seem overjoyed to have them there and was continually imposing new rules governing their passage through the theater. But La Scala's resident ballet company, with whom Balanchine had worked the prior January, was most welcoming.

The tour marked a brief and ill-fated return by Marie-Jeanne Pelus. A decade earlier she'd been Balanchine's adored muse, but was now perceived by him as an unreliable albatross. Soon after joining NYCB in 1948, she had left to marry her second husband. Now, four years later, it was not Balanchine but Lincoln Kirstein who asked her to accompany them to Europe. She told Kirstein she needed a year to get back in shape; he told her it was now or never. Yet Wilde was quite aware that her friend and ex-colleague "was not ready to dance." In Milan she pulled a muscle onstage and needed help to get to the wings. "You'd better go home," Balanchine told her, "You're like Joe Louis, you can't make a comeback." At age thirty-three, she decided it was time to bring her glorious but checkered career to a close.

Wilde now began to accept Bardyguine's invitations to eat after the performance. He regaled her with stories of the French Resistance under the Nazi occupation, when he had been doing things like sabotaging railroad tracks to derail enemy trains.

At the end of September, NYCB was leaving Como for Naples, changing trains in Rome. They had been told that their railroad car would be shunted onto the connecting train, so the dancers left all their things in the car. Wilde and Mounsey took advantage of several hours of free time to secure accommodations for their appearance in Rome two weeks later. When they got back to the station, they looked for a train destined for Naples, not realizing that the posted destination was instead "Amalfi Coast." Indeed, all of their colleagues seemed lost as well. Finally they spotted Bardyguine trying to muster a group of reluctant dancers, convinced that he'd gotten on the wrong train. The train was pulling out. Bardyguine was yelling at an attendant to pull the emergency brake, but he was refusing.

The dancers feared they'd lose all their belongings, because they'd been told that thievery was rampant in Naples. Cameras had been left on the seats, freshly washed tights hung out to dry. Finally they found the next train to the south. When they arrived in Naples, Bardyguine and company manager Betty Cage were there to greet them. Their luggage was safe and sound. The two company officials had packed up everything themselves and taken it off the train. In Wilde's eyes, Bardyguine was a hero.

At Naples's historic Teatro di San Carlo, Wilde experienced one of the most mortifying moments of her performing career. Backstage there was a tribe of cats maintained to keep rats and mice away. They descended en masse to greet the dancers at the stage door, but the administration assured them that the cats never, ever strayed onto the stage in performance.

One night during their week at the San Carlo, however, Wilde was dancing *Concerto Barocco* to the unprecedented and inexplicable hilarity of the audience. Was something sticking to someone's costume? They eventually discovered that a cat had indeed wandered onstage. It provided a riveting display of felinity, grooming itself, then finally strolling across the stage and back into the wings. Wilde wondered if the cats did routinely wander onstage but were usually disguised by opera's voluminous sets and costumes.

FROM TODAY'S PERSPECTIVE, it seems incredible that Wilde at twenty-five was practically the last unmarried NYCB ballerina, most of whom were around her age. Marriage, of course, was what women in their twenties generally did in the 1950s, what conferred the emblem of respectability and social integration. Celebrated female performers might generally be allowed a certain additional amount of sexual and romantic license, but that does not seem to have been eagerly grasped by NYCB's leading women. "We all had boyfriends or lovers," Wilde recalled, but holy matrimony was usually the not-too-delayed or remote culmination. Balanchine notoriously objected to his female roster getting married, which might have made them all the more determined to place an intermediate man somewhere in the orbit of their omnipotent boss.

Although Gordon New was waiting for her in New York, Wilde thought she had succumbed to Bardyguine's attentions in Genoa, at the end of October, when he bought her a dark brown poodle she named Brandy. Strolling one cold night with Bardyguine after a performance Wilde couldn't resist a curly brown face, cradled in a street vendor's jacket. They were sure that he had been stolen from a kennel, however, and so Bardyguine insisted she take the dog to a veterinarian early the next morning to verify the state of its health. She gave the dog's putative owner her hotel address and told him to meet her there the next morning.

A vet told her that Brandy was a male, contrary to what she'd been told, and was less than a month old, months younger than his purported owner had claimed. But he was healthy. After agreeing on a price at the hotel, Wilde needed certification that the dog was indeed her own before the company headed to Germany. In Italy as well as other European countries at the time, it was possible to go to a local chemist's to arrange for legal papers.

In Munich and then Stuttgart, Wilde brought Brandy to the dressing room she shared with Le Clercq. Wilde was feeding him warm milk and an egg every two hours. Le Clercq augmented his diet by handing him her old pointe shoes to chew on. After the performances in Stuttgart, Wilde and Bardyguine ate at a restaurant that delighted the couple by giving their poodle a bowl to feast from under their table.

One night she left him in her hotel, and he relieved himself on the carpet. The hotel didn't make an issue of it until, as they were checking out, Wilde got to the front desk as roommate Mounsey was handed a bill including the cost of a new carpet—more than the dog itself had cost. "I'm not paying that!" she insisted. But Wilde was.

The tour closed with a week in Brussels ending November 17. Wilde was now cooking ground beef for Brandy on a Sterno stove in her hotel room. She and Bardyguine wisely secured the papers necessary to get the dog through U.S. customs. (Birds that other dancers brought home to

New York were exterminated by the customs officials because they lacked proper papers.)

They were scheduled to fly home from Paris, and Wilde decided to take the night train after the closing performance in Brussels. She'd get an extra day in Paris, where she and her dog could stay with Roger Shattuck's friend Baucion. Reaching the United States, however, proved much more difficult. Fog settled in and they waited several days in Paris for it to lift; finally they were told to board the boat train to England and fly from London.

On September 9, Wilde's sister Nora had given birth to a son, Marc, her second child. The Shattucks were living in Cambridge, Massachusetts. As Wilde flew over Boston on the way to New York, she thought how nice it would be to get off and see her new nephew. Her sentiments found fruition when they turned back from Idlewild in New York, lacking sufficient gas to circle the stacked airport as many times as would be required before landing.

They flew back to Boston for refueling, landing at two in the morning. "I'm getting off here," Wilde announced, even though it meant leaving her luggage on the plane.

The customs people had all just gone off duty and were not pleased at having to come back to their desks. But she got through with Brandy and got out and called her sister. She saw her nephew and stayed a few days. Marriage was on her mind as she returned to New York, while New York City Ballet was about to launch a production that would prove of inestimable value to its future fortunes.

23

WEDDING

NIGHT

Wilde waited to accept Bardyguine's offer until she had put behind her the unpleasant task of facing Gordon New with the news that their love affair was over. It was not music to his ears. But she believed that he had developed a taste for ballet-dancing women; her peripheral impression was that he was dating NYCB colleagues of hers for some time to come.

Adventurous as usual, Wilde was marrying a man of the world and a man of experience. Eight years older than she, Bardyguine was divorced and was the father of a young son living in France. He spoke and read Russian but identified culturally with France. He had been only a toddler when his mother took him out of Russia to join his father in Berlin, before they joined his paternal grandparents in Nice. Bardyguine had previously been involved with NYCB's Edwina Fontaine, but Wilde dismissed his philandering as the bad influence of André Eglevsky, who would, however, remain a close and important figure in both of their lives.

Anya Davis, Wilde and Bardyguine's daughter, wonders today whether Wilde's marrying a fellow Russian with whom Balanchine was friendly could indeed have buffered and thus helped her mother's relationship with the choreographer. While in the long run that may be true, Balanchine's initial reaction to the marriage was anything but propitious.

Balanchine had decided to stage *The Nutcracker*, Tchaikovsky's final ballet score, choreographed at its premiere in St. Petersburg in 1893 by Petipa and Ivanov. This would be the first full-length ballet staged by NYCB. Onstage in St. Petersburg, Balanchine had danced the act 2 "Kingdom of the Sweets" hoop dance, which he now re-created verbatim for Robert Barnett. Everything else he rechoreographed.

Monday, December 14, 1953, was the first day of *Nutcracker* rehearsals. It was also Wilde and Bardyguine's wedding day. After going down to city hall to pick up a wedding license, she had told Bardyguine that they could be married either on Saturday, December 12, or on Monday, the 14th. "Everything bad that has ever happened to me has happened on the 12th!" Bardyguine replied. So December 14 it was.

First they went to see NYCB company doctor Mel Kiddon for the requisite check-up, then down to city hall to tie the knot, then back to her apartment for a glass of champagne. From there Wilde went to the School of American Ballet for rehearsal. The marriage was not unexpected, but the anxieties of the harem vis-à-vis pasha prevailed. She walked in to the school wearing her wedding corsage and nearly everyone in her vicinity asked, "Does Mr. B. know?"

Wilde didn't tell Balanchine directly; instead she told rehearsal director Vida Brown. When Brown informed Balanchine, his response was, "I'm so glad 'cause I was worried about Brandy." "So you don't need Pat?" Brown asked. "Oh, yes," Balanchine corrected her. "It's very difficult music." Balanchine was going to create the Dance of the Marzipan Shepherdesses for Wilde and four corps women. Their music was, however, hardly very forbidding, even to a choreographer less musically tutored than Balanchine.

Wilde's two-hour rehearsal call was for seven o'clock that night. "Everything he gave me to do that night was ridiculously difficult." Among the tasks assigned was repeated *entrechats six* landing on pointe. "He can't do this, he can't do this," the four women behind her whispered. "He's doing it," Wilde affirmed.

It went on. It got worse. She was very angry. "I thought, OK, he cares about my dog, but what about me?" To herself she vowed that Balanchine was not going to give her anything that she couldn't do. The battle of wills lasted not two hours, as originally scheduled, but instead no fewer than three. It was ten o'clock that night before he called a halt. Wilde's colleagues were as furious as she. She duly reported to her in-laws' apartment for a wedding supper that had started much earlier. But by then she wasn't in the mood to eat anything.

Difficult as it had been, the marathon rehearsal was something in the nature of a wedding present, since for the next two weeks Balanchine effectively banished Wilde from the company. Every day she took class but was not scheduled for a single rehearsal. Eventually his point sank in: her new marital status was not going to change anything in their relationship. He was, as if there could ever have been any doubt, still the boss.

Having made that perfectly clear, Balanchine now signaled forgiveness. He ushered in 1954 by bringing her back into the fold. She and Diana Adams, partnered by Magallanes and Moncion, would lead part one of the new ballet to which he now turned his attentions. Performed to and titled after Arnold Schoenberg's Opus 34, it would premiere January 19, two weeks before *The Nutcracker.*

Schoenberg's eight-minute *Accompaniment-Music for a Motion Picture* was played through twice. Schoenberg's deconstruction of melody produced an anticlassical movement palette. Dressed in white leotards, Wilde and colleagues stood in turned-in positions and wrapped their arms around their knees. As always, Balanchine was meticulously observant. A habitual gesture of Wilde's in class was shaking her calf out to loosen her muscles. And as the curtain went up on part 1, that's what she was now doing onstage. But at the end, all present collapsed in a heap.

Part 2 was set in a nightmarish operating theater, in which Le Clercq and Herbert Bliss were seemingly flayed by unspooling layers of gauze, then exposed in skeleton-printed unitards. A cadre of men crawled under a black tarpaulin to invisibly transport her across the stage while she performed what Robert Barnett recalled as "contortions." At the very end of part 2, five klieg lights from the back of stage shone right into the audience. "I think a couple of people had to be carried out," recalled NYCB's Jillana Zimmerman, who later danced Le Clercq's role. "It was not pretty." The two leads walked upstage and disappeared as if they had disintegrated.

The ballet's rehearsal period became fraught for Wilde as she realized that she was coming down with a fever. As the premiere approached, during breaks she resorted to lying down at the back of the City Center stage, shaking and sweating.

A "Balanchine weirdie," in the words of Robert Sylvester in the *Daily News*, *Opus 34* was highly regarded in some critical quarters, but shocking and provocative to all. As with so many intriguing ballets from these early years of the company, it was gone from the repertory soon after its premiere—in this case, a year later.

Soon after *Opus 34* opened, Le Clercq was hospitalized with appendicitis—"It was one of those seasons when everybody was getting things," Wilde recalled. Wilde herself was now definitely on the sick list as well, although she continued to perform. As so often, it didn't seem to occur to her that she could request some relief. Balanchine recommended a particular doctor, who was stumped by her symptoms. The NYCB company doctor, Mel Kiddon, told Wilde that her suspicions of mononucleosis were unfounded. During the war he'd conducted experiments on the disease in London. Finally she went to her own doctor, who wasted no time: "You've got mono."

Le Clercq recovered in time to dance the February 2 *Nutcracker* opening, but Wilde was forced to sit it out. During Wilde's two weeks in limbo, Balanchine had choreographed a new version of Marzipan for Janet Reed. If Wilde couldn't be onstage, she could still prove her mettle. Recuperating in bed, she was not idle, but was fully occupied in the all-hands-on-deck Zeitgeist of NYCB's earliest years. It fell to her, perhaps on her husband's suggestion, to paint props for *The Nutcracker:* musical instruments that were going to look gilded.

The Nutcracker immediately proved itself the cash cow the company might have been praying for. Eventually, repertory for the final two of the season's nine weeks was canceled and more *Nutcracker*s substituted.

Wilde recovered quickly and on February 18 was able to dance the premiere of Jerome Robbins's *Quartet*. She enjoyed Robbins's work, but he did not frequently cast her. In his 1950 *Age of Anxiety*, she had succeeded Melissa Hayden as an authoritarian fantasy shadowing the heroine, who was one of a quartet of protagonists seeking answers amid the postwar landscape.

Quartet was set to Prokofiev's second string quartet; Wilde and Herbert Bliss led the first movement. The composer had written the music while living in the Russian Caucasus, and it had something of an indigenous flavor. The ballet was mildly received by critics, then pulled either by the ever-skittish Robbins or by NYCB's administration so quickly that any chance it might have had to build a following was scanted. Wilde, however, remembered his steps as original and enjoyable. And all the cast loved the costumes, designed by Irene Sharaff in Thai silk (three years after she'd dressed *The King and I* on Broadway). They approximated contemporary fashion, below the knee and draped in a princess line—"they would have made lovely cocktail dresses." When the ballet was shelved, the women wished they could take their costumes home with them; instead they were sent to a warehouse and eventually ruined in a flood.

During the two-week *Nutcracker* reprise at the end of the season, Wilde was happy that the "ridiculously difficult" choreography for Marzipan that Balanchine had set on her on her wedding night never saw the light of performance. Instead, when she reached the stage as Marzipan she danced what Balanchine had created for Janet Reed, which was "perfectly charming, and just difficult enough."

It had been a tumultuous but also triumphant season for Wilde. Reviewing for London's *Ballet Annual*, Ann Barzel declared her "always a joy to watch," observing that she was "very popular with the public, as well as a dancer's dancer."

Wilde took her husband on a quick trip to Ottawa to introduce him— separately—to her parents. Bardyguine and John White got on famously. Eileen was not pleased that her youngest had married someone she'd never met, nor that she hadn't been present at the wedding. Nevertheless, her introduction to her new son-in-law was also amiable.

Wilde and her husband laughed that Brandy was the first member of their new family to become an American citizen. Bardyguine was still stateless, because the French government had not naturalized Russian refugees, insisting they stay confined to the Nansen passports that the League of Nations began issuing to refugees in 1922. He was able to work in the United States because Balanchine and company manager Betty Cage had supported his application for a work permit.

Wilde herself now came to the reluctant conclusion that she would relinquish her Canadian citizenship, a condition at the time of American naturalization. Every time she left the United States, she had been required to report to the IRS and undertake the rigmarole needed to certify that she was free of tax arrears. An additional motivation was the fact that her husband could now join her: both husband and wife's work with NYCB was sufficient support to their request for citizenship. Naturalization meant a crash course in American history and a private interview with an official.

Bardyguine was living with his parents in a small walk-up in Hell's Kitchen. Wilde's apartment was too small for two. In the search for a new place to live together, Bardyguine relied on Wilde's ability to make decisions firmly and quickly. She found a two-bedroom apartment on West Ninety-Fifth Street between Central Park West and Columbus Avenue. It also included a large combination living/dining room and a maid's room with separate bathroom off a good-sized kitchen. It was by far the biggest living space she'd yet had; combined incomes made possible a commensurately higher rent.

Both Wilde and her husband liked to read and, when work schedules permitted, relax with a cocktail while spinning an LP on the turntable. At home, Bardyguine was the master chef, serving guests culinary specialties that were sometimes Russian but more often Mediterranean. Wilde was customarily sous-chef, doing chopping and other preparations. But her own cooking was the spark that incited one of the adult Wilde's rare explosions of temper with her husband or anyone else. By now, the girl who had been prone to erupt when thwarted had "learned to control my temper." But living on Ninety-Fifth Street, she was once expecting Bardyguine home from Philadelphia, where he had gone on business with NYCB lighting designer Jean Rosenthal. She now prepared a special dinner to welcome him home. Bardyguine, however, was very late: "Oh, we stopped and had dinner," he explained. She was livid.

Several times the Balanchines were dinner guests at Ninety-Fifth Street.

Discussion was about anything and everything except ballet; Balanchine never liked to talk shop during leisure hours. Wilde and her husband also began spending weekends with them at their new country house in Weston, Connecticut. In 1946, Balanchine had bought a seven-acre parcel from Alice De Lamar, a close friend of Russian émigré Lucia Davidova; both women were wealthy and cultured. Balanchine had befriended Davidova soon after his arrival in the United States. He had spent time on her estate recovering from one of the attacks of tuberculosis that began in Russia and recurred throughout his youth. His condition had relapsed with a vengeance as soon as he reached the United States.

Only after marrying Le Clercq, however, did Balanchine erect a home at 10 Ridge Road in Weston, a one-story prefabricated house of no particular style. Kitchen, dining room, and living room were combined into one big open space. There were two bedrooms. The front door opened directly into the kitchen; a second door led outdoors to a terrace.

A half mile or so before they'd gotten to 10 Ridge Road, the Bardyguines would let Brandy out of their car, and he'd race all the way to the front door, announcing their imminent arrival. The Balanchines were busy taming a property that was forest when they first arrived. Their land was level, but uphill from Davidova's estate. They planted roses along the driveway and along a pathway in back of the house. A separate garden had been established near the house. It was perfumed by lilacs planted near one of the doors, and the property further Russified with the introduction of birch trees.

As closely as they did in the ballet studio, choreographer husband and ballerina wife collaborated on planning the gardens and maintaining their household. Nevertheless, the constrictions of their common ground prompted Wilde's opinion in hindsight that Le Clercq "was just happy to have other people around.

"I'm sure she loved him in her way," Wilde said. "But part of it was respect for what he was doing, what he had done, what he was going to do. They were for each other, absolutely," theirs was "a very caring relationship," but Wilde couldn't help seeing Balanchine as the prototypical older man. As far as Wilde was concerned, "it wasn't romantic love." On Balanchine's part Le Clercq's function as vehicle and inspiration for his choreographic exploration was of course first and foremost.

He was more than willing to do everything he could to make it possible for her to put her feet up. "It was Mr. B. who really did everything around the house," Wilde recalled. Le Clercq did some light housekeeping when so inclined. A cleaning woman came in regularly only when they were in residence longer than the occasional weekend.

Wilde knew that Le Clercq was under a different quantity as well as intimacy of professional pressure, but neither ballerina during Wilde's short visits ever undertook any balletic practice. Exertion consisted of going out to trim the roses or washing the dishes together.

Wilde was a logical guest because "I was definitely for him the expert on country life." Balanchine always seemed particularly aware of her rural Canadian upbringing. One day in class, he turned to her as he assigned pliés: "What's that vegetable that we grind and it's hot? You know, it's root." "Horseradish?" she volunteered. "Yes. That's what you look like," he said to one of the company's men. "You look like that going down."

Along with a country house had come Balanchine's interest in home improvements. He was taking courses in carpentry, and he and Bardyguine were jointly engaged in various projects around the property.

Another couple that visited frequently was Balanchine's first wife, Tamara Geva, and her then-husband, actor John Emery. Geva and Balanchine had married as teenagers in postrevolutionary Petrograd. They divorced while both were in Diaghilev's troupe, but remained intermittently close over the next six decades. Geva and Emery also had a country house nearby.

After Diaghilev, Geva had gone on to make a great success in Broadway musical comedy before turning to straight acting. She had an ego to match Balanchine's; she was ambitious and manipulative, and also highly intelligent and verbal—"always putting on a good show," Wilde recalled. "Certainly holding up her end of the conversation!" Handsome Emery was impeccably mannered but more diffident.

Wilde declared Balanchine "a very good host. He wanted to take care of everybody. That was his pride: he had you in his home and he was going to treat you right." He ran a tight household. "He was a disciplinarian, certainly," said Frederic Franklin, recalling times when they were roommates on Ballet Russe tours. Their routine was "all choreographed: 'Now we go to sleep. Now we wake up.' Room service would come in. 'You go to the bathroom; I go to get dressed.' . . . All laid out."

Balanchine had developed a consuming interest in cooking, inevitable perhaps given how frequently he recalled his desperate hunger in Russia during the Revolution and its aftermath. Together he and Bardyguine collaborated in the kitchen, while delegating table-setting and other chores to the women. Brandy the poodle proved useful as well as adorable. Canine garbage disposal obviated the need to clean up scraps: "Green peppers, anything that fell on the floor, he'd eat," Wilde recalled.

Le Clercq "never seemed to need to diet," Wilde said. "She was very hyper." For Wilde, though, weight had suddenly become problematic. In her very early years with City Ballet, "she was quite thin and looked gorgeous," Robert Barnett recalled. Immersion in a repertory that was athletically demanding in the extreme certainly built muscle mass, but Wilde was also prone to blame the life she'd led with the Ballet Russe as a teenager. Irregular hours on tour had meant that "you just didn't eat properly."

The attempt to keep her weight within balletic conformity would vex her throughout her remaining years onstage. "She struggled with her weight and I struggled with her weight," a frequent partner said. "She had a terrible time," Barnett recalled. One time Wilde completely omitted salt from her diet, resulting in severe leg cramps.

Together with Bardyguine and Mounsey, Wilde had once visited a celebrated pasta restaurant in Rome, where the chef cooked specialties tableside. Her husband and colleague availed themselves happily, but Wilde insisted on turning down the chef's offer, much to his evident offense.

Turning down Balanchine was a different story. During working hours, he frequently admonished her to be more vigilant, and "if Mr. B. thought I was a few pounds overweight, I knew it, because there went my performances!" Yet if Balanchine himself was doing the cooking, he wanted her to partake of everything, including sampling each bottle of wine he'd selected from his wine closet. "You've got to have this Château," he'd insist. And Wilde was happy not to resist too strenuously.

24

EXPANDING

HORIZONS

A favorite motto of Balanchine's was "No one is indispensable—including me." Confirmation of that insofar as New York City Ballet was concerned occurred when Maria Tallchief, its de facto prima ballerina, signed a contract as guest artist with her alma mater, the Ballet Russe de Monte Carlo, for the 1954–55 season. She was paid the almost unimaginable sum of two thousand dollars a week, ten times what she made at City Ballet. One suspects that it was her salary as much as her artistic attainment that landed her on the cover of *Time* magazine that fall. Lucrative as it was, her temporary defection from Balanchine's company was "a mistake," Tallchief admitted in 1981. When she returned to NYCB a year later, Balanchine immediately made two marvelous new ballets for her, but her subsequent career with her home company turned into something of an anticlimax.

Tallchief's return to the Ballet Russe became an artistic windfall for Wilde, who now made her debut in both Balanchine's *Firebird* and *Sylvia Pas de Deux*, created for Tallchief in 1949 and 1950, respectively.

Wilde had been on the road with NYCB all during the summer, while the company embarked on its second tour to the West Coast. En route they performed a season in Chicago opening May 26, adding a debut in Seattle to their return to San Francisco and Los Angeles.

Wilde and her husband wanted their poodle with them on the road, even if it meant staying in inferior hotels, where they frequently were neighbors of NYCB's Richard Thomas and his wife, Barbara Fallis, who also traveled with their dog. Usually Wilde brought the dog to the theater, which suited him fine. But if they wanted to go out after a performance, they'd have to confine him to their hotel rooms, and retaliation often followed.

Once in Chicago they locked him in the bathroom, only to find when they returned that the carpet looked as if it had been plowed: he had escaped and pulled apart seams in the carpet. Bardyguine bought a big bunch of tacks to nail them down again. In San Francisco, they once did the same thing and came home to find a corner of the bathroom door chewed away. Bardyguine bought wood and reconstructed the door.

On tour, Balanchine began choreographing two new ballets, *Ivesiana* and *Western Symphony,* that would premiere at City Center, where they reopened August 31. After they closed in Los Angeles on August 15, Balanchine needed to get back to New York immediately, so he and Le Clercq flew home, while Wilde and Bardyguine drove the Balanchine car cross-country. They eschewed diversionary expeditions and so had time for a short visit to Nora and Roger before going back to work.

On Monday, September 6, Martin in the *Times* declared it "distinctly Patricia Wilde's weekend at the City Center." She had "covered herself with glory," debuting in *Sylvia* on Saturday night and in *Firebird* the following night—"two stunning performances."

Sylvia was one of the rare occasions when Balanchine used French music—here excerpted from act 3 of Delibes's full-length ballet—for Tallchief. He seemed to be asking her to lighten the emphatic attack that was so much a hallmark of his style, but was also an innate part of her dance temperament. The pas de deux was paced as a gradual buildup to fireworks: their entrance a gracious preface to prolonged balances in the supported adagio that followed and to the pyrotechnics of both man and woman's variation and then their coda. For Wilde it may have served the same purpose. In his review, Martin described her *Sylvia* as a breakthrough in which "the familiar, refreshingly tomboyish brilliance that has made her one of the most exciting of dancers gave place to a new daintiness, a new elegance, as if she had suddenly glimpsed for the first time the ballerina's transcendent world."

In *Firebird*, Wilde admired and had learned from Tallchief's iconic interpretation. The role was designed by Balanchine to highlight the smoldering aloofness that was quintessential Tallchief. Wilde wanted to bring something of her own, an acknowledgment of humanity in the mythical creature, even though this was counter to Balanchine's idea. For one thing, she emphasized an enhanced feeling of wonder when the Firebird discovers Prince Ivan in her magic forest: "It's your territory, but you're always discovering something new there," Wilde explained. Later on, having saved Ivan and his future bride from the wizard Kotchei's tribe of monsters, she wanted to illustrate the regret she heard in Stravinsky's "Berceuse." Wilde's Firebird was "pulled away" from the humans she'd shielded, but the composer's lullaby told her that she "didn't entirely want to go." The romantic, erotic aura of Moncion's Prince had perhaps penetrated her feral autonomy. Martin described the way she "found a strong dramatic line as well as a vividly realized characterization. In the final scene, indeed, there appeared colors that had never been seen in the work before that added to its advantage dramatically."

Walter Terry in the *Herald-Tribune* seemed to miss Tallchief's glitter: "Miss Wilde executed the extremely difficult steps with authority and, frequently, with brightness but she didn't really shine. The shimmer—a very special kind of brightness—was missing. The technique was there, an understanding of style was discernible, touches of grandness emerged from time to time. It was a good performance by an exceptionally fine dancer. All that was needed was an artist's command of movement colors as will surely come." Wilde would dance both *Sylvia* and *Firebird* many times up to the very end of her career. Indeed, her very last performance, a Paris charity gala in 1966, would be *Sylvia*.

Balanchine's two new ballets both accessed provinces of starkly different American lore. *Western Symphony* was performed to Hershey Kay's orchestration of Western folk tunes, while *Ivesiana*, like the Charles Ives music Balanchine selected, enveloped echoes of Native culture in eerie dislocation.

Premiered September 7, *Western Symphony* had no sets or costumes. This time, spareness was due not to aesthetic manifesto but financial constraints. Each of the lead dancers went to Bloomingdale's basement to select different color sweaters, the women's tying in back. Eglevsky, who would be Wilde's partner in the third movement Scherzo, went onstage in something lavender that Wilde found incongruous on the husky danseur—she imagined that his wife had picked it out for him.

The four lead ballerinas—Adams, Reed, Le Clercq, and Wilde—decided to fashion themselves to look like a combination of saloon girl/Toulouse-Lautrec dance hall denizen, settling on a common hairstyle with bangs. Each constructed her own version of the hairdo, sometimes more, sometimes less elaborate depending on how much time they had to get ready. *Western Symphony* was always programmed as the closing ballet and the ballerinas might very well be dancing something else as well, earlier in the performance, that had required a totally different look.

Barbara Walczak recalled that the corps women were then told that Balanchine wanted them to wear bangs as well. That posed a problem for some, since they had hair that was cut long all the way around. A solution was found at Woolworth's: gag party hats with simulated bangs, which they bought, removed, and pinned to their heads.

Western Symphony "was not André's thing at all," recalled Robert Barnett, who followed him in the part. Balanchine's attempts to diversify Eglevsky's repertory with frolicsome pieces often met with resentment by the classical premier. But for Wilde, the Scherzo was too much of the same kind of thing, filled as it was with beats and pertness. "Go-go-go, pick up your feet and be that little pony, again—everything I'd ever done was right there." Eventually she would dance the lead in all three of the flanking movements, succeeding Adams, Reed, and Le Clercq. Their sections were gay and funny but more womanly, less soubrette, and more to her own liking.

Ivesiana is a Balanchine masterpiece, in which Wilde's contribution eventually became murky. Together with the very young Jacques d'Amboise, Wilde at the September 14 premiere danced to Ives's "Halloween," in which tonal scales went haywire. Twenty years later, Le Clercq recalled the sight of Wilde "sort of rocking in a rocking chair, like Whistler's Mother, rocking with Jacques . . . peculiar." Wilde herself retained the haziest memories of anything she did: going across the floor on her knees (in the ballet's final movement, "In the Night," the ensemble also moves that way), a passage with d'Amboise where she was upright and he supported her from a prone position.

Six months later, Balanchine substituted Ives's "Arguments," a longer, harder-driving piece, and choreographed a new duet for them. In November 1955 Balanchine replaced that with "Barn Dance," another one of Ives's fracturings of American cultural inheritance. *Ivesiana* fell out of repertory; revived in 1961, "Barn Dance" was out, as were Wilde and d'Amboise, and as was "Over the Pavements," originally danced by Adams and Bliss. Today the ballet is considered one of Balanchine's greatest, but it is rarely performed. Perhaps its particular anomie is forbidding.

Such had been the success of *The Nutcracker* in its premiere season at City Center, and on tour in Los Angeles over the summer, that on November 3, 1954, NYCB opened a six-week season devoted entirely to the evening-long ballet.

In addition to dancing Marzipan, Wilde now made her debut in Tallchief's created role of Sugar Plum Fairy, presiding over act 2's Kingdom of the Sweets, and as well in Le Clercq's original role of Dewdrop, leading the Waltz of the Flowers, one of a series of entertainments over which the Sugar Plum Fairy presides.

Adams, who had danced a few Sugar Plums at City Center earlier in the year, now made what was reviewed as her official debut, as did Le Clercq. Of the three, Wilde "seemed the most at ease in her initial performance," P. W. Manchester wrote in *Dance News*, "largely due no doubt to the sure and sensitive partnering of Magallanes." She was "brilliantly precise in some additional choreographic frills" that Adams and Le Clercq were not doing. Wilde didn't recall what they were, but Balanchine frequently tinkered with his steps to suit a different talent and personality.

Writing in the *Times*, Martin found her, however, "not yet free to devote herself to anything except the sheer execution of the choreography. As a result she seemed too strong, too vital, too business-like." The "utterly winning vision" she had presented in *Sylvia*, "she has not accomplished here," but "in all probability," the same luminosity would eventually manifest itself.

Dancing the pas de deux, Wilde's own goal was to make her performance very soft and gracious. Sugar Plum is chatelaine of her kingdom, welcoming the two visiting children as well as a host of entertainments. "No, no," Balanchine corrected—she was to be more magisterial, more in command, more reminiscent perhaps of the Imperial ballerinas he'd seen in the role when he himself had danced Candy Cane.

Where this is constructed along the lines of the traditional pas de deux, Dewdrop is a solo role, darting, coursing, spinning through, around, and in front of a large corps of female flowers. The role was filled with big jumps. Le Clercq's high extension and the "nice open quality" to her movement could convince an audience—and even Wilde—that she was more aerial than she actually was. For Le Clercq, Dewdrop was perhaps a push by Balanchine into a new pinnacle of athleticism. Wilde, coming at the role with a different physique and temperament, fulfilled it instead by moving into a diminution. She needed to ensure that she treated the space-eating exertions with the utmost finesse: "This was jumping that you wanted to do very lightly, not pushing it, flying on top of the music."

No tutu here. Instead she wore a very short skirt—"You pulled your stomach in!"—lightly and expertly boned by Karinska to create the most flattering contour of the ballerina's midsection. And no tiara, but instead a freeform headpiece of rhinestones. Classical trappings were jettisoned, classical decorum unbuttoned a bit. Dewdrop was "not any ballerina-ing around, but really going out there and shining. I loved it, more than Sugar Plum."

That fall, local opera production returned to Chicago with the formation of the Lyric Opera of Chicago, which mustered an extraordinary three-week season, opening November 1. It featured the American debut of Maria Callas as well as the participation of other international superstars. Chicago-based choreographer, teacher, and author Ruth Page knew Wilde from the Ballet Russe, where Wilde had danced corps roles in Page's *The Bells* and *Frankie and Johnnie*. She invited Wilde to perform a pas de deux in *La Traviata*, which Callas would sing twice. Wilde was an interpolated *bonne bouche* to the act 2, scene 2 gambling scene.

During the act 2 curtain calls, Wilde had been bowing in standard ballet style, which meant a more opulent acknowledgment than Callas, who opted for an exceptionally minimal curtain call. Together in front of the Opera House curtain, Callas was "glaring and muttering," her vocal colleagues "pretending not to notice," reported Seymour Raven in the Chicago *Daily Tribune*. Wilde was more or less oblivious until more muttering was sent her way via management from Callas's husband and manager, Giovanni Meneghini. Nevertheless, Raven liked the "clean thrusts from Ruth Page's choreographic inventiveness," while in the *American*, Wilde was described as "one of the great ballet technicians of our time."

As so often when Wilde made guest shots, her *Traviata* appearances gave her no time to look around. She was in, out, and then headed back to *The Nutcracker* without the chance to sample any of the operatic riches.

MOVING

ALL OVER

Following its all-*Nutcracker* run, NYCB returned to City Center on February 12 for a monthlong season. Immediately before that, though, Wilde was again saluted in *Cue* magazine, in the "About the Town" column: "In her Pony dance in Cakewalk, in a remarkable Swan Lake passage, and especially in Caracole, Miss Wilde reveals herself as one of the best dancers in the land. Her leaps and turns are spectacular, her movement is vivid, enormously musical. Hers is not a gentle lyric style, rather a brittle, joyful allegro movement. . . . Each season offers further proof that hers is a unique talent."

On February 27, *Western Symphony* returned, now outfitted with a décor designed by John Boyt as well as costumes by Karinska. On March 1, Wilde, Hayden, and Eglevsky introduced what became known as Balanchine's Glinka *Pas de Trois* to distinguish it from his earlier pas de trois to Minkus's *Paquita*. Short as it was, the new pas de trois was one of the very few ballets Wilde in retrospect would allow herself to concede was "hard!" Thinking back on one particularly difficult combination in her variation, a series of turning beats—*brisés volés en tournant*—she confessed, "I still can't quite figure out how I did it."

The music was laden with significance for Balanchine. It was the same ballet music from act 3 of Glinka's opera *Ruslan and Lyudmila*, a staple of the Russian repertory, that Fokine had choreographed for a production of the full opera at the Mariinsky in 1917. Balanchine would have been familiar with that choreography. It was thus music that evoked his youth, that established a point of connection both with the Mariinsky and with Fokine, whose work Balanchine admired, as well as an opportunity for appropriation.

That spring, New York City Ballet embarked on its third tour to Europe. By now, Wilde and her husband had made a habit when touring overseas of kenneling their poodle with Bardyguine's parents. Madame Nevelska already had her own poodle, but it was old and happy just to stay at home, whereas Brandy loved going to Nevelska's ballet studio in Carnegie Hall. When she taught class, he stayed decorously by her chair. But once he saw that her class was performing a repeated sequence of *changements*, he knew that the jumping students meant that class was about to end, and he would again be doted upon. Now he gave vent freely to his jubilation.

NYCB's tour began in Monte Carlo on April 9. The city and its tiny, ornate opera house were important to Balanchine: it was here that he'd joined the Diaghilev company in 1925, during their annual residence in the opera seasons. NYCB made return appearances in Florence, Rome, Paris, Stuttgart, Lausanne, Zurich, and The Hague, along with debuts in Amsterdam, Bordeaux, Lyon, Marseilles, and Lisbon.

Balanchine's *Roma* had premiered in New York in February, created for Le Clercq and Eglevsky, set to Bizet's *Roma Suite*. Wilde was scheduled to alternate with her on the European tour. *Roma* was one ballet of Le Clercq's that Wilde was not enthusiastic about inheriting, so much did its choreographic design evolve definitely from her long, loose limbs. Wilde was particularly reluctant to tackle *Roma* because no one had ever taken the trouble to teach her the full choreography. Only when they arrived in Rome did Le Clercq teach her the part prior to the May 11 season opening.

Rome declared itself offended by *Roma* at the first performance; the ballet's scenic depiction of an Italian town strewn with hanging laundry was thought to be clichéd and derogatory. Wilde was to make a flying entrance onstage; at her first performance she didn't stint on energy and wound up flat on the ground. Nevertheless, she continued to alternate with Le Clercq over the next and final year of the ballet's lifespan.

Staid Zurich went wild for the company, as it had during their first visit three years earlier. On June 22, *Western Symphony* provided farewell to their three-night season. "We bowed and bowed," Wilde recalled, and she was taking the pins out of her headdress as the audience was still stamping their feet. The dancers were told they'd have to go out for another bow. Together with Balanchine, they went out through the little door in the fire curtain, the ballerinas holding their headpieces in place.

On July 8 they concluded their European tour in The Hague; twelve days later, they were back at the Greek Theater in Hollywood to begin a two-month West Coast tour that concluded with another season in Chicago. On November 8 they reopened at City Center, closing January 1, 1956, and then beginning a new season there on February 28. The workload was grueling, but the dancers were ever grateful for as many employment weeks as possible.

Wilde was always a willing body when any choreographer she respected wanted to experiment. Robbins was preparing his new *The Concert* for its March 1 premiere and was, as always, indecisive about how to resolve a matter of his own competing ideas. One of the ballet's many zany episodes had Le Clercq and ensemble engaged in a quixotic chase after butterflies. The ballet wasn't on her docket, but Wilde was happy to submerge herself into the rank and file during rehearsals. They tried performing the butterfly hunt various ways, none of which seemed to please Robbins. But he fiddled and fiddled until they achieved a version that satisfied him.

On May 1, together with Eglevsky, Adams, Le Clercq, and Moncion, Wilde performed in San Juan, Puerto Rico, in a ballet program sponsored by the Pro-Arte producing group. The dancers had the day free and wandered down to the beach. Soon they were taking a short ride on a glass-bottomed boat. Short, but not short enough—the dancers were broiled by the time they got back to shore. That night Wilde was dancing *The Duel*. Onstage under the lights, she looked down and saw that sunburn plus black tights equaled a purple tone that was decidedly freakish. Her colleagues commented, but she never found out whether the audience could notice.

At the end of May, NYCB took part in a salute to Mozart on the occasion of his two hundredth birthday held as part of the American Shakespeare Festival in Stratford, Connecticut. Balanchine created a new ballet to Mozart's *A Musical Joke*, which was never seen again after the two Stratford performances. But he also created *Divertimento No. 15*, a partly rechoreographed response to the same music that had powered *Caracole* four years earlier. The company's dizzying array of ballets might indeed have meant that significant portions had already been forgotten. In any case, the solos for *Divertimento* stayed true to *Caracole*, but the duets seemed to Wilde to be newly imagined by Balanchine. In *The Nation*, B. H. Haggin would write that the new version was more musical because each duet was longer, preserving the continuity of Mozart's Andante. Now, however, young Allegra Kent would dance the solo Wilde had created in 1952.

During the days before the May 30 premiere, Balanchine and Le Clercq once again hosted Wilde and Bardyguine in Weston. They stayed in the guest bedroom, while sleeping on the living room couch was Diana Adams, who was now drawn ever more closely into Balanchine's orbit. For one thing, she was Le Clercq's closest girlfriend in the company. Just as important, she had parted company with the Ballet Theatre contingent with whom she had joined NYCB in 1950–51. Laing and Tudor left NYCB after the fall 1953 European tour to return to Ballet Theatre. Kaye followed a few months later. Adams, however, decided to stay, and she and Laing divorced.

Bardyguine was up and out earliest, with chores to attend to at the theater. Balanchine at that time was also an early riser, putting time in on his plantings. The hard-working ballerinas preferred to sleep in a bit before they all drove to the theater. Balanchine was of course cooking. After a rehearsal, the dancers stayed at the theater while he went back to the house to prepare dinner. He made ham with pineapple and brown sugar, sweet potatoes with marshmallows—a true American meal, so far as he was concerned. When they got back from the performance, they all ate it. It made them so thirsty, however, that "all night long we kept meeting each other," pouring glasses of water and visiting the facilities: "Mr. B., what did you do to us?"

A Musical Joke featured Wilde and Francisco Moncion as one of three lead couples engaged in aristocratic indulgence in rustic mating rites—apposite to Mozart's time and place. *Divertimento No. 15* had new costumes by Karinska, replacing the Christian Bérard tutus the ballerinas had worn in *Caracole*. Also gone were the feathered headdresses that, together with the 1952 title itself, had lent a flavor of dressage. Now their tutus had tiers of ribbons, arranged ladder-like in the eighteenth-century embroidery style called *échelle*. Karinska's costumes for *A Musical Joke* were also described by the *Times* as very beautiful. For that ballet, the men wore period wigs and breeches, while the women's flaring skirts, trimmed with silk blossoms, suggested Baroque skirts as much as balletic tutus.

From the perspective of her later career, Allegra Kent would seem an odd choice to have inherited in *Divertimento No. 15* not only Wilde's *Caracole* solo, but also a few other of Wilde's powerhouse parts. Vicissitudes eventually made Kent technically unreliable, although she always manifested a movement quality that was mesmerizing.

Wilde immediately recognized that Kent was someone very special when she first joined the company in 1952. Le Clercq and Tallchief were also among Kent's biggest boosters. By 1956, Balanchine had already made a haunting role for Kent in *Ivesiana* in 1954. In "The Unanswered Question," Kent was kept in the air by a phalanx of men, thereby preventing a lone man from ever being able to reach her. Balanchine had exactly distilled Kent's enigmatic, elusive presence. But casting Kent in Wilde's old *Caracole* solo, Balanchine was making a point of contrast and congruity. Kent hadn't the methodical training that Wilde had, but, like Wilde, she had a huge jump.

For Kent, dancing Wilde's role was daunting; she omitted the *gargouillades* that Wilde had danced. A circle of jumps also taxed her, and she wasn't moving with the amplitude Balanchine wanted. "He really wanted you to step way out and then really travel," recalled Wilde. He delegated her to rehearse it with Kent: "Get her to move that!"

In *Divertimento No. 15*, Balanchine gave Wilde the solo that Tallchief had danced first, which Wilde had already taken on in London in 1952, when the ballet was still *Caracole*. Her performance was preserved on video when NYCB recorded *Divertimento* for Canadian television in 1961. Seen today it remains astonishing. She invites comparison with the mythical

Amazon Camille, who could run over blades of grass without bending them. Her strong classical foundation is apparent in the way that speed and abandon blend with precision. Even at this speed, she's able to introduce a second of retard in places, exactly the kind of rhythmic flexibility that Balanchine preferred. Her performance remains unsurpassed.

NYCB had worked almost unceasingly over the past two years, and Wilde enjoyed having the early summer of 1956 off. Soon, however, she and the company were rehearsing for their next European tour. On August 21, 1956, NYCB flew out of Idlewild to begin its fifth tour to Europe, which would last eleven weeks. Once more they would perform in France, Germany, Italy, Belgium, and Holland. They would also be making debuts in Salzburg, Vienna, Copenhagen, and Stockholm.

This tour was to prove particularly fateful for the company. It saw the psychological disintegration of Herbert Bliss, which culminated in his death in 1960 in a car crash that some who knew him were convinced was suicide. Still more cataclysmically for NYCB, it was at the end of the tour that Le Clercq, who had just turned twenty-seven, was stricken with polio, never again to walk, let alone dance.

26

LE CLERCQ'S
LAST DANCE

Reportedly Le Clercq was afraid of becoming ill from the inoculation, particularly apprehensive before a fourteen-hour trip by propeller plane. At this time polio inoculation was in transition from live to dead polio vaccine. The live vaccine carried some risk of negative reaction, even of inciting an actual case of polio. Decades later, Le Clercq would tell a friend of hers, the writer Holly Brubach, that she and Balanchine had read about an instance in which that worst-case scenario had actually played out.

Perhaps half the dancers had not been vaccinated, primarily those who, like Le Clercq and Wilde, were just past the age when vaccination was prescribed. Robert Barnett, at thirty-one, had not been vaccinated, while his wife, Virginia Rich, ten years younger, had been—her mother even summoned her home to Atlanta to ensure that she received the inoculation before the tour.

The possibility of contracting polio was something to which Wilde herself never gave a thought. For her, any eventual future, short or long term, without dancing was completely unimaginable. The fact that she might be taking her life and career into her hands never occurred to her; indeed, even the inevitability of eventual retirement seemed inconceivably remote. "You mean we're not going to be able to dance forever?" is the way the octogenarian ridiculed her twenty-eight-year-old self.

The dancers were accustomed to living in a state of perpetual peril. Ballet is always a perilous business. NYCB had more safety nets in place than Ballet Russe, but not all that many more. One night Wilde was scheduled to perform *The Duel* and another ballet. She'd been dancing even more than usual: "It was one of those seasons when I was in for everybody doing everything." A soft corn on her foot had become infected, and she asked the company physician, Mel Kiddon, to please show up at City Center before curtain and administer some treatment. But he didn't appear until after *The Duel*, which requires constant drubbing to simulate combat on horseback. Blood poisoning was now climbing up her leg. Kiddon said she couldn't dance the next ballet, and the infection was drained. For several days, she then had to soak it for thirty minutes every two hours with Epsom salts. "I could have killed him for not coming and putting me out of my misery." At the same time Wilde wouldn't have imagined consulting the boss: "I wouldn't bother Mr. B. with something like that."

It might not have been just that a life without dance was unthinkable; such a life might even have seemed unbearable. For Melissa Hayden at that time it apparently was. Hayden frequently said "she hoped she would die onstage," Barbara Walczak recalled. "That's really what she wanted. Go with her shoes on."

The tour would be not only long, but particularly grueling. The company junketed back and forth between disparate climates. It was summer when they played Venice in late September, cold in Germany when they arrived ten days later.

They opened August 26 in Salzburg. The city's special intimacy was lovely, Mozart's house a required destination. From there they spent a week in Vienna, and on September 12 they opened a four-day season in Zurich, at which point Maria Tallchief left the tour. Tallchief had recently married her third and final husband, the Chicago businessman Henry Paschen. She discovered that she was pregnant before NYCB left New York. She was intending to dance up through the company's return to Paris the third week of October, but doctors feared complications and ordered her to bed.

As far as Tallchief was concerned, she remained NYCB's prima ballerina. "Maria was still expecting it be centered around her," Wilde said. "She was telling Mr. B. what she wanted to do, what she wanted changed. He let it go for a while, but . . ." Tallchief's dispensability would increasingly be impressed upon her, and she would take longer and longer time off from NYCB before her retirement in 1965.

Yet Tallchief was still prominent on this tour, and her absence naturally put an extra burden on all the ballerinas. In Tallchief's hotel suite in Zurich, overlooking the lake, she taught Wilde her role in *Pas de Dix*, which Balanchine had made for her a year earlier. Tallchief's ambitions often grated on Wilde, but nevertheless, as she looked back, she had to admit that most often "Maria was very helpful to me."

Company-wide there was not a question of withholding any information that could enhance a rival's performance. This was a point of honor among the ballerinas. "You feel responsible for your part, that it has to be right," Wilde said. "If you're passing it on, then you've got to give it all that you can. It's a pride in passing it on, part of your professional ethics and obligations."

Le Clercq wrote to Arthur Gold and Robert Fizdale, her pianist friends in New York, that Eglevsky was now "in a snit as he speaks to neither Pat nor Milly [Hayden]," but now with Tallchief absent he would have no choice but to partner them. Wilde didn't recall what Eglevsky's snit with his two frequent partners had been about, but he certainly was subject to such peevish sulks. Whatever it was, it passed. He partnered Wilde in *Pas de Dix* over the remainder of the tour, to her great enjoyment. It was both new and old, a restaging of the act 3 wedding celebration in *Raymonda*, a decade after Balanchine and Danilova's staging of three three-act ballets at Ballet Russe.

Tallchief's absence meant more *Swan Lake*s for Adams and Le Clercq, but neither relished the prospect. It was seemingly the perfect showcase for the two lyric, long-limbed ballerinas, but "they were both wrecks about doing it," recalled NYCB's Jonathan Watts. The mystique of the role lay heavily upon them. "They let that baggage get in their way." On more than one occasion since Le Clercq's 1952 debut as Swan Queen, Wilde found herself reassuring her: No, it didn't look bad; yes, she could do it.

On September 18, NYCB opened a week's season in Venice at the eighteenth-century Fenice. Night filming for *Around the World in 80 Days* was taking place in the Piazza Venezia next to the opera house. After performances, they'd leave the stage door to find the piazza ablaze with klieg lights.

On this tour, NYCB had received increased funding from the State Department, funneled through the American National Theatre and Academy (ANTA), which had been founded by congressional charter in 1935. Certainly the U.S. government understood the power of NYCB to advance cultural diplomacy. But in Berlin, where they spent a week at the end of September, it seemed to Wilde that as cultural emissaries they might be hitting a brick wall.

For a week they alternated between the opera house and the Art Deco Titania-Palast theater. West Berlin had begun to rebuild, but Wilde found the atmosphere more ominous than it had on the company's previous visit. They could hear gunfire from Russian maneuvers in the Eastern sector. They stayed at the same excellent hotel where they'd been four years earlier, but the staff's attitude was radically different. In 1952, "they couldn't do enough for you," she recalled. Every woman in the company was "Madame" and the staff understood every word the dancers spoke in German or English. This time, their requests were often greeted with a show of incomprehension; the prevailing attitude had become "What are you doing here?"

Herbert Bliss had been a colleague of both White sisters at Ballet Russe. "Herb was a very dear friend," Nora White said, and she was aware of his psychological frailty. Bliss suffered from depression. "I wish I could have helped him." At NYCB, he was a confidence-inspiring partner to Wilde, "gentle, thoughtful, and intelligent," off- and onstage. Another NYCB dancer recalled that in Berlin a knock on his hotel room door brought him face to face with a distraught Bliss. "Would you mind just holding me?" he asked. "He was as cold as ice," his colleague recalled. "It was frightening." Bliss continued to dance on that tour, but was distracted; one time he went onstage wearing a sweater from his own personal wardrobe.

Returning to Paris, the company now finally was able to take the stage of the Opera for an entire week, beginning October 17. In Paris, Wilde's dressing room was always festive, filled with old friends and former colleagues from her year living there. The Opera's lavish dressing rooms made for a congenial salon. Pouring the champagne was Wilde's stepson Michel, product of Bardyguine's first marriage. The boy had come up from Monte Carlo, where he lived with his mother, to spend a few days with them. His mother doted on him. She managed a restaurant and had remarried, but neither her second husband nor Bardyguine was encouraged to exert too strong an influence. Nevertheless, Bardyguine saw him whenever he could.

While they were there, *Western Symphony* was filmed for the United States Information Agency, another indication of the State Department's growing interest in them. The conditions were terrible: a frigid television studio with a cement floor. It was the dancers' day off and they were furious, although they had the right to refuse to participate.

Balanchine's decision to give Wilde's Scherzo to Kent for the filming didn't bother the older dancer, since she had never been very attached to the role. Nor was Kent, however. She again felt technically overwhelmed inheriting a Wilde role. The stamina required made it "a punishment," Kent recalled, but hers as well as the entire company's recorded performance remains an eloquent testament to the verve and spirit that were enchanting Europe.

AS THE TOUR PROCEEDED, Wilde had begun to have the distinct impression that the Le Clercq–Balanchine marriage was now close to the end. Dressing with Le Clercq in a number of German cities, she was convinced that by this point Le Clercq was ready to achieve independence from a yoke all the more onerous for being inextricably both professional and personal. "Tanny was raring to blow out!"

To Wilde it seemed odd that, whereas the Le Clercq mother and daughter had been Balanchine's constant companions on earlier tours, Edith's place was now frequently taken by Diana Adams, even though Mrs. Le Clercq had once again accompanied them. "Diana was always around," Wilde recalled. "It was always Diana, Tanny, and Mr. B." Being flanked by the two was certainly a provocative and visible sign of a transition, albeit an ambiguous one. Adams and Le Clercq "enjoyed it in a way," Wilde recalled. "They were helpful to each other." With a man as enigmatic and mercurial as Balanchine, having "a third person along can be helpful; it took off some of the responsibility on each one of them."

Le Clercq said more than once that she was very tired and hadn't wanted to go on the tour. From Venice in mid-September, Le Clercq had written her friends in New York that she had come down with not one but two infected toes and might not dance the opening night, which would not, she added, have been a great loss. That could have helped to seal her eventual fate, since such infections can go into the bloodstream, thus weakening her resistance.

On their night off in Venice, Peggy Guggenheim invited the entire company to a party at her palazzo, across the Grand Canal from the Piazza San Marco. Dusk was coming on and lanterns were strung everywhere. Lavish platters of hors d'oeuvres were arrayed throughout the rooms, filled with Guggenheim's fabled collection of modern art. There were also interesting guests from outside the ballet world.

Dressed to the nines, Wilde and Le Clercq went by gondola together. As they were crossing the canal, Le Clercq dipped her fingers in the water and then licked them. "Oooh, Tanny," Wilde scolded, "don't do that!"

It was indeed, as Wilde recalled, "such a stupid thing to do," but Wilde saw it as of a piece with a moth-to-the-flame quality inherent in Le Clercq offstage and on. "She was always trying to be a little daredevil," sometimes deliberately for effect. But was that how she contracted polio? Wilde didn't necessarily think so. Her old friend Ethel Van Iderstine, with whom she'd gone to Mexico City in 1945, was living in Stuttgart, married to her West Point boyfriend and mother of three children. She contracted the disease that same summer. She returned to the United States once she could travel, although she was never again able even to sit fully upright. But even in that condition, she still wanted to see ballet. Wilde arranged for her to able to attend a NYCB performance in Washington, DC. Several years later, Van Iderstein died of pneumonia.

Near the end of the tour, on opening night of the company's season in Cologne, they were fêted by the American attaché and his wife. Barnett was shocked the following summer when he went to visit Le Clercq at the polio rehabilitation center in Warm Springs, Georgia. Their Cologne hostess of a year ago was now a patient in a nearby room.

After Cologne, they traveled to Copenhagen on Thursday, October 25, and opened the following night. When the queen of Denmark attended a performance, the company was told to bow as one in the direction of her box before bowing directly to the public. On the Sunday matinee, Le Clercq danced *Swan Lake* and Robbins's *Afternoon of a Faun*. Wilde was opening the evening performance in *Pas de Dix*, while Le Clercq was closing the show dancing her famous role in *Bourrée Fantasque*. After Wilde was done, she came by Le Clercq's dressing room to ask how she was feeling, knowing that *Swan Lake* could make her physically unwell.

"Oh, Pat, come in. Look at my back. It feels strange." "Well, I don't see anything." Wilde asked if she wanted her to replace her in *Bourrée*. "Oh, no, I've got my makeup on," Le Clercq said. "I'll do it." She stayed in bed on Monday. By Tuesday Le Clercq was immobile and was taken to Blegdam Hospital, where her fever spiked horrifically.

After the closing performance Wednesday night, a dazed Balanchine went to the hotel room shared by Vida Brown and Melissa Hayden and told them that Le Clercq had just been diagnosed with polio. Most of the company, however, including Wilde, did not know about it. But when they gathered to leave for Sweden, the absence of Le Clercq and Balanchine meant that something was terribly wrong. The tragic irony of her final ambulatory days is that, at the first sign of a polio symptom, patients were immediately sent to bed. Le Clercq had danced day after day after being exposed, thus aiding the virus's spread.

The ferry ride "was like *Outward Bound*," NYCB's Marian Horosko recalled. In Sutton Vane's 1923 play the passengers on a vacation ship come to realize they are in effect sailing the River Styx—they are in fact dead. "We were just floating in some kind of world that you never knew existed, and that was so sad," Horosko remembered. Adams, who must have been informed, was in tears.

From Malmö they boarded a train to Stockholm, and en route "the rumors started," Wilde recalled. Then health officials came through the train telling everyone that Le Clercq had been diagnosed and that vaccine was being sent in from an army base in Wiesbaden, Germany. Anxiety about the vaccination still riddled the company. Although "everyone was frightened about getting polio themselves," NYCB's Walter Georgov recalled, they nevertheless "didn't know if they should get the shot." As it turned out, corps member Annie Inglis came down with a slight case—in Stockholm she was onstage when suddenly she couldn't lift her arm. She recovered fully, however.

During their week in Stockholm, ballet mistress Vida Brown did her best to pull the company together. Together with Edith Le Clercq, Balanchine stayed in Copenhagen with Tanaquil, whose survival remained in doubt for a number of weeks.

27

ZENITH

Interviewed in 1973 by John Gruen for his book *The Private World of Ballet*, Wilde became "visibly moved" recounting what had happened in Copenhagen in 1956. She wondered then and continues to wonder today if a delay in diagnosis had made the damage Le Clercq suffered more extensive than it might have been. She hadn't been placed in an iron lung until three days after being admitted to Blegdam Hospital's polio center. According to Wilde, Le Clercq's doctors there thought she might have come down instead with a virus then plaguing Malmö in southern Sweden that produced temporary paralysis. During their last days in Copenhagen, the dancers discussed reports that it was this virus that Le Clercq was suffering from. But Le Clercq's doctors told reporters that it was her near-fatal fever which had made it impossible for her to be put immediately into an iron lung. Had her breathing been eased earlier, less damage would have ensued, or so Wilde believes. Such speculation is of course impossible to verify.

But there was no doubt that Wilde missed Le Clercq's sharp intelligence and their dressing-room capers; nor could her place onstage be filled. "Everyone had a unique talent," Wilde told Gruen in 1973 about those early years of NYCB. "Especially Tanny." Even today, Wilde doesn't see any other ballerina being artistically related to her.

If it had been she who had been stricken with polio, she said, "I don't think I would have been defeated," as indeed Le Clercq was not. Wilde had never wanted to do anything other than dance: "I just loved to move. If I hadn't been able to, I would have gotten some kind of a job. I might have gone into something totally different. But I didn't have an alternate plan—ever!"

In early December the company reconvened for rehearsals; Wilde, Adams, and Hayden were photographed in the Eighty-Second Street ballet studio receiving polio shots that were follow-ups to the ones they'd been given in Sweden. Now established as annual tradition, the company's long winter season, combining repertory with weeks of *The Nutcracker*, was in 1956–57 "miserable" for Wilde and her colleagues. "None of us knew what was actually happening, how they were doing. We were missing a real director. Nobody kind of knew what should be going on." By Christmas 1956, Le Clercq's survival seemed assured; however, it was uncertain whether she would ever regain full use of her legs or right arm. The queen of Denmark, who had watched her dance two months earlier, now visited her bedside. Balanchine staged *Apollo* and *Serenade* for the Royal Danish Ballet to show his gratitude for the medical care his wife was receiving.

Divertimento No. 15, which NYCB had performed throughout Europe, now received its New York premiere. But for the first time since City Ballet's inception in 1948 there was obviously not going to be any new work from Balanchine. The breach was filled by a number of disciples: company members Todd Bolender and Francisco Moncion, as well as the modern dance choreographer John Butler. Balanchine's invaluable lieutenant Vida Brown ran the company the way she thought he wanted it run, aided by corps member Una Kai, now a rehearsal director. Also taking up the slack was Janet Reed, now transitioning from performance to rehearsal responsibilities.

Balanchine's absence, however, encouraged dancers to make claims to his deputies about repertory they coveted. There was a shortfall of Swan Queens in the company: not only was Le Clercq out of commission but, as her doctors had feared, Tallchief had indeed miscarried and was now performing only sporadically. Melissa Hayden was furious when her good friend Vida Brown had to tell her that Balanchine wanted Allegra Kent, not Hayden, to be the company's newest Swan Queen.

Balanchine, Le Clercq, and her mother finally returned to New York in March 1957, when she entered Lenox Hill Hospital and then went to Warm Springs, Georgia, for months of rehabilitation. It wasn't until the summer that Balanchine was turning his attention to ballet again, planning an extremely ambitious return. In 1945, Wilde had watched Balanchine in Mexico City work through his suffering over his divorce from Zorina; now she saw him return to work with a vengeance. He would contribute no fewer than five new ballets during the 1957–58 season.

For Wilde he now had an idea that would prove one of his most novel and gave her perhaps the greatest triumph of her career. *Square Dance* would offer a caller and musicians onstage and would use square dance patterns, but the steps would be neoclassical. The music would be gorgeously melodic and rhythmic selections by seventeenth- and eighteenth-century composers Vivaldi and Corelli.

What perhaps inspired Balanchine was a *New Yorker* profile earlier that year of Elisha Keeler. Fifty years old, he owned a small wholesale flower business in South Salem, New York, forty-five miles due north of Manhattan. On weekends, aided by his wife and two teenage children, he conducted square dances across Westchester and Connecticut, calling the group the "Happy Humdingers." As much as Wilde and Magallanes, Keeler would be the star of the new ballet.

As Balanchine prepared his fall comeback, Wilde and her husband began spending most weekends with him in Weston. The house was being outfitted with ramps to await Le Clercq's return. Although divorce remained inevitably on the horizon, it certainly was not something broached for years into the future. In fact, Balanchine would spend the next several years in a quixotic effort to bring back to life the muscles that he had tutored for so long.

Over the summer, Balanchine and Bardyguine also built a tool shed. Wilde baked bread and sampled the men's culinary collaborations. Without Le Clercq, she took charge of domestic arrangements: More guests were expected during the week? She'd make up the beds.

In *Square Dance*, Balanchine's original approach was going to be boldly free-form: Keeler's script would have nothing to do with what the dancers were actually doing. That eventually began to seem too obscure, and instead Keeler's patter would comment directly on what the dancers were performing. The only time that Wilde remembered ballet intruding into her sojourns to Weston was a few times when Keeler visited and in the living room she would show him some ballet vocabulary. But after *Square Dance* reached the City Center stage November 21, Keeler's daughter Mollie recalled that her father was routinely stricken with stage fright before the rise of the curtain. Once in a while he would give a heads-up to the audience about Wilde's batterie—"Watch her feet go whickety-whack"—but at that moment she would instead be turning. (Perhaps an involuntary reversion to Balanchine's original idea of disconnectedness!)

Twenty-three-year-old Virginia Rich was one of six mixed couples Balanchine used in the ballet, assigning them steps nearly as challenging as what he gave Wilde. Nevertheless, when Balanchine began working out Wilde's solos, "our mouths were hanging open," Rich recalled. "I'd never seen a woman dance like that. I remember being totally amazed."

Even for Wilde, *Square Dance* was exceptionally demanding; when she first reached the stage, "I could hardly get through it." Today the role is often given to women who are shorter and more easily able to move very fast. Wilde was five foot four and three-quarter inches, relatively tall for that era. (Ballerinas have gotten taller and taller since then.) She looked taller than she actually was because her legs were well proportioned. She also had long feet, which enhance the elegance of a ballerina's silhouette but are usually more difficult to move quickly and brilliantly. Wilde's feet combined length with extraordinary facility; the fact that they were flexible enough but not exceptionally so also gave them additional strength.

More challenging than all the complicated steps she performed in *Square Dance* was the short adagio Balanchine choreographed for Wilde and Magallanes. In *Balanchine Variations*, Nancy Goldner writes that this duet "brings to mind the elegance, simplicity, and long singing line" of the slow movement in *Concerto Barocco*. But Wilde found it far more taxing. She understood what he was asking from her: making it happen was not easy, however. Helping her to sustain these lines and movements was a deep plié controlled by her very strong feet, but she needed to use extra control to keep her foot expanding into the plié.

Throughout *Square Dance*, Wilde wanted to convey joy. "It doesn't mean grinning all the time, but that feeling through your body, which I tried to get across." Her performance exemplified Balanchine's special way with balletic bravura. Pyrotechnics can be oppressively bombastic or life affirming, a celebration of human potential, as it was here. The exhibitionistic impulse must be present in all performers. Yes, Wilde agrees today, everyone who gets on a stage is saying, "I'm up here; look at me!" But there are myriad degrees and intonations: "It's also *how* you say it."

As the "ballerina of the barn," Wilde was widely perceived to have reached the apex to date of her career. Jonathan Watts said that from Wilde onstage a particular warmth appeared "when she was most at one with a role and a partner, at her greatest suitability to a role. She was very warm, beautiful, and luscious in *Square Dance.*"

Some of her performance is preserved in excerpts broadcast on TV's *Bell Telephone Hour* in 1963. Giving all her movement, fast and slow, an organic quality was her ability to make movement breathe, facilitated and coordinated with actual breathing. Essential to her interpretation of Balanchine technique and style was "that pulse: the intake up to go down to go up again." Rising in relevé before descending in a plié as preparation for beats, "I'd take a breath as I was up, then as I went down I'd breathe out, then breathe in as I jumped. It creates a real explosion as you go up"—lifting and expanding her muscles, her movement, her presence in space.

It wasn't something that Balanchine had worked on with her, just something that seemed to come naturally by then after working with many different teachers. Spending so many hours as a girl running and playing on her mother's estate didn't hurt, either: "You learn to use your breath to help you do things."

Over the past four decades I've seen *Square Dance* many times. I've seen it done beautifully. I've also seen the steps done expertly, but without the spring and buoyancy in the muscles, which seems to make all the difference. Yet beyond those criteria, what cannot be replaced is Wilde's playful and passionate spirit. As he did so often, Balanchine created a great work that would endure indefinitely, but was so much a portrait of its original interpreter that it could never live quite as completely onstage with anyone else.

Wilde's own interest in rural and athletic pursuits remained as much a constant as its signal exploitation by Balanchine in *Square Dance*. She continued to ski whenever she could, something Balanchine would have frowned upon, but "I think he trusted me not to do anything stupid." In any case, she never injured herself. Whenever free time loomed, she liked going up to Vermont and staying with her sister Bet. Once Wilde was visiting when their father also came to stay. Somewhat unexpectedly, her mother showed up as well—Eileen's visits were usually timed a little approximately. Everybody was very nervous about how they would tolerate each other, but "they were fine," Wilde said. "They just talked and chatted away." They remained married until he died in 1960.

With Le Clercq permanently sidelined, Balanchine now turned his attention back to Adams. Over the years, she both submerged herself in the most doctrinaire belief in his principles as well as a defiant resistance, conscious and/or unconscious. His inability to observe boundaries paid diminishing artistic returns in his relationship with both Adams and Allegra Kent, with whom he was also entranced.

Balanchine was determined to pull dancers out of their comfort zones. Applied to Wilde this meant the incentive to become more supple and develop greater continuity of movement. Where Adams was concerned, Balanchine wanted to make her "luscious," Wilde recalled. Ironically, it had been her pursuit of the nonluscious qualities of speed, precision, and attack—all foreign to her earlier training—that perhaps made more stringent an innate guardedness. Stage fright also hampered her. Blurred boundaries may have made her more resistant to Balanchine's encouragement to manifest the emotional exposure that came much more easily to Tallchief, Le Clercq, Wilde, and Hayden. "He wanted Diana to open herself up like she didn't want to do," Wilde said. "It scared her." Adams began to suffer frequent injuries that kept her offstage for long periods. She also forestalled any personal pursuit by the master with her marriage to NYCB stage manager Ronald Bates.

Kent has said that her mother "was becoming anxious about Balanchine's interest in" her, and insisted she acquire a husband. At twenty-one, she began a long and largely unhappy marriage to photographer Bert Stern. Soon after that she gave birth to the first of three children. She, too, would prove elusive professionally as well, resisting the single-minded, all-consuming focus that Balanchine preferred.

Sexual as well as artistic politics of a different sort were evident in Balanchine's treatment of Alexandra Danilova. Ten years earlier, Wilde had been a novitiate satellite to Danilova's dominance of the Ballet Russe. Now the remarkably enduring prima ballerina ventured the occasional guest performance but, in her mid-fifties, was finally having to plan her exit from the ballet stage. Danilova had taught a variations class at the School of American Ballet intermittently since the 1940s. She was now teaching freelance out of financial necessity and would have loved a full-time position at the school. That was not forthcoming until 1964, and then only after much lobbying by Danilova's friends. Balanchine eventually valued Danilova's presence at the school, and they collaborated on a new *Coppélia* in 1974. But his initial reluctance may have been in part due to her indiscreet comments about her married life with Balanchine thirty years earlier, made rashly when Danilova had imbibed some champagne. Instead, Balanchine invited Danilova to teach company class—on Mondays, the dancers' day off. When Wilde took Danilova's class the elder ballerina invariably thanked her for attending; almost no one was there. Wilde assured her that it was only exhaustion that was keeping them away.

In November 1957, Wilde, Adams, and Yvonne Mounsey recorded standard-setting performances of Balanchine's *Serenade*, filmed in Montreal for the Canadian Broadcasting Corporation. NYCB had begun filming repertory there in 1954. By now Wilde had performed each of what became the three canonic leads after years of shuffling by Balanchine: the Waltz ballerina, the Russian Ballerina, and the Dark Angel. All three streak across the opening movements, but in the final *Élégie*, Waltz ballerina is vanquished by Dark Angel, who takes possession of her ostensible romantic attachment, danced here by Jacques d'Amboise. The Russian Ballerina provides a form of makeweight, threading through their entanglements. This was the role that Wilde performed most frequently, the role she dances here, flanked by Adams's Waltz ballerina and Mounsey's Dark Angel. They were often cast together this way onstage as well.

Bereft in the triangle, Waltz Ballerina throws herself into the arms of a corps member. At Ballet Russe, Wilde had been the ensemble woman who catches her: "Look at her like she's your mother," Balanchine would tell successive Waltz ballerinas. And the entire CBC performance is infused with this type of lushness, together with Balanchine's signature fleet, spacious possession of space.

Invaluable as performance record, the Montreal tapings were not optimum venues for the dancers. Chalk marks controlled their progress across a small performing studio space: they had to conform to the precise camera angles selected by Balanchine. He knew exactly what he wanted the camera to see. Sometimes he changed choreography to suit what he glimpsed through the viewfinder. Music was live on the soundstage, but the conductor and musicians were out of sight of the dancers. "You were kind of on your own," Wilde said. When she filmed the Sanguinic variation in *The Four Temperaments* in 1964, he decided he wanted to tweak the musical timing in the finale as well. He fiddled and fiddled, until "it must have been a mess when we finally did it," Wilde speculated. But those changes remained when they got back to City Center.

These tapings meant a great deal to Balanchine, as a way both to preserve his work and to bring it to the widest possible audience. Filming two Stravinsky ballets, *Agon* and *Orpheus*, in Montreal in the spring of 1960, Balanchine phoned Le Clercq in New York. He sounded depressed. He had done all he could, and his work was finished: "It's in the hands of machines."

28

THE FAR EAST

Again sponsored by the State Department and ANTA, New York City Ballet toured Japan, Australia, and the Philippines from March through August 1958. Balanchine elected not to accompany them; instead he remained in New York tending to Le Clercq. Robert Barnett and his wife had visited her in Warm Springs, but Wilde recalled that for months after she returned to New York Le Clercq "didn't want to see any of us" except Diana Adams. Yet Balanchine kept her informed about the company. Wilde was "thin and dancing beautifully," she wrote to the pianists Fizdale and Gold later in 1958.

During their months away, Vida Brown was his principal deputy. Liked and respected by the company, Brown "held the company together," Wilde recalled, but it was their loyalty to Balanchine above all that made them determine to represent the company at its best even without his presence.

Their flight to Japan was a two-day sequence of multiple stages. On one leg the cabin ran out of drinking water. Almost as irksome for Wilde was the little cold box lunches that were distributed. She found the combination of raw fish and rice so unpalatable that it turned her off Japanese food forever.

In Tokyo the company was given a lavish reception at a fantastic garden. There were photographers everywhere; one of them had his camera trained on Wilde just as she'd made the mistake of picking up a cold rice ball wrapped in seaweed. "You love oysters," she told herself. "You can swallow it; you can swallow it. Pretend it's an oyster." It worked.

Another reception for the company was held on the afternoon of a performance at the Imperial Silk Factory. That evening, Wilde was scheduled to dance the first movement of *Western Symphony*, partnered by Roland Vazquez, a pal. En route to the theater, they visited the reception. Vazquez was drinking martinis as he walked down long halls drinking in beauty. Onstage later that evening, he was decidedly not himself, unsteady as he fielded Wilde in her many jumps into his arms. It felt to her as though she barely had a partner onstage at all. He had recovered by the finale, and apologized after the curtain came down. "Oooh, I could have killed you," she told him. Closing night of their three weeks in Tokyo, the audience saluted them with the traditional celebratory blizzard of streamers and confetti.

They spent three nights in Osaka, where they performed under the aegis of the International Festival of Music and Drama at the brand-new Festival Hall, built to inaugurate the event. Backstage had been constructed to American measurements, which meant that pipes on which scenery was to be tied were too high for the Japanese stagehands to reach unaided. Each stagehand thus kept his own stool in the wings, running out with it onto the enormous stage during intermission scenery changes.

Four nights after closing in Osaka they were opening an eight-week season in Sydney. Wintry August in Australia meant that the Empire Theater was so cold that the American embassy had to round up heaters to raise the temperature in the wings. Wilde's workload was extra heavy because Tallchief had left the tour after Japan after finding out that she was again pregnant. In addition, Mounsey had just retired. Adams was injured for most of their months in Australia, but chose to stay on with her new husband, NYCB stage manager Ronald Bates. Kent was also shouldering much of the repertory and had begun to buckle from the strain.

When NYCB moved on to a six-week season in Melbourne, Hayden injured herself, which meant that Wilde was now dancing three ballets at practically every performance. Often she did *Firebird*, the Glinka *Pas de Trois*, and one of the four movements in *Western Symphony*. But *Firebird* made everything particularly sticky, since the amount of extra face as well as body makeup it required was not easy to strip off quickly. She tried to enlist Kent as a substitute in the Glinka. Kent proved elusive, although she later danced it in New York.

They closed the tour with a short and perspiration-drenched season in Manila, performing in the University of the Philippines theater, which was shaped like a Quonset hut. Tubs of ice were set up backstage to relieve the dancers. By the time they'd finished applying their makeup, it was already starting to run. Pointe shoes suffered similar meltdowns.

The curtain went up on *Serenade* and the dancers were hit with a hissing sound that engulfed the auditorium. "What *is* that noise?" they asked themselves and each other. Finally they could make out the sight of en masse fanning: every single spectator was cooling him- or herself off. Before long the stage was swamped with pools of sweat.

Bardyguine was not a great fan of Hayden, who was now back onstage after her injury in Melbourne. "He thought she was always pushing me around," and in addition, "Millie was always loud," which ran contrary to Bardyguine's Continental upbringing: "He didn't think that was the way ladies should behave." Nevertheless, as he watched the Manila opening, he couldn't help but sympathize as he watched the ballerina leave pools of perspiration on the ground every time she rose from a kneeling position.

Immediately upon their return NYCB was reopening at City Center. Tallchief was pregnant and Adams still injured; as Doris Hering noted in *Dance Magazine*, "a super-human performing burden" again fell upon Hayden and Wilde. Wilde's reward for continued stoic soldiering arrived September 8, six days after the New York season began. She starred opposite Eglevsky in *Waltz-Scherzo*, a new and quite special duet, performed to Tchaikovsky's piece of the same name written for violin and orchestra. It was short and flowing. There were no lifts.

Hering wrote that their duet "created an image of sophisticated flirtation—of light innuendo and casualness. The casualness was a somewhat new element in Balanchine style." In the *Times*, Martin also recognized it as a departure, giving Wilde "a chance for a change to lilt along as if there were not a technical problem in the world. She did it enchantingly, and

Karinska, to boot, has dressed her most becomingly in the simplest of white, beautifully cut."

Over the course of the five-minute duet, Wilde and Eglevsky shifted solo roles without any definite or formal stops or breaks. "You can't even say it was an adagio section," Wilde said. "One section we were dancing together. Then I took over, then he took over, then we got back together again." She was very happy with it. Nancy Reynolds, writing in *Repertory in Review*, recalled Wilde's ability to "skim across the stage, skirts billowing windblown behind her, with something like the speed of light."

They closed in New York September 28, and two weeks later began a two-week tour of the middle United States that concluded at Philadelphia's hallowed Academy of Music. At the end of November they opened their annual two-month season back in New York, which reached its culmination for Wilde on January 19, 1959, when she could show off another new Balanchine vehicle, *Native Dancers*. The new work could be seen to crystallize Balanchine's equal interest in making works that would click instantly with the public as he was in pushing forward the frontiers of ballet. *Native Dancers* cashed in on the public's love for the champion Thoroughbred of the same name—by now an established television celebrity. Balanchine loved horse racing and loved bringing equine vocabulary onto the ballet stages. "He was always giving me pas de cheval," Wilde recalls about the pawing step named for its equestrian inspiration. The new ballet's namesake raced on flat ground, but with Wilde and d'Amboise as stars lots of jumps were almost mandatory. Anatole Chujoy in *Dance News* noted the presence of "jumps, turns, lifts and supports usually associated with the Soviet ballet." Those moves had been articulated by Balanchine himself in his earliest choreography at the very dawn of Soviet ballet. Now the cultural exchanges between East and West were again making them common coin. Moscow's Bolshoi had made its British debut in 1956; it was now going to bow in New York in April, three months after *Native Dancers* did.

In the central, Adagio movement, however, Balanchine returned to the device he had used in Kent's role in *Ivesiana* four years earlier. Wilde never touched the ground; she was borne aloft by a small men's ensemble, transferred, sometimes thrown from one man or small group to another.

Native Dancers certainly prompted lively newspaper copy; in the *Daily News*, Douglas Watt proclaimed that "running five furloughs on a dry track, Wilde and d'Amboise finished lengths ahead of the other starters." But the ballet didn't endure in the repertory as long as it might have. Choreographed to a symphony by Vittorio Rieti, with whom Balanchine had collaborated since Diaghilev, he was never satisfied with Rieti's third and final movement. He lost interest in the ballet when the composer could not modify it to his satisfaction.

BARDYGUINE FREQUENTLY handled companies presented by Sol Hurok. When the impresario presided over the Bolshoi's Metropolitan Opera debut, Wilde sat with Hurok in his box while her husband monitored backstage. Stage rehearsals leading up to the opening night had been problematic. Bardyguine did a great deal of troubleshooting about production values, ranging from lights to the order of curtain calls. "They felt like they wouldn't have had a season without George," Wilde said. After the opening, Hurok threw a party for the company in the St. Regis hotel ballroom. When Wilde and Bardyguine walked in, the dancers stood up and cheered him.

Prima ballerina Galina Ulanova came over to kiss him; she was not always so demonstrative. However, she and Wilde became quite friendly during this New York season. The Bardyguines entertained Ulanova and her husband in their apartment. Ulanova was ending her long career with a string of spectacular triumphs in the West. Onstage she alchemized a rather earthy physique to suggest a filmy creature of air and spirit, but she told Wilde that during layoffs she liked to suntan and build up her arms rowing. "Oh, you must come to Russia," Ulanova insisted—an invitation that would serve Wilde in good stead the following year.

Cultural exchanges were inevitably a jockeying for national preeminence. The Soviet authorities' comments on contemporary art in all its manifestations, ballet prominent among them, were withering; likewise, Balanchine was not averse to putting down the Soviets' reliance on nineteenth-century three-act warhorses. Few companies embodied as much as Balanchine's the capitalist West's perpetual search for the new. What the United States might celebrate as a quest for innovation, the Soviets could castigate as a frenzy of built-in obsolescence. In addition, few companies embodied as totally as NYCB the Soviet-reviled taste for the aesthetic of abstraction.

Yet human appetite had its universal component. The Russians took every opportunity in New York to acquire creature comforts not readily available in the USSR: Ulanova purchased a top-of-the-line refrigerator. And personal ties could, if not transcend, then certainly supplement doctrinal manifesto. Wilde recalled that Balanchine was very friendly with Leonid Lavrovsky, whose 1940 full-length *Romeo and Juliet* to Prokofiev's score was seen during the Bolshoi's visit. Balanchine and Lavrovsky were contemporaries and fellow students in Leningrad. Lavrovsky had danced in what was then Petrograd with Balanchine's Young Ballet in 1923. Wilde's husband frequently joined his two fellow Russians. Together they went to see the film of Ulanova's *Giselle* that had been made in Britain during the Bolshoi's 1956 debut; it was showing in Manhattan.

Rapprochement of a sort also held sway at NYCB a month later, when Martha Graham created a work for the company. It was above all at the instigation of Lincoln Kirstein, eager as always to diversify NYCB's repertory, that Graham was invited. Kirstein's prolific writings on dance usually reflected his bias toward ballet and his assertion that modern dance techniques did not exist as codified systems apart from the idiosyncrasies of their creators. Nevertheless, polemical utility aside, he was an ardent admirer of Graham's, as was Balanchine himself. Balanchine "told me he thought she was the most marvelous dancer," the School of American Ballet's Muriel Stuart recalled, and he had not been shy about borrowing her vocabulary from time to time.

In *Episodes*, Graham and Balanchine would not only share the program but would also each offer an original interpretation of the works of Anton Webern, whose entire small canon of orchestral pieces Balanchine apportioned between himself and her. They each worked with their own companies, but exchanged a single dancer: NYCB's Sallie Wilson joined Graham's troupe, while Graham's Paul Taylor was in Balanchine's.

Graham's *Episodes* was characteristic in its depiction of strong women from history and myth: here Mary Queen of Scots and Elizabeth I. Graham's debt to Noh theater determined the way the work spooled backward in time, projecting out of the mind of Mary prior to her execution. Her power struggle with Elizabeth was abstracted to play out in the form of a ritualized tournament or tennis game. Balanchine's half of the program typified his interest in paring down theatrical appurtenances, severing traditional continuities between ballet steps, and, once again, borrowing from modern dance and melding it into ballet.

Wilde was already an admirer of Graham and her work, as was Nora, who had studied intermittently with Graham for years after leaving Ballet Russe. Wilde's husband frequently worked with Graham's company on tour as well as in New York, and Wilde attended every performance that she could. Graham herself was yet another of their poodle's admirers. "Where's Brandy?" Graham would ask in her dressing room. "He didn't come to visit me. I need to see him before I go onstage!"

Bardyguine would let the dog venture onstage, where it took to scrambling up and down ladders screwed into the back wall of the stage. Bardyguine used their dog's prowess to reap a flutter of betting wagers. "My dog can go up *and* he can go down," Bardyguine boasted to skeptical stagehands working Graham's performances. "'Oh, I don't believe it.' 'All right; I'll give you ten to one.'"

Theater and theatricality interested Wilde, who was frequently escorted to Broadway shows by Saul Goodman, a ballet lover and sometime writer, whose family owned a Seventh Avenue hosiery business. She studied Graham's manipulation of theatrical qualities that by this time were not the primary emphases at City Ballet. Graham was as dynamic when standing stock-still as when she moved. The tension in her body, the angle of her head, her shoulder, all were filled with meaning. Naturally, the ballerina wanted to apply it to her own work: "I could have used some of that in *The Duel.*"

At NYCB, Wilde watched as many of Graham's rehearsals for *Episodes* as she could. No less than Wilde, Balanchine himself was "astonished" at Graham's Mary, Muriel Stuart recalled, at the power discharged by a woman in her sixties—something unheard-of in ballet.

A month after *Episodes* premiered, Wilde had some time free and approached Graham about the possibility of taking some classes at her school. Graham invited her to take company class with her dancers. No, Wilde insisted, she wanted to take a beginner's class; but no, Graham insisted, that was not appropriate for a reigning ballerina. Instead, Graham assigned several of her dancers—Mary Hinkson, Bertram Ross, Matt Turney—to tutor her privately.

But while Adams, Tallchief, and Hayden had all danced before Hollywood cameras, Wilde herself was not interested in trying to break out professionally from her specialized métier. Approached by Broadway producers about the possibility of doing a Broadway musical, she assured them that she could not sing. They assured her that anybody could sing. She was set up in a rehearsal studio with a pianist and a voice coach. Every time she said, "No, it's not going to work," she was met with, "You're not letting it come out." Finally a truce and a halt were called.

29

A BALANCHINE

SWAN

The Bolshoi's American debut emboldened Balanchine. His company was one-fourth the size of the state-supported Soviet troupe, but had to be every bit as impressive on its own terms. After the Bolshoi's visit he began teaching company classes that could easily last three hours or more. They were "very, very technically precise," Allegra Kent recalled. "He refined everything," said Mimi Paul, who had trained at the school of the Washington Ballet. She had won a scholarship to the School of American Ballet in the fall of 1959, and a few months later joined NYCB.

Felia Doubrovska, for whom Balanchine had created Polyhymnia in *Apollo* and the Siren in *The Prodigal Son*, had been teaching at Balanchine's school since 1949. He now asked her to begin teaching a special class for a small group of young women just entering the company who he thought were potential future soloists and principals.

Balanchine also began culling older members of the ensemble. As a ranking ballerina, Wilde did not believe that her position was threatened—for the moment. She did find slightly disconcerting a remark that Balanchine made to her husband to the effect that Wilde was now so familiar with the way he worked and choreographed that she knew what he was going to do before he did it. "I don't know whether he was saying, 'It's no fun anymore,'" she muses today, but he had an insatiable need for new stimulation as well as a need to impress the next young dancer with something new to her as well as him.

Wilde would find company events during the 1959–60 season distressing. But the season would also mark her debut as Balanchine's Swan Queen—a role she had long coveted.

As so often, Hayden and Vida Brown had been roommates during NYCB's tour to the Far East in 1958. That was why, Wilde deduced, Hayden did get to make her debut as Swan Queen in Australia, despite Balanchine's having denied her the role a year earlier. That stiffened Wilde's resolve to finally ask Balanchine if she could finally do it as well. She'd wanted to for a long time. By now, the pas de trois she'd created at the 1951 premiere had been retired and the waltz music used for the Prince's solo.

It was the first time, she says, that she ever requested a part from him. Direct appeal might work; as Allegra Kent pointed out, "If he really didn't want it he'd say no, but he might consider it." Yet Wilde's customary attitude had been that it was an exercise in futility: "What for? He wants it or he doesn't want it. And if he doesn't want it it's not going to happen. And then there's the question: If he doesn't really want it to happen, do *you* want it to happen?" ("By all means!," many others dancers would have said.)

But after her onerous schedule during the 1958 Far East tour, she also felt as entitled as she ever allowed herself to feel in Balanchine's company. In New York she approached him nervously: "Mr. B., I would really love to do *Swan Lake*." Balanchine didn't seem very enthusiastic, but was as usual equivocal. "Well, you know, some people are soprano and some people are alto. . . . You don't sing the same things." All right, she said to herself, she was not Odette in his eyes—which, no matter how visionary, belonged simply to one human sensibility.

But now a year later, he suddenly told her that she was dancing the role. "My voice had changed," she quips today. Of all the world's *Swan Lake*s, this would have been the one she was perfect for, since her natural tempo and Balanchine's were rapid. Balanchine's *Swan Lake* was faster than the *Swan Lake* she'd danced with the Metropolitan Ballet in 1950. She liked Balanchine's restoration of Tchaikovsky's allegro coda to the pas de deux.

Whether he was rewarding her for years of devoted service, or whether he actually wanted to see her in it, it would be difficult to say. But *Swan Lake* was one of the ballets on which he lavished unusual attention. Each ballerina danced a different variation tailored to her talents, as did the Princes who partnered them. Rehearsing Wilde, he mentioned Olga Spessivtseva often. "Oh, Spessivtseva was always so great in this..." He wanted Wilde to really move in her first entrance: "Oh, Spessivtseva used to fly!" She was to be anything but static in her arabesque poses—instead, she was to alight in a suspended breath, as if electrified by fear.

Wilde's partner in her September 1959 debut was Jonathan Watts, who had joined the company in 1954. He was then twenty-two, a graduate of the High School of Performing Arts, where his training was much more in modern dance than in ballet. When NYCB had reached Copenhagen in 1956, Watts told Balanchine that he wanted to leave the company and spend time working with Wilde's former teacher Vera Volkova, who had moved there from London. Balanchine insisted that he stay; true to his credo, he impressed upon Watts that only by functioning as a principal dancer would he actually become one. That is a precept subject to question, but the fact is, Balanchine needed him. He had an unusually beautiful balletic physique, was medium tall, and was a good partner. "You could become American's first male classical dancer." During the company's seasons in Australia in 1958, Watts would remain in the theater after performances, working alone until two in the morning.

Watts "wasn't an ebullient dancer," Wilde said. "He was very serious and very secure." She sometimes missed the panache of an Eglevsky, but Watts danced "well and cleanly and musically." They enjoyed working with each other, and each exerted some influence over the other. For Watts, "intricate pas de deux were a great pleasure," he said, "more interesting to do than the solos. I immensely enjoyed working things out with whomever I was working things out with."

Wilde eventually became godmother to Watts's son; their mutual trust and respect was sufficient to survive some vicissitudes. Dancing the Grand Pas de Deux in *The Nutcracker* at one performance, she was upstage, running into his waiting arms downstage, where he was meant to lift her into a perch on his shoulder. But that shoulder seat never happened; instead she toppled him in a flying tackle. Flat on the floor, he managed somehow to lift her back onto pointe. When they came offstage, Lincoln Kirstein was in the wings, white with shock, asking how they were.

As White Swan Odette, Wilde wanted to plumb the role's emotional potential; she wanted to live it onstage. Indeed, she didn't see how it was possible to dance a role, with so patent an emotional arc, in any other way. To be effective, the ballerina has to show—has to experience, even—a hint of insecurity: her reticence, fear, and awareness of the Prince as a possible threat, but then the gradual accumulation of trust and security and rapture as Odette entertains hope of possible redemption.

"She was doing it on her own terms," said Watts, who was grateful that she was at her thinnest. "She wasn't trying to do something that she couldn't do." Wilde's eyes were sad and her body spoke "in the simplest way," Mimi Paul recalled. "It was clear. Not like you see today: not mannered at all." Nora White made a point of seeing her sister's debut.

"She seemed whole, somehow," Nora said. "It was very moving," both her younger sister's performance onstage and the fact that she was getting to do something that meant so much to her. "I think I probably cried."

Reviewing her Odette in March 1961, John Martin wrote that her debut a year earlier had been "highly impressive," but her performance now was "no less than great.... breathtaking. With her fantastic technique apparently as easy for her as breathing, she devoted herself to matters of character, drama and style. . . . She has studied the role with patent love, and has found endless colors for it, by her personally illuminating phrasing, and a wealth of dynamic shading." In the *Herald-Tribune* Walter Terry wrote that her Adagio was "soft and lyrical . . . defined in the most stylish terms."

Wilde danced the Swan Queen until the end of her career in 1965, and Balanchine stayed involved in her performance. It was rare that he would come onstage and ask her to rehearse something that she had just danced, but it happened once after a *Swan Lake*. She was happy to work on the role as long as he wanted; "I loved doing *Swan Lake*!"

SUPERSTAR ERIK BRUHN did not in any way fit into Balanchine's agenda, yet Balanchine found Bruhn foisted upon him as the opening of the two-month winter season approached in early December. A product of the Royal Danish Ballet, Bruhn had since the mid-1950s established himself as an international presence, guesting with many of the world's great companies.

Bruhn was on the NYCB roster due to the insistence of Kirstein as well as company manager Betty Cage, who could only dream of what his participation would bring to the box office. Wilde imagined, however, that it was Bruhn who had initiated the offer by telling them how much he wanted to work with Balanchine.

"How can you hold someone's own talent against him?" Wilde bemoans today. But it seemed to her as the season progressed that Balanchine was doing exactly that. "Poor Erik suffered," Wilde recalled. Balanchine's treatment exacerbated a neurotic temperament. His perfectionism could drive Wilde to distraction: after a great performance he might tell her, "I can't ever do that again," or itemize everything he thought he could have done better.

It fell to Wilde to teach him his variation in *Divertimento No. 15*. They were dancing the ballet together, and no one had seen fit to ensure that he knew the steps. When Bruhn was scheduled to make his debut opposite her in the third movement of *Symphony in C*—a bravura exercise with a tint of folk flavor—Balanchine called a stage rehearsal for the afternoon of the performance. He started changing choreography with the evident desire to make Bruhn look foolish. During the rehearsal Wilde sprained her neck and was told by a doctor that she couldn't dance that night—"the smartest injury I ever had." She didn't want to be onstage in what she considered Balanchine's degradation of his own choreography.

The worst was yet to come: a new ballet called *Panamerica*, which premiered at City Center on January 30, 1960. It was performed to a medley of music by South American composers, and choreographic contributions came from four other creators in addition to Balanchine. One day Tallchief came to rehearsal with her hair down, as if to inspire his theatrical venture to sultry climes. "She looked gorgeous," Barbara Walczak recalled. But when it came to the production, Balanchine "put her onstage in something unflattering and had Diana appear with her hair down." The trio he made for Adams, Magallanes, and Moncion suggested a covertly pornographic speculation on Adams's relationship with ex-husband Hugh Laing and ex-mentor Antony Tudor.

Each section was named after a South American country. In John Taras's "Argentina," to music by Alberto Ginastera, Wilde was featured with Violette Verdy and Edward Villella, and an ensemble of eight women. But it was Balanchine's "Colombia" that remained in her memory as one of her most trying experiences on the ballet stage. Wilde and Bruhn were dancing a duet to music by Luis Escobar that she found interesting, scored for drums and tympani. Balanchine rehearsed them extensively and was quite pleasant to Bruhn, but the partnering he assigned him was perverse, to Wilde's way of thinking. Bruhn was never able to support Wilde in any of the conventional holds: he never took her hand or put his arm around her waist. Throughout the entire duet, they instead locked arms, often his hand circled her wrist. "It was so awkward for him," Wilde said. Bruhn didn't complain to her, but she could see that he was uncomfortable, as was she, and more so when she saw her costume. Her midriff was bare, and on her head was a big hat reminiscent of Carmen Miranda. She didn't wear tights under the very short skirt; instead she wore body makeup on her legs. She was afraid that she looked ridiculous.

Wilde thought that Balanchine was "doing us all in in *Panamerica*." His malaise and belligerence, if that's what it was, was perhaps a reflection of a home life with Le Clercq that could only have been torturous. Balanchine needed a muse, and "my muse has no legs," he told SAB's Natalie Molo. But Wilde gritted her teeth and, as always, got on with it: "Just another one of those things that you have to do." As much as Wilde found her duet onerous, Allegra Kent found her "incredible" in it. "Her section was amazing" because of its "fire, timing, complexity," and power of native evocation. The full ballet was critically panned and immediately dropped, but Wilde's duet was among the pieces perpetuated as stand-alone repertory items for a while. She also succeeded Tallchief in her "Cuba" section.

Bruhn did have something to be very grateful to Balanchine for. On

January 6 he had danced the Poet in Balanchine's *La Sonnambula* (formerly *Night Shadow*) when the ballet entered NYCB's repertory, fourteen years after he'd created it for the Ballet Russe. The role suited Bruhn's theatrical persona, which subsumed some of his own driven, tortured edge. After the winter season ended in February, however, Bruhn departed, although Wilde danced with him again when he returned to NYCB for a few performances in the fall of 1963.

RAYMONDA

VARIATIONS

Bardyguine was hired by American Ballet Theatre to supervise production on a long tour of Europe in the spring and summer of 1960. The tour would culminate with five weeks in the Soviet Union in September and October. Wilde was going to be free, and she determined to take what might be her only chance to see the Soviet Union, the homeland of both her husband and Balanchine.

Bardyguine was two in 1922 when his mother devised a plan to sidestep the infant USSR's tightening emigration regulations and join her husband in exile in Europe. She procured a doctor's note to the effect that her son missed his father so desperately that he was wasting away. The gambit worked, and of course mother and son never returned to the Soviet Union. Now, in 1960, Bardyguine's parents were nervous about the prospect of him traveling behind the Iron Curtain. But both he and Wilde were excited at the idea.

She could join Ballet Theatre's tour in August, once NYCB finished a monthlong tour to Bear Mountain in New York, Los Angeles, and Chicago. Ballet Theatre left the United States in May, opening their tour in Lisbon.

Heading ABT's tour was guest star Maria Tallchief, who had danced with ABT as a guest a decade earlier, together with Erik Bruhn, who had been a permanent guest with it over the past decade. They had been a success together at NYCB the previous fall, but according to Wilde, "Maria was a mess" on the ABT tour, at least the part of it she witnessed. She did not think Tallchief was dancing at her best, and both she and Bruhn, with whom Maria was having an affair, were very demanding. "They didn't want this, or they wanted a different program, and the stage was never quite right." Wilde resented it because (a) her husband was often the one having to mediate, (b) Tallchief's displays of what Wilde considered grandiosity always grated on her, and (c) Wilde herself was not a complainer. "It's always easy to complain about things, not always easy to fix them."

The French impresario Anatole Heller, whom Wilde had known when she lived in Paris, was managing the tour. After Wilde arrived in Europe, she kept reminding him that she wanted to go on to Russia and he needed to get her papers in order. But he seemed lukewarm, complaining about problems caused by orchestra wives when he had taken the New York Philharmonic to the Soviet Union a year earlier. Finally they were in Bulgaria, the final stop before Moscow, and still he hadn't made any headway about getting her the entry visa she needed to be admitted to the USSR. Wilde went to the Soviet consulate in Plovdiv to inquire about a visa and played her trump card: "Madame Ulanova invited me." Told to come back the next day, she found her visa waiting for her. Bardyguine left a day ahead of the company to ready the first stop in Moscow. Wilde traveled with the company. In Moscow, Gosconcert, the Soviet performing arts bureau, gave her red-carpet treatment. Ulanova's fabled name meant that she had an interpreter and a car at her disposal.

She also had tickets to any performance she wanted to see: the grayness of Moscow was belied by the splendor onstage at the Bolshoi. She attended a memorable *Boris Godunov* starring guest artist George London and also saw the Bolshoi's Rimma Karelskaya dance *Raymonda*. Wilde admired her performance and was thrilled by a moment in act 2 made possible by the trap doors in the massive old stage. At one point, the Saracen Abderrachman ran from upstage right to downstage left and dropped out of sight, seemingly off the face of the earth, in an instant.

But for both Bardyguine and Wilde, the highlight of their stay was visiting his aunt, Madame Nevelska's sister Sonia, who had also danced at the Bolshoi and now taught in its school. The Russian restrictions on socializing with foreigners meant that their visit to her Soviet-era apartment block in one of the newer sections of the city had to be clandestine. There was no question of just getting into a taxi from their hotel; instead they boarded a city bus, got out, and then caught a cab.

Lafiera now occupied a single room in the apartment she'd originally been assigned, which currently housed at least two other families. But she served them a lovely dinner. They had been told that gifts to Soviet citizens were *verboten*, but Bardyguine's mother had laden them with many presents for her sister. That was another reason they wanted their visit kept secret. She never mentioned her daughter, but they had heard from other friends of the family that she had spent time in a prison camp.

In the years before the Revolution, Bardyguine's family had grown prosperous from a fleet of fabric mills and once owned a mansion overlooking the Moscow River. When he went with Wilde to visit the family's old home, they discovered that it was now a navel officers' residence. He pulled out his camera. Guards pounced immediately. Bardyguine pretended he didn't speak Russian—otherwise, he feared, they would have confiscated the film. Posing as one more American tourist, he managed to hold on to the camera as well as film.

Tallchief's performances would be erratic for the remaining half decade of her career, although she did impress Russian audiences. Watching her on the tour, however, Wilde began to ponder how much of Balanchine's remaking had been superimposed. Had he created a false dependency? Or was the pinnacle Tallchief had achieved at NYCB possible only with his constant maintenance? Wilde also considered the possibility that somewhere deep within, Tallchief was fighting his influence and dominance—was rebelling against him.

Tallchief was indeed interested in striking out in new directions. When ABT reached Tblisi, capital of Georgia, she was coached in *Giselle* by Vhakhtang Chabukiani. Tallchief had been enthralled watching Balanchine coach Toumanova's Giselle at the Paris Opera in 1947, but he had discouraged Tallchief from trying the role herself. But Chabukiani, a prewar star of the Kirov, choreographer and flamboyant partner to the reigning Dudinskaya, thought she should try it. Whether she was right for the role is open to question; she never performed it onstage.

Throughout the Soviet Union, getting food served seemed a monumental chore. Each meal seemed to take forever to appear, and as she sat in hotel dining rooms, Wilde filled up on bread or smoked even though she wasn't a smoker. "You only smoke when I can't get any cigarettes!" her husband complained.

NYCB COULD CLAIM a great deal of credit for the unprecedented popularity that ballet was now achieving in the United States. Its promotion by polymath Kirstein, its use of difficult music, and its embrace of abstraction all gave it an intellectual cachet that was almost unique in the dance world. In 1957, the Ford Foundation began putting money into the school and into the cause of ballet nationwide, funding scholarships to SAB and to the school of the San Francisco Ballet.

NYCB's leading dancers were sent out across the United States on inspection and scouting tours, awarding scholarships to SAB and evaluating the caliber of instruction nationwide. Certainly sufficient numbers of students were pursuing ballet seriously that bodies approximating the ideal—flexible muscles; beautiful feet; thin, shapely, well-proportioned limbs—were more and more common. "Millie Hayden and I used to talk about that all the time," Wilde said. "Neither of us had perfect bodies"—and very possibly, they realized, that would by now have prevented them from reaching the positions they had.

Sometimes Wilde would have to decide whether or not to award a scholarship to a girl whose neck was slightly short or shoulders slightly broad, and yet "you could see the will and the little spark there . . ." But give it to her only to have her be pushed aside further down the line? It was a dilemma.

Sometimes bad training distorted the dancer; across the country Wilde would see "horrors" perpetuated in local schools. It sometimes seemed that nothing had changed in decades around America: Tallchief had been put on pointe at age five, with deleterious results to the shape of her feet and the way they articulated that she was still bitter about when writing her memoirs. Now Wilde watched a girl around eight whose legs were already misshapen from being given too much to do too early. "How long have you been on pointe?" "Oh, four years, I think." Another time, Wilde followed a teacher armed with lesson book into the studio, where the woman taught an hour-long class that comprised four equal parts: tap, acrobatics, jazz, and ballet. It was certainly not the concentrated focus from which professional dancers were made.

IN A COMPANY DEDICATED above all to the glorification of the ballerina, Balanchine's belief that a man could only improve his partnering by doing a lot of it made him surprisingly oblivious to the possible hazards. When Le Clercq had made her debut as Sugar Plum in 1954, *Dance News* reported that twenty-year-old Jacques d'Amboise, dancing his first classical premier role, was handling her so roughly that he was "putting her safety in jeopardy" with every supported promenade.

Wilde didn't quite feel that way when it came to being partnered by young Edward Villella, but dancing opposite him in the early 1960s was "no fun," she recalled. In his mid-twenties, Villella's training had been interrupted for four years after his father insisted that he give up ballet and go to college. Wilde wasn't the only guinea pig. Violette Verdy was assigned the young dancer when Balanchine brought his *Theme and Variations*, originally created for Ballet Theatre in 1947, into NYCB's repertory in 1960. "He's not completely ready, but he's going to learn," Balanchine told Verdy, who had performed *Theme* as a guest with ABT in 1957: "You know the ballet, so I expect it will not be too bad for you."

Balanchine had a similar comment for Wilde. "Oh well, he has to learn how to do it," he said when she complained. "You're strong; you can help him."

Allegra Kent found the Wilde-Villella coupling aesthetically strange as well. "The proportions were so off," Kent said. "It was just totally wrong." But gradual mechanical improvement on Villella's part meant that Wilde was willing to stick with the partnership through additional guest engagements. In the summer of 1961, they danced together at Jacob's Pillow, at the newly convened dance seasons at the open-air Delacorte Theater, in Central Park, and as guests with the New England Civic Ballet, forerunner of the Boston Ballet. By the mid-1960s, however, Villella was embarked on a more compatible partnership with his contemporary Patricia McBride. "They were great together," Wilde said.

Up to the very end of her career, Wilde was interested in finding new ways to do ballet steps, even those she was most famous for. In 1960, Balanchine imported Stanley Williams from the Royal Danish Ballet as guest teacher for the company. He was an immediate hit and was asked to return for another season-long residency.

Wilde had been turning like a top since she was a girl, but Williams changed her pirouettes. "He made me very aware of getting up there into the position immediately." It was an idea she later incorporated into her own teaching. "The moment you're on your pointe or demi-pointe you have to be in position. I think that's giving you pictures you want to have in your mind, that you want to create."

Williams was also excellent at developing the foot's responsiveness. He'd have them perform small jumps followed by a quick relevé and then a slow descent. "That is exactly what you want landing from a jump," Wilde said, "through the foot. Balanchine wanted you to roll through the foot, but he never gave us that kind of exercise."

Wilde and NYCB loved Williams's classes too much, in fact. Balanchine "got very upset," she recalled, as the company wanted Williams to take on more and more teaching responsibilities. They even asked if he could teach a special warm-up class in the evening before a performance. Balanchine's response was to move Williams out of the company and into what became in 1964 a full-time position at the school, where he remained until his death in 1997. Why couldn't they have Williams at the company? "He's busy," they were told. NYCB dancers continued, however, to migrate to his classes at the school, and he remained a formative influence on many of the company's leading dancers. Although Balanchine may have found Williams a threat, a measure of gratitude might instead have been in order. "Stanley was the one who helped you to understand Balanchine's choreography better," recalled John Prinz, Balanchine's favorite young male dancer at NYCB during the mid-1960s. Prinz's comment was supported by any number of similar testaments by leading NYCB dancers.

In the fall of 1961 Balanchine created his last role for Wilde: the lead in *Raymonda Variations*. For her it was a Janus-faced ballet. It looked back—glancingly—at the 1946 full-length *Raymonda* Balanchine and Danilova had staged at Ballet Russe. But *Raymonda Variations* now had an entirely different approach to the score. The ballet saluted the horizon as well. Wilde at age thirty-three was one of NYCB's senior ballerinas. She dominated the ballet, but Balanchine also included solos for five rising young women in the company. She was queen of all she surveyed, but the future was racing in tandem with her, with Balanchine, and with the aesthetic lineage.

Wilde had been touring domestically with NYCB from July though October 1961. At the end of October, she was in the studios NYCB shared with the school on Eighty-Second Street and Broadway. They had moved there in 1956 after their Madison Avenue premises were sold and demolished. Balanchine appeared unexpectedly. "Oh, Pat, do you have time?" They worked for an hour on a variation to music from Glazunov's score. But he never said that this was going to be part of a new ballet for her. Several weeks later, she was back to work, beginning rehearsals for the winter season. She saw on the rehearsal board: "Wilde *Raymonda*." He asked if she remembered the variation. She didn't, because she hadn't made a point of remembering; she didn't think he was doing anything except choreographic doodling. And so on the spot he created an entirely new one to the same music, a lyric piece originally intended for Raymonda's companion Henriette. In the finished ballet she danced a second solo as well, performed to Raymonda's act 2 variation: a much more plangent exhibition piece.

As always, Balanchine used the dancer's talent to create new steps, new combinations. Wilde's strength and resilience made possible a moment in her first variation when she landed from a jump and immediately without any pause or preparation relevéed on the landing leg and performed a pirouette.

It might be said that Balanchine in his new ballet now consumed *Raymonda*, eliminating not only the story but most, if not quite all, of the ballet's iconographic attributes. In Wilde's second variation, however, he preserved some flavor of the original when he specified that the arms should look slightly like a Czardas. But in the context of Balanchine's new ballet, the score meant something else almost completely: d'Amboise danced to music composed for a woman's variation.

Wilde made her first entrance midway through the same waltz she had danced in in the first act of Balanchine and Danilova's 1946 *Raymonda*. Stepping out from upstage right, she ran on pointe all the way to downstage left. Without a special lightness and delicacy, it could have looked plodding. It was important that "you fly out there like there's no stage underneath you!" Wilde said. "I'd take a deep breath and fly."

Now a much more able partner than he'd been partnering Le Clercq's debut, d'Amboise was nevertheless not the most sensitive. Rehearsing their duet in *Raymonda Variations*, Wilde was in tears. D'Amboise "didn't have me on my leg'"—he couldn't stabilize her equilibrium on pointe to enable her to lift her leg as high as she could. "Just get your leg up!" Balanchine barked. It was clear to her that Balanchine did not want to ruffle her partner. For one thing, Balanchine needed d'Amboise to partner his tall ballerinas. For another, although Balanchine was as much an alpha male as d'Amboise, Wilde was also aware that Balanchine could be intimidated by very tall men. "But I'm so small," Balanchine had told Vida Brown in 1950 when they were dancing the Mazurka from *A Life for the Czar*. Ballet's leading men at the time were considerably shorter than today's. Nevertheless, over the course of Balanchine's life ballet's men had gotten much taller and he had shrunk. He was now, in his fifties, not the same man Wilde had known fifteen years earlier: "He wasn't flying around in class doing *tours en l'air* anymore."

"Jacques could be exciting to dance with," Wilde said. She had danced with him not only at NYCB but also in concert appearances. "There was no question of him not holding up his end of a performance." Few dancers could hit the stage and immediately engage a public at his peak level of excitement: "He'd go out there and he went *boom*!"

Valse and Variations, as it was called at first, premiered December 7, 1961. Scenically it recycled the Horace Armistead backdrop used for Tudor's *Lilac Garden* in 1951—another sign that Balanchine had no intention of perpetuating a Tudor legacy in his company. It was enormously taxing for both principals: each one had two solos, and together they danced an adagio and two codas. The supporting solos were danced by Victoria Simon, Suki Schorer, Gloria Govrin, Carol Sumner, and Patricia Neary.

"I was nervous as all hell," recalled Simon, who had joined NYCB in 1958. In the solo Balanchine made for her, he challenged her with hops on pointe, a step she had trouble with. But aspiring as well as reigning stars all triumphed when the ballet premiered on December 7, 1961.

In the *World Telegraph and Sun*, Louis Biancoli reported the next day, "It was obvious that the solo dancers, thanks to the amiable Zvengali who coaches them, had moved a few paces beyond their own self-assumed limits. They all seemed inspired last night." In the *Journal-American*, Miles Kastendieck noted, "A pas de deux made evident what a lyric dancer Patricia Wilde has become, though Balanchine has not overlooked her special brand of preciseness." A month later, the ballet was performed with d'Amboise's variations, which had been omitted at the premiere because he was injured. Wilde was "dancing enchantingly," Martin wrote in the *Times*, "with all her phenomenal gifts as a ballerina."

THE USSR

Publicly and privately Balanchine frequently articulated his belief that work should come before anything else in the life of a ballerina. True to form, Balanchine told Wilde to wait and have children after ballet, but she was confident she could combine dancing with children, as Hayden and Kent were doing. Conception was proving difficult, however, and her doctor recommended she try fertility treatments at a clinic in Switzerland, outside Lausanne. Following a week there, she was invited by Eleanor Barzin, wife of NYCB's music director, Leon Barzin, to stay with the Barzins in Paris.

Barzin was a Post cereal heiress, twenty years older than Wilde. She had a long association with the arts: at twenty-one she had eloped with the screenwriter and director Preston Sturges. Barzin was her fourth and final husband. By now she and Wilde had shared many excursions around Europe. Barzin often accompanied NYCB tours, and inevitably wanted to visit every point of interest, museum, historical site, and botanical garden. She'd get a driver, and any time that Wilde could get free, they'd go off together. Wilde went with the Barzins for the occasional day at their country house outside Paris, which had every conceivable amenity, including a private theater. At Easter in 1962 they were cutting stacks of lilies, which they brought to a church in Paris. Wilde's medical issues turned out, however, to be the result of her dieting. It was only a year after her final performance that she at last conceived.

She was back in harness by April 24 when NYCB opened a new season at City Center. Balanchine's evening-long *A Midsummer Night's Dream* had premiered two months earlier, and now was given its own week of performances. Act 1 told the story, and act 2 was celebratory dancing commemorating the multiple weddings. The highlight was a long, intricate adagio, created for Violette Verdy and Conrad Ludlow. Now Balanchine assigned it to Wilde and Watts as well.

Together with the *Square Dance* duet, this was the hardest adagio she ever danced. But by now she had developed resources to enable her to move through a lyric passage with an ease that bore no semblance to the strain she might experience. Allan Hughes, who succeeded Martin at the *Times* after he retired, wrote: "The part seemed to have been made for her as much as it had seemed to have been made for Miss Verdy. The qualities brought to it by the two dancers are quite different, but it would be difficult to express a preference for one over the other. Miss Verdy accentuated the vivacity to be found in it, while Miss Wilde stressed elements of nobility and grandeur that she discovered."

Another new assignment allowing Wilde to demonstrate her mature artistry was the "Ricercata" originally danced by Melissa Hayden in Balanchine's 1959 *Episodes*. It also gave Wilde the chance to do things that she wasn't usually expected to do—not perform pyrotechnics. Unusual for Balanchine, each of the movements in *Episodes* was completely self-contained; the dancers didn't return for a finale. And so it fell to the two leads and corps of the concluding "Ricercata" to manage on their own a statement of recapitulations and summary. The music helped, being the most tonal of the Webern pieces, an orchestration of Bach. Wilde's solo contained weight shifts, small steps in place, condensed but significant pauses.

The fall of 1962 would bring a month in Europe as well as the company's debut in the USSR. Balanchine had not been back since leaving in 1924 and was rabidly anti-Communist. NYCB had first been invited in 1956, when Kirstein told ANTA's Dance Panel that Balanchine was "anti-Stalinist, and he thinks he might encounter difficulties if he appears in Russia." Since then, however, the Bolshoi had made its U.S. debut in May 1959, followed in September 1961 by Leningrad's Kirov.

Certainly, acceptance in his homeland meant something to him. "Oh, my God!" Balanchine exclaimed when Wilde handed him a jar of homemade marinated mushrooms. During her visit to Russia with ABT, a friend of his youth had given it to her to present to him. Balanchine appreciated the gesture. But it was the State Department that was most determined that NYCB would advance the cultural front of the Cold War into the home ground of the enemy.

It was going to be an eventful fall after an eventful summer, when the company toured the West Coast for a month, including appearances at the World's Fair in Seattle. Wilde, however, didn't feel the need to rest as the fall tour approached, so she fit in some summer gigs with NYCB's Ludlow, a favorite partner.

Before Russia, NYCB spent September touring Europe. In Hamburg, they got off to a terrible start. D'Amboise and Victoria Simon were hit by a streetcar, and he spent weeks in a hospital there. Balanchine's *Liebeslieder Walzer*, performed to Brahms's song cycle, turned into a disaster in the city of Brahms's birth. It was "well played but badly sung," Watts recalled. "This doesn't sound right to me," he told partner Hayden at the dress rehearsal. "Oh, honey, you know how singers are; they're just saving their voices." But in performance the singers were booed. Balanchine was white-faced. He decided to pull the ballet from the Russian repertory.

Moving to Berlin, they now played the big, spanking-new opera house, followed by seasons in Zurich, Stuttgart, Cologne, Frankfurt, and finally Vienna, where they opened a week's run on September 29 at the historic Theater an der Wien. Preparing for its fall reopening, the theater had just scoured and polished its stage, making it treacherous to the ballet. Any number of the dancers took falls.

Throughout her NYCB career, Diana Adams had sustained more than her share of spills, "and Mr. B. loved it," Wilde said. What better way to demonstrate how fearlessly and completely she was committed to his movement, his aesthetic? Opening night in Vienna, she took commitment a few steps too far, falling not once but three times, and "after the last one she didn't get up." She had seriously hurt her knee. It was with Adams that Balanchine descended the gangway stairs when their plane touched down in Moscow a week later. But, to his disappointment, she performed very little in Russia.

All around Europe Wilde roomed with Jillana Zimmerman, who used only her first name professionally. In 1948 she had been a teenage charter member of NYCB. "Pat and I had a lot of fun," she recalled. Four years later, when she gave birth to her son William, she asked Wilde to be his godmother. "I felt that she would do a good job with him if I wasn't around."

In every city the two ballerinas treated themselves to one dinner at a first-rate restaurant, lifting but circumspectly their self-imposed restrictions on what they could eat and what they could spend. In Vienna's expensive stores, they looked at beautiful objects and didn't buy. In Russia, their lodgings and food were going to be paid by the company, but they knew there was no guarantee they'd be adequately fed. Wilde had no intention of repeating her previous trip to Russia two years earlier, where she had filled up with bread waiting for meals to arrive. Grocery stores in Vienna did a thriving trade catering to mountaineers, and Wilde bought tubes of cheese and dried soups.

When NYCB opened October 9 at the Bolshoi theater in Moscow, Wilde danced the Russian Ballerina in *Serenade,* together with Kent, Jillana, Magallanes, and Watts. Despite this lineup, the audience was "perplexed and fairly indifferent," reported John Martin, who was sent by the *Times* to cover the Russian tour. It was a matter of their unfamiliarity with non-narrative ballet. Composer Aram Khachaturian's statement could be taken as a word from officialdom: "The only trouble with the American ballet troupe is the absence of a story line. But this shortcoming is made up by the brilliant technique of the artists." *Western Symphony* was much easier to take and was enthusiastically received.

The Bolshoi was in season, so for the rest of the month they alternated between that venerable citadel of red and gold, and a red citadel of a different sort: the six-thousand-seat Palace of Congresses within the Kremlin, which was as much meeting arena as theater. It had a very wide stage, not that deep. Awkwardly placed wings stretched long, so that Wilde knew she was visible to the audience before she'd actually stepped onstage.

She was rehearsing the adagio in *Concerto Barocco* in an upstairs studio at the Bolshoi when her foot jammed during the repeated sequence of slides supported by her partner. She performed as scheduled that night but was in agony. She kept on performing, but was receiving regular massages and some therapy from the Bolshoi's helpful rehab staff. Meanwhile, Watts, who took over d'Amboise's role in *Raymonda Variations*, suffered a terrible back spasm during one performance in Moscow. Wilde and Watts "kept meeting at the therapist," she recalled. Fortunately for Watts, d'Amboise arrived from weeks of hospitalization in Hamburg and was able to dance some performances.

As the Cuban Missile Crisis unfolded during the second half of the month, the dancers were briefed as a group. Wilde attempted to quell her colleagues' anxiety. At that moment, Bardyguine was touring the United States with the Bolshoi, which had arrived in San Francisco. Wilde didn't think the moment was just right for nuclear confrontation. "Don't you think the Bolshoi in San Francisco is in exactly the same position?" Mutually assured ballet-troupe destruction would hinder Armageddon. She believed that her words had some positive effect.

By the time the company moved on to Leningrad at the end of the month, the geopolitical threat had abated. Most of the Leningrad season was at the mammoth Lensoviet Palace of Culture in the Petrogradskaya district across the Neva. But Balanchine insisted that they open at the Mariinsky. The sun still hadn't risen when Wilde arrived for class in the late morning, but as performance approached the theater was a blaze of chandelier-lit blue and gold. Its great old stage gave Wilde a lot to think about. To varying degrees, every member of NYCB, no matter how wide his or her experience, was tempted to refract ballet history through the lens of Balanchine. As Wilde warmed up on the stage where *The Sleeping Beauty* and *The Nutcracker* had their first performances, she thought about how this was where he had performed children's roles as a student, then danced with the company as a young man. Later during their week in Leningrad, Wilde visited the 1830s school on Rossi Street where Balanchine and so many of the émigrés Wilde worked with had trained. The School of American Ballet's Felia Doubrovksa had entrusted her with presents for a childhood friend, who was now an administrator there.

NYCB was a spectacular success in Leningrad. As Martin tabulated in the *Times*, there were fifteen-minute ovations after every performance, cut short only by Balanchine himself requesting the public to finally leave so that the dancers could rest. But Balanchine's return home traumatized him. The inevitable emotional toll was aggravated by the Soviets' evident attempts at surveillance and even harassment—his hotel phone ringing inexplicably in the middle of the night.

As the company prepared to leave for Kiev, it was told that Balanchine had returned to New York for a week. Wilde today suspects that SAB's Natalie Molo, who was also returning to Russia with them, had something to do with his sudden leave-taking. Molo was a close friend of Le Clercq's mother, Edith. As Wilde said, "Edith and Tanny were *not* the same person." Le Clercq was now trying once more to establish her own independent identity, albeit a far different one than she could ever have imagined during her earlier prepolio estrangement from him. Edith, however, was emotionally invested in keeping her daughter's marriage viable. Le Clercq told company manager Betty Cage that she'd prefer not to see her husband before he returned as originally scheduled at the conclusion of the Russian tour in December. Nevertheless, Balanchine did spend a week with her in New York while the company went to Kiev. After Kiev, Balanchine returned and NYCB fulfilled its engagements in Tbilisi in Georgia, and Baku, capital of Azerbaijan.

Impresario Leon Leonidoff's tours were generally well organized. The company played prestigious theaters. But on this tour he was not present and had instead sent a deputy, whose treatment of the dancers aroused resentment. Tbilisi's southern climate ensured fresh fruit and vegetables in an abundance unknown in the North. For dinner, however, the dancers were served chicken necks with Russian dressing. "Nobody ate it," Wilde said, but it kept coming back, being served night after night, until finally the dancers were squashing cigarette butts in the plat du jour. Meanwhile they saw plates of shish kebab and other appetizing specialties going to the table occupied by Leonidoff's lieutenant. This tour would be the last time that Leonidoff presented the company.

After winding up the Bolshoi's U.S. tour, Bardyguine had now come to Europe to join a tour of the young Robert Joffrey Ballet, which was bankrolled by Rebekah Harkness, a very wealthy dilettante in her forties. Later she and Joffrey would part company and Harkness establish her own company, for which she funded months-long rehearsal periods in the South of France, where Bardyguine had grown up. Working for Harkness was for him a good job all around. Wilde did not mind spending long periods of time on her own—getting back in touch with a love of solitude dating back to her reading while perched in one of her mother's apple trees.

Nevertheless, she was happy to reunite with her husband after NYCB finished its Russian tour. She needed time to rest her foot and, rather than return to New York with her company, where they would reopen December 14 at City Center, Wilde joined her husband's tour. Flying with her were Watts and his wife, corps dancer Diane Consoer. They were leaving NYCB, as they had informed Balanchine before the tour began. Although no one was indispensable, Watts was a definite asset, and Balanchine did try to forestall his departure by promising him new repertory. But Watts had reached the point of disillusion experienced by many around Balanchine.

By now, Wilde had read enough and lived enough to be reconciled to the fact that Balanchine was not a substitute for the paternal presence she'd been denied as a girl—no matter how patriarchal his authority and control. "If I ever had a problem, he wanted to know," but that didn't guarantee he had the time or inclination to address it. Wilde accepted that their relationship was quid pro quo. "He used me and I used him," she said. "And I was happy to be used!" she laughs. "What else would I be there for?" Looking back, it disturbs her a bit that "Jonathan let everything get to him."

Watts and his wife were going to dance with the Joffrey, where he had danced before NYCB. From Baku, they flew to Moscow, caught a flight to Copenhagen and then another to Lisbon, where the Joffrey was performing. Their tour, again subsidized by ANTA and the State Department, took in the Middle East and the subcontinent; sometimes Wilde and her husband traveled with the company, and sometimes they would fly ahead if Bardyguine had advance business to conduct for the next booking.

At New Year's 1963 they were in Tehran. Harkness was at that time married to Dr. Benjamin Kean, a parasitologist. From Tehran they and the

Bardyguines took a chartered plane south for the day to a city in southern Iran plagued by health issues that Dr. Kean was interested in. When they subsequently reached Jerusalem, Wilde and her husband visited the convent of the Order of the Holy Sepulchre. Bardyguine's childhood nurse had left Russia and resettled in Europe with him and his parents. She spent her final years in the convent, and he wanted to see the people who had taken care of her. He and Wilde explained that they were traveling with the ballet, and the convent staff told them that Alexander Glazunov's widow was now living there too. "I'm sure she would like to meet you." "Oh, Mr. Balanchine!" Madame Glazunov exclaimed, when Wilde informed her about *Raymonda Variations*. Balanchine would reminisce to the company that the composer was very involved with the life of the Rossi Street school, sometimes playing for classes. "She was in heaven to hear all of that."

Rising in the West Sixties in Manhattan, Lincoln Center's Philharmonic Hall had opened in April 1962, the first theater in the complex to be completed. A month earlier, Wilde and Ludlow had danced excerpts from *Swan Lake* as part of an all-Tchaikovsky program, one of the Philharmonic's final performance before leaving Carnegie Hall and moving to Lincoln Center.

The following spring, conductor Andre Kostelanetz asked them back to dance on his newly launched Promenades program at the new theater, when the concert hall was transformed into a nightclub setting. Then in 1964 and '65 she returned not only to dance but also to make her debut as choreographer, working on herself and a small group of young dancers from the fledgling Joffrey Ballet. Balanchine came to see what she'd done and offered encouragement. "You know, you want music? I help you find music." Wilde had no interest, however, in following in his shoes. Totally unlike Balanchine, choreography for her was "like pulling teeth and nerve-racking."

Opposite the Philharmonic, the New York State Theater was being readied for Balanchine and his company. "I designed it for George," architect Philip Johnson declared. Balanchine wanted a stage so cushioned that the dancers' feet would not send any sound out into the audience. Sometimes Balanchine asked Wilde to help him test flooring materials. They'd walk over from City Center and report to a half-finished studio in the new building. She would stand on a big piece of sample material, trying little jumps and some traveling steps to gauge spring and resilience. He did get what he wanted, which did not work out so well for the New York City Opera, which was also moving from City Center. Johnson's endeavors to muffle the dancers' steps made for exactly the wrong acoustical environment for an opera company.

Nursing her knee injury, Diana Adams had performed hardly at all in Russia. Her mind was on having children, which was proving elusive after more than one miscarriage. In the spring of 1963, Balanchine choreographed *Movements for Piano and Orchestra* for her, but she bowed out on discovering that she was again pregnant. Balanchine was furious, but was mollified by the replacement Adams, d'Amboise, and ballet master John Taras came up with: seventeen-year-old Suzanne Farrell. Adams had discovered her in Cincinnati during an audition tour in 1960 and awarded her a scholarship to SAB; a year later she joined the company.

Farrell was exactly what Balanchine was looking for: she was young, malleable, and his for the molding. She had a great natural facility for movement, an unusual sensitivity to melody and rhythm. But she had started serious ballet training only at age fifteen, when she entered SAB. She needed a Pygmalion, and he, as always, a new Galatea.

Balanchine's attention to his latest muse soon became obsessive. It initiated a period at NYCB unlike anything else Wilde had ever experienced, helping to make her final years onstage—as well as the ongoing careers of many colleagues—fraught, chaotic, bewildering.

32

"YOU CAN ALWAYS
COME BACK"

In August 1963 the Ford Foundation announced a $7.7 million grant to upgrade ballet training throughout the United States, putting a colossal new infusion of cash toward an expansion of programs it had been supporting since 1957. More than half the money would go to New York City Ballet and the School of American Ballet. Wilde was pleased to attribute its final approval to a benefit for the Pennsylvania Ballet in which she had had danced a month earlier. Balanchine attended, as did McNeil Lowry, the point man for cultural giving at the Foundation, and his wife. It was held on a private estate, where a temporary stage was erected. It had rained earlier in the day, and the temperature dropped by night, but still Wilde and colleagues contributed their services, and a full audience turned out to watch them.

On the train back to New York, Wilde listened as Lowry told Balanchine that the grant was going to go through. Wilde thought that the performance had had some influence. Lowry "saw that people cared that much. They came for it, were willing to support it: we were out there dancing in the cold."

Although *Raymonda Variations* was the last ballet Balanchine created for Wilde, she was treated by NYCB with a certain amount of deference during its final seasons at City Center. On September 5, 1963, *Square Dance* was revived after an absence of several seasons. Terry in the *World-Tribune* opined: "The performance itself found its center and its peak in the dancing of Miss Wilde. She never looked prettier (sometimes she can look quite stern) nor happier and her grand pas de whickety-whack deservedly earned her a batch of roaring bravos."

Wilde was certainly happy to have *Square Dance* back. Six years older than she'd been at the premiere, Wilde nevertheless found it easier to dance because "I had learned how to pace myself." During her remaining two years onstage, Balanchine would eliminate the caller and orchestra. It diminished the vernacular flavor that made the original so charming as well as unique, but allowed the dancers space in which to move.

During the winter season, Balanchine revived his 1959 *Waltz-Scherzo*, which had been one of Wilde's favorite creations. This time she was partnered by d'Amboise, Eglevsky having long since left the company. And for the revival Balanchine added some lifts, the absence of which had made the original singular. Again, however, the duet didn't last long in the repertory. Once again the reason was musical: Balanchine was not happy with the way it was being played. Only a particular Russian violinist could produce results that satisfied him. "That's the way it's got to be!" Balanchine said. Wilde thought the work remained something original in Balanchine's canon, even with the inclusion of lifts, and regretted that he'd dropped it.

The company was going to inaugurate the New York State Theater in spring 1964. It was with an eye toward the much larger stage of the new theater that a stylistic shift began. Balanchine always privileged an assertive conquest of space, but now he was wanting everything "bigger and bigger," Wilde said. Classical niceties that Balanchine had long insisted on could suffer as a result. "There aren't *real* fifth positions anymore," she would tell John Gruen about the state of NYCB in 1973. Fifth position, the legs tightly crossed together in turned-out position, is one of the essential punctuations of classical ballet grammar.

Suzanne Farrell epitomized the new style—and then some. She took liberties that he wouldn't tolerate in others, but what Balanchine adored most about Farrell's dancing was its recklessness. He didn't seem to care if the chances she took overrode a prudent threshold of stylistic integrity as well as physical probity. Bacchic abandon as evidenced by Wilde and her contemporaries was still based on a foundation of methodical training and judicious proportion. Wilde disapproved of how uncontrolled Farrell's movement was. Performing a pirouette to arabesque *penché*, her leg would sail over her head heedlessly, without any circumspective braking. "Just *whack!*"

Farrell's mother was a nurse and often traveled with the company in a professional capacity. Wilde was in a ladies' room on tour when Mrs. Ficker—Farrell was born Roberta Sue Ficker—walked in. "Oh, I don't want Suzanne to be another Tanny," she blurted out to Wilde, but seemed as much to be saying it to herself. Le Clercq above all could seem like a living symbol of the hazards of musedom; there had been rather widespread apprehension about the wisdom of their union. "She's playing with fire," Pat McBride, Le Clercq's closest friend, said when she found out they were dating. But the celebrity and artistic glory Le Clercq and others in the lineage experienced were very alluring indeed. Mrs. Ficker soon came around, switching to a mode of pushing her daughter into Balanchine's arms.

For a number of years, Farrell herself found a way to get exactly what she wanted from Balanchine without submitting personally. Undoubtedly she realized the extent to which sexual capitulation and particularly marriage itself—Balanchine became intent on marrying her—could actually mean the beginning of the end. In any case, the more elusive, capricious, and demanding she became, the more his obsession grew. Farrell was "warm, caring, and attentive," d'Amboise writes in his 2011 memoirs, "then cold, distant, and rejecting, juggling him masterfully between the two."

It certainly seemed to many in NYCB that, in the words of another principal dancer, "Suzanne was running the company." Nothing quite like this had happened with Balanchine before, and the susceptibility of age as well as his ghastly experience with Le Clercq both have to be taken into account. His inability to somehow make Le Clercq walk again was a blow to his ego that added to his anguish over the fate she had been dealt.

It was certainly unprecedented for Balanchine to take Farrell to administration meetings and allow her to tell him what ballets should be on the programs as well as which ones she wanted to dance. And "she wanted to do everything," Wilde said.

On April 23, 1964, Wilde danced *Serenade* at the State Theater's gala opening night—she loved the expanse of the big stage, and that night was "at her greatest," according to Edwin Denby. Reviewing the opening season in the *New Yorker*, Winthrop Sargeant described her as "the company's great female trouper, and a dancer, who, one feels, would take on anything, no matter how difficult, and do it to perfection."

Tallchief, who had returned to NYCB the previous fall after an absence of three years, requested Wilde as her dressing-room mate in the new theater. "When Maria was in a foul mood you didn't want to go anywhere near that," Wilde said, but mutual respect kept things on an even keel. They were now the two final company veterans of Balanchine's years at the Ballet Russe two decades earlier.

Studio space at the new theater was generous enough that for the first time in the company's history it was no problem for a principal dancer to request a rehearsal beyond what he or she was scheduled for, although a pianist wouldn't always be supplied. Lavish as the new theater was, Balanchine again insisted that ticket prices be kept under control, and indeed they were until he died in 1983.

Wilde would spend eighteen months with NYCB at the State Theater. Looking back, however, she believed it had been three years—so trying did those months become for her. Balanchine's company class had now turned very strange. He and Farrell would usually arrive together, and often late, having met for coffee on the way—and sometimes lingering in his office to talk. Class would wait for them. Class was not only muse-centric but also muse-indulgent. Demi-plié was a problematic area of Farrell's physical capabilities, but rather than find a way around it, Balanchine stopped assigning pliés altogether, as well as jumps after Farrell injured her knee.

His experiments in class could seem bizarre and unnecessary to Wilde. The most musically trained and attentive of choreographers, he now entertained the idea of running class with only piano chords or bare rhythms as accompaniment. Wilde instead began taking Stanley Williams's class at SAB.

NYCB had numbered sixty-three dancers in August 1963, a good fifteen or so more than it had employed when Wilde joined in 1950. Now, with the move to Lincoln Center, the company was rapidly expanding and would eventually reach over ninety dancers. There was no longer any need for principal dancers to be saddled with the workload of previous years; and of course there were many new, young, talented dancers whom Balanchine wanted to sample in prominent roles. Yet it proved impossible for Wilde to rewire herself. She was used to dancing at most performances, and often more than one ballet per performance. As she danced less and less, she looked for ways to stay in shape, to stay performance-ready, but most of all a way to compensate for the disorientation she felt. Wilde was soon taking two classes a day, to make up for the performances she wasn't giving. With so much downtime between performances, her stage fright started to become severe. She no longer felt like a true part of the company.

In the interests of conservation and longevity, reduced workload might have seemed prudent to a senior ballerina, but some dancers believe they need to be onstage continuously to stay stageworthy. In Russia, principal dancers never, except on tour, performed more than four times a month, and they usually enjoyed very long careers.

Balanchine was giving her very little attention, but he did insist she now perform a new variation in *Swan Lake*. She thought his new choreography—including an emphatic swing into attitude—derivative from, and more suitable to, Balanchine's *Sylvia*, lacking the breadth of what she'd originally danced. "I hated it."

Other avenues, more satisfying at the moment than performing, were opening up as the regional movement in American continued to advance. In the spring of 1965 Wilde was adjudicator for the Southeastern Regional Ballet Association's annual festival, which was now a decade old. She went to cities all over the South to evaluate local companies, which were usually attached to their own schools. "In general, the level of the technical ability existing in the dancers observed was not sufficiently advanced," Wilde wrote in her report. "It is therefore recommended that all companies insist that at least four classes per week are made mandatory for their dancers. Whenever possible more than four classes would be advisable."

Each little company converged for a weekend in Memphis in April to participate in workshops and perform at a gala evening. Wilde produced a treat for the workshop weekend: a lecture-demonstration on choreography conducted by none other than Balanchine himself. Wilde selected students from the various schools—nearly twenty in all. Teachers and spectators watched as Balanchine demonstrated how he deployed an ensemble, how he used music. "The kids were in seventh heaven," Wilde recalled. "The teachers learned a lot."

A month later, in May 1965, Suzanne Farrell was crowned as NYCB's reigning divinity. At a gala preview performance, she was Dulcinea opposite Balanchine himself in the title role of his new three-act *Don Quixote*. Onstage, the physical frailty of the sixty-one-year-old Balanchine was evident even in this pantomime role, and he seemed utterly naked emotionally. Wilde went to the performance and found it all so unseemly that "I was sick about it."

That summer NYCB was again embarking on a long European tour that would culminate with two weeks at Covent Garden in September. NYCB's return to London after thirteen years was enormously ambitious: in the space of less than two weeks, it would showcase no fewer than nineteen different ballets. Previewing the season for London's *Dancing Times*, Lillian Moore wrote that Wilde had "gained enormously in authority and artistic stature since she last danced in London." But Wilde almost never got to London. She had put on weight and wasn't cast for much as the company performed across Europe. The less she danced, the more the weight stayed on and the more frustrated she became, which in turn didn't help her weight. In Athens she was summoned to company manager Betty Cage's office and told that Balanchine said he couldn't use her at her present weight. SAB's Natalie Molo had accompanied them on this tour and was present for the conversation, which didn't make it any more comfortable for Wilde. She told Cage that in that case she was going to Cannes on the Riviera to take class at Rosella Hightower's studio. Would she be able to join them for London? She would certainly try her best.

In Cannes she swam, took one class a day, but only sometimes two. She was careful about what she ate and drank but, just as important, it was a relief to be away from the company, away from the atmosphere surrounding Farrell and the stress of being sidelined.

"Thank you!" Balanchine cried when she appeared in class in London, considerably thinner than she'd been in Athens. But dressing again with Tallchief, both women believed that the message he was really giving them was quite different: "You're here, but I'm not going to use you. You're taking up space, marquee space, and I have to keep thinking of something to give you to dance."

Wilde was just happy to get through the season, but Peter Williams, reviewing for Britain's *Dance and Dancers*, concluded that NYCB's senior ballerina roster had seen better days. "Her glory is dimmed," he wrote about Tallchief. "To remember that crisp attack and clean line, with the warm femininity which matched them, and now to see her out danced by others, was sad.

"The other two veterans," he wrote, referring to Wilde and Hayden, "came out better, although unevenly." If Wilde was thin enough for Balanchine—she danced a half-dozen lead roles in those two weeks—apparently she wasn't for Williams: "What Patricia Wilde lacks now in line she largely disguised by the speed she still retains."

At age thirty-seven, was Wilde past her prime? Judging by her *Four Temperaments* filmed in Montreal in 1964, as well as the praise still given her by New York reviewers, her technique was certainly still intact. But weight may have become intrusive, although in *Four Temperaments* she looks very slim and long-legged—"My dream!" as Wilde says today. Certainly any performer's malaise, hers included, can often take a toll on performance.

NYCB's senior ballerinas had spent their company careers shouldering herculean workloads. They were "always rushed," Wilde recalled, "too much to do, not enough time." And they were plying what was very likely the most taxing technique in the world. "Immersion in Balanchine technique does not necessarily lead to longevity," Margot Fonteyn writes in 1979's *The Magic of Dance*. As much as Wilde believed and continues to believe in Balanchine's aesthetic, she would agree: "There's no relaxing in Balanchine."

But she believed that it was above all the infrequency with which she now danced that was impairing her.

Back in New York, Wilde began to seriously consider an offer extended by Rebekah Harkness to direct what sounded like a fabulous new school. To house it, Harkness had purchased an 1890s mansion just off Fifth Avenue on Seventy-Fifth Street. Money would be no problem, and Harkness promised that Wilde could design exactly the kind of program she wanted. Harkness confided to her diary on October 12 that she'd talked with Wilde and "it seems perfect person."

Wilde decided to accept. The job sounded too good to turn down, and it was time to cut short a foundering coda to a glorious fifteen years at NYCB. She proceeded to her exit interview with her director. "Mr. B., I'm not used to working this way. One performance here and there—I'm a nervous wreck." He was not going to adjust his priorities to accommodate her, but he was understanding, so much so that he extended the ultimate blessing: "You can always come back." That was a very rare response by him to any dancer's decision to leave his company. "My reward for not complaining all those years!" Wilde laughs today.

Tallchief, too, had now left, reportedly after Balanchine's response to critical comments she made to the press: "Dear," he told her, "we don't need a museum piece in this company." Wilde was about to dance her final performance by the time *Newsweek* ran an article in its October 25, 1965, issue, describing a company-wide crisis. "Perhaps the only solution for the New York City Ballet, overcrowded with superb dancers, is to form a second company, as England's Royal Ballet has done. But, in any case, the current situation is not calculated to aid the morale even of the younger dancers. One, who dare not be named, said: 'Is that what we can look forward to, after all the training and hard work—abbreviated careers?'"

On November 1, 1965, Wilde danced *Raymonda Variations* for the final time. In the *Herald-Tribune*, Terry reported that "at the curtain calls, all of the dancers onstage led by Mr. d'Amboise, applauded the ballerina as she took her bows before a cheering public."

Wilde was feeling some residual disgruntlement later that year when she told Harriet Johnson of the *New York Post* that Balanchine "doesn't want to create for anyone over 23. He gets his creative impulse working with very young, unformed dancers. When he works with mature dancers, he feels imposed upon."

Yet Balanchine's parting words encouraged Wilde to tell the press that she was not retiring as a dancer, but instead hoped she would be asked to make guest appearances, whenever schedules permitted, with her old company. But staying in shape to do the occasional performance would have been a very tall order. Wilde realized this as she prepared early in 1966 for one more performance she had agreed to give. Months earlier she had said yes when NYCB's André Prokovsky asked her to dance Balanchine's *Sylvia* with him at a Red Cross gala at the Champs-Élysées in Paris. Getting herself in shape after two months off was daunting enough to put the idea of future guest performances out of her mind. After working at Harkness all week, she began taking private class on Sundays with Héctor Zaraspe. Wilde had already started giving herself class, but realized the necessity of "having somebody see what you need rather than just what you felt you needed." She certainly wanted to be on top of it as she danced Balanchine's difficult pas de deux. And with all the responsibilities she was assuming in her job, it was nice to be someone else's responsibility.

On February 11, 1966, Wilde stood in the wings of the Champs-Élysées, nervously crossed herself, and said a customary "God help me." She determined she would give as best as she could, and reminded herself, despite her nerves, to enjoy this one last performance. Prokovsky was a good partner, and the performance went well; Wilde got through all the supported and unsupported balances, and also "those goddamned hops on pointe" in her solo, made more difficult because the ballerina had to traverse the entire depth of the stage, from upstage down to the footlights.

The next day she put on a pair of diamond earrings, a Christmas present from Bardyguine, and took herself to dinner at Lasserre, a chic restaurant near the theater. Now she could eat whatever she wanted, and now she felt free to toast herself not only to a farewell performance well done, but to the two decades of performances that had preceded it.

CHILDREN

Wilde says that even in the months immediately following her retirement, leaving the stage was not very painful. She was ready for a different life and identity, which the new Harkness school could certainly provide. She toured the United States holding auditions at schools she'd visited and vetted on behalf of the Ford Foundation and the School of American Ballet. She was looking for students ages fourteen through sixteen who would benefit from an eclectic program encompassing all disciplines of dance. She certainly was not looking to prepare students for New York City Ballet—that was the job of SAB, which was now headed by Diana Adams. Eventually, however, Wilde added some children's classes aimed at beginners age seven or eight.

The students Wilde selected were going to receive full scholarships as well as room and board. The Seventy-Fifth Street facility was splendid, and Harkness's deep, deep pockets meant that "we gave the kids everything," even paying for students' orthodontia.

Harkness herself dabbled in many art forms. She studied painting and composed music—the Joffrey had commissioned a ballet to one of her scores. She was also, although over fifty, studying ballet. Mikhail Fokine's nephew Leon would give her a private class every day. But she loved to have somebody else in class with her, and "she roped me in," Wilde recalled. Harkness wanted to know what dancers experienced, "but I don't think ever did." For one thing, the classes weren't very demanding; there weren't, for example, any big jumps. That made it good but not overly taxing exercise for Wilde as well.

The school's faculty was "fantastic," Wilde said. Harkness was all for Wilde hiring anyone she wanted. Teachers were engaged on a freelance basis, which gave Wilde freedom to suggest virtually any guest who might have some extra time. Wilde herself taught as well, which she had started doing when touring schools for the Ford Foundation. "I enjoyed teaching right from the beginning."

The students experienced different genres as well as subgenres. Frank Wagoner taught what might have been called classic Broadway jazz dance vernacular. Also on the faculty was Evelyn Krafft, who had teamed up with sister Bernice and Jack Cole in a nightclub act that launched Cole's career in the 1930s. At Harkness, Krafft taught Asian Indian dance, which was a major influence on Cole's movement vocabulary. Matt Mattox, another Cole veteran, taught Cole's technique, which involved a demanding emphasis on strengthening and stretching the pelvis. Both Krafft and Mattox talked up Cole to Wilde, who, with Harkness's blessing, called him in Los Angeles. He came east for more than one stint of guest teaching. Cole's class was even more demanding than Mattox's, but "the kids loved him."

In summer the school continued to operate in Manhattan but Harkness also brought some students to her estate in Watch Hill, Rhode Island, where the Harkness family mansion overlooked the Atlantic. Wilde would work Monday through Thursday in Manhattan and then drive up on Friday mornings. In Rhode Island she had a room in the "West House," another Harkness inheritance in the adjacent town, next to the Harkness ballet studio, a converted firehouse. Wilde swam in Harkness's pool and sometimes took class with visiting summer instructors, among them Stanley Williams and Vera Volkova, whose class in London she had attended regularly in 1950.

Harkness's personal orbit was increasingly populated by dissipated courtiers and sycophants, while Harkness, who recorded in her diary frequent bouts with depression, herself became steadily more drug-dependent. But Harkness "was not at all malicious," Wilde said, "not an evil woman at all." Yet her propensity to interfere in matters artistic ultimately proved fatal to every dance project she sponsored. That was why she and Robert Joffrey had parted company in 1963, at which point both had founded new companies. Now the Harkness Ballet was headed by ex–premier danseur Yura Skibine and managed by Jeannot Cerrone, both long-standing acquaintances of Wilde's. Relations between school and company were good.

Harkness's susceptibility to slickly presented ideas meant that she was constantly proposing new plans, insisting they be implemented, but then failing to do any follow-up or ensure that checks and balances were put in place. She was all ears when a dance educator presented a method she'd developed that was designed to work with students who had real technical and physical issues to overcome. "'We can make anybody dance,' this is what they were saying," Wilde recalled. The method "had some good points," and there were indeed students who could benefit from it. Wilde's selection criteria were wide enough to include talented and individualistic students who, classically speaking, might have been called diamonds in the rough. Their feet might not be beautiful or articulate, their turnout not optimal. However, she objected when the method—which included videos and other learning tools—was applied to students who "were doing fine and just needed more practice, more work, more refining."

She felt a pressing responsibility to the teachers she had hired, whose work was now being superseded, and to students being experimented on needlessly, and perhaps, she felt, not to their own benefit. She also felt responsible to the regional schools that had produced them. "Teachers around the country said, 'Oh, well, Patricia Wilde is there. We have faith in her. She'll take care of them.'"

In summer 1967, the educator proposed an experiment: a sizable group of students would remain in New York and continue their tutelage in her method. Wilde would supervise the more advanced students at Watch Hill, where they would work on new pieces with a number of young choreographers.

She drove up on a Friday morning only to find that the plan now functioned in reverse: the more proficient students were going to be working on the method, while the more problematic had been sent up to Watch

Hill. That seemed like cheating to Wilde. She was tired of fighting and felt anyway that she'd lost control of the entire situation. She threw up her hands and drove up to her sister Bet's in Vermont. Bet lived in Hartland, but had built a cabin on a lake much farther north, close to the Canadian border. Together they loaded five hundred bricks onto a truck, drove up to the lake, and built a fireplace in Bet's cabin.

Wilde was breaking her contract, without asking for severance; nevertheless, when she returned to New York she was contacted by Harkness's personal lawyer.

"I do not believe in this, and I'm responsible for these students. No way my name's going to be associated with that." Wilde's departure did not affect her husband's working relationship with Harkness, nor ultimately her own social one. Harkness subsequently bought a house in Sneden's Landing on the Hudson, near where the Bardyguines were by then raising two children in nearby Tappan. She invited Wilde and her husband to parties, where all was friendly.

As soon as she returned to New York from Vermont, Wilde called Balanchine, who remained a guru. He advised her not to give the press any reasons about why she'd left Harkness and not to criticize what had been going on at work. He immediately asked whether she'd like to come back to NYCB. "What do you want to do? Do you want to dance? Do you want to teach? Coach?" It didn't take her long to decide. Reviewing her repertory, she realized that some of it, particularly after eighteen months offstage, was just going to be too strenuous. And the dissension in the dancing ranks generated by Farrell had, if anything, grown worse in the months Wilde had been away. Teach and coach it would be.

She then joined Bardyguine for a short vacation in France, where he had just returned from a Harkness company tour. She met up with him in Cannes, where the company maintained one headquarters. They drove through Switzerland and wound up in Paris. All through the trip they went to superb restaurants, but Wilde couldn't eat much because her stomach was chronically upset. They thought she had food poisoning, but back in New York she soon discovered that she was four months pregnant. She wondered if her decision to leave Harkness had been triggered by hormones, but remained convinced that it was the right one.

At NYCB, she was more or less a free agent, making her own schedule. "Do whatever you want," Balanchine said when she started teaching company class on an intermittent basis. He sometimes came to watch her teach, which fluttered her nerves, but he was quite hands-off. He'd restrict himself to a few suggestions privately after class. Sometimes he asked her to stress some aspect of technique that he was planning to explore in a new ballet—which was what he often did in his own company class.

On January 17, 1968, Wilde gave birth to her daughter Anya at Doctor's Hospital on the Upper East Side of Manhattan. She wanted a natural childbirth and studied the Lamaze technique, finding its exercises and breathing routines extremely helpful. Two weeks before the baby's scheduled arrival, Wilde was experiencing labor pains and timing them; very early in the morning, Bardyguine drove her to the hospital, where her spasms immediately stopped. She was told, however, to stay overnight just in case. Sure enough, at eleven that night, she was alone in her room and the spasms started all over again. This time they were for real. Lamaze did not eliminate pain altogether but did eliminate need for an anesthetic. The birth was comfortable enough, but she was frustrated by the medical habit of those days, which didn't allow the mother to spend long periods with her newborn. Instead Anya was brought in to her for brief visits. Bardyguine had the opportunity to hold her only when they were leaving the hospital and Wilde was being wheeled to the door.

On Ninety-Fifth Street their extra bedroom now became the baby's room. Wilde was soon back at work, leaving every weekday morning after the arrival of a nurse. With her usual thoroughness, Wilde boned up on books about childhood stages and ages.

In New York, the entire ballet community was rocked by the endgame of the Balanchine-Farrell folie à deux. In January 1969 she married NYCB dancer Paul Mejia, which resulted in Balanchine taking away as many of his performances as he could. Finally, in May, Farrell gave Balanchine an ultimatum about putting her husband back onstage. This time she had gone too far: Balanchine refused, and Farrell and Mejia left the company. Ulti-mately, even Farrell was not indispensable, particularly in the state of holy matrimony. But then again, at least as creative partner, she possibly was. Balanchine did allow her back—without Mejia—in 1975. Until he died in 1983, Balanchine continued to create vehicles for her that were superior to those he'd made in the throes of infatuation, which now had passed.

Wilde herself was slowly moving away from Balanchine's orbit. Leon Danelian, a long-ago colleague from the Ballet Russe, now directed Amer-ican Ballet Theatre's school. Unlike NYCB's, it was run for profit, and ad-mission was open to all who could pay. There were also classes strictly for gifted scholarship students. She accepted Danelian's invitation to teach those scholarship students. Then Robert Joffrey, with whom Wilde had toured when her husband worked for his company, also invited her to teach his scholarship students.

When Balanchine asked her to start a school attached to the Geneva Ballet, which had named him artistic adviser, Wilde accepted immedi-ately. Now expecting her second child, Wilde and her twenty-month-old daughter arrived in Geneva in September 1969. Erik Bruhn, then directing the Swedish National Ballet, had also asked her to come to Stockholm the following January to rehearse Balanchine's *Symphony in C.*

While establishing the Geneva school, she taught the company, then, once the school was in place, taught at both places. Finding an apartment as well as a nursemaid proved very difficult as she attempted to negotiate Swiss protocol for foreign visitors. Finally she told the opera house admin-istration that she was leaving the next day unless they gave her some help. An apartment was immediately procured as well as an exemplary nurse with whom Wilde is still in contact.

Bardyguine had been scheduled to travel with Martha Graham's company on a long tour, but it was canceled, and he arrived in Geneva close to the baby's due date. Three weeks before her husband's arrival, Wilde had re-alized that her strength was ebbing and arranged for a substitute for her classes at the school; she still taught the company. Two weeks passed and no baby. "He was ready. He was just not willing to come out." On a Friday she told Dr. Mattern, a prominent obstetrician, "Look, I have only this next week, and then I have to be back in school, so this baby has to come." He promised to induce labor if she hadn't delivered by Monday.

The Bardyguines invited the Geneva director Alfonso Cata and his assistant Wilhelm Burmann for the traditional European Sunday lunch. At two o'clock that Sunday morning, October 26, her contractions started. Bardyguine took her to her doctor's private clinic, too comfortable to resemble a hospital. Her room let out on the garden. He went back home to wait for Anya's nursemaid. Although it didn't take him long to get back to the hospital, by then she had delivered her son Youri. But Sunday's lunch preoccupied her until Bardyguine assured her it would take place as scheduled—and would be brought to her.

Wilde toured the garden with her daughter and new baby, pointing out to Anya the rabbits shooting through the greenery. "It was fantastic," she recounted, "so much pleasanter than when Anya was born." The lunch did go on as planned. They set up plates in the garden, Anya served the champagne, and Wilde did as much hostessing as she could. By the end of the week, she had resumed all of her work responsibilities.

Balanchine arrived to watch a program of his ballets, in which NYCB's Kay Mazzo would make a guest appearance. Mazzo had assumed much of Farrell's repertory. Balanchine eagerly awaited her arrival.

Wilde and Bardyguine had asked Balanchine to be the child's godfather. The morning of the baptism, Balanchine was recovering from a late night partying with Sophia Loren. At the Russian Orthodox church, a priest asked Balanchine if he wanted a Russian Bible to recite a long prayer earmarked for godfather. "No, no, I know, I know," Balanchine assured him. But soon after he started off, he abruptly stopped. It seemed that he had said one word incorrectly. He went back to the beginning and this time was word perfect right through to the end.

Wilde remained in Geneva through the final day of 1969, but agreed to the company's request that she return after she was finished in Stockholm. In Sweden, the company supplied her with a hotel suite plus kitchenette. Stockholm in January was pitch-dark at ten in the morning, when she taught company class, but streetlights blazed as if a gala premiere was in store. After class, she rehearsed *Symphony in C*, then in the afternoon taught class at the school. This kind of schedule was nothing new for her, but union restrictions meant that the Swedish company had a different way of doing things. They would rehearse until two in the afternoon, then were free unless they had a performance that night. The women thus were able to balance ballet and motherhood with less complication than American ballerinas. But the hours they clocked in were just not sufficient to achieve the results that Wilde wanted. She did sometimes manage to get two of the principal dancers to come back in the evenings to rehearse.

A few of the women dancers were in their mid-forties and not required to do anything on pointe anymore. However, some put on their pointe shoes for the end of Wilde's class. She thanked them. When she'd finished her time there, a dancers' committee took her to lunch. In the highly unionized theater they were powerful. "What can you tell us to make the company better?" "Well, you have to get used to really working. Rehearsing two and a half, three hours a day is not going to do it."

"That didn't go over well," Wilde recalled. They wanted the company to reach its full potential, but the prospect of sacrificing a comfortable lifestyle was daunting.

After her six weeks in Stockholm, she was back in Geneva for several months, until Lucia Chase, American Ballet Theatre's co-director, suddenly phoned. The company would be performing at the New York State Theater that spring of 1970. Chase, whose powers of persuasion were legendary, all but pleaded with Wilde to return to the United States to teach company class before and during their season. After six months in Europe, Wilde made plans to return to New York with her family.

34

AMERICAN

BALLET THEATRE

Wilde was grateful to Balanchine for immediately offering her a berth at New York City Ballet after her breakup with Harkness. She came to believe, however, that it was better for her not to work at New York City Ballet. No matter how accommodating Balanchine was, NYCB was a world unto itself, Balanchine's self-contained fiefdom. She again wanted to venture outside the walls.

Before long, ABT was keeping her very busy. She not only taught company class frequently, but at the school taught both scholarship classes as well as an open class at one o'clock. Wilde didn't mind teaching classes open to anyone. There were people who used the class simply for exercise: "They stayed in the back," Wilde recalled, and she didn't pay much attention. But amateurs who really wanted to progress could expect some comment and correction from her. Most stimulating, naturally, were professionals, who came from Broadway and modern dance as well as ballet. Wilde's ex-NYCB colleague Allegra Kent frequently attended, because Wilde's classes were "fantastic—the organization of the class, the steps, the corrections."

The Bardyguines' home on Autumn Drive in Tappan was a pre–World War II house on a small lot. One side of the property climbed uphill and received abundant sunlight; here Wilde planted roses and a few shrubs, but dedicated most of the plot to an extensive vegetable garden. There were long periods, however, when Wilde's teaching schedule became so busy that she felt as though she barely saw her home.

For one year during the early 1970s, Wilde found herself teaching beginners for the first time at the school of Dance Theatre of Harlem (DTH) after ABT's school was forced to cut back its schedule. DTH had been founded by Wilde's ex-NYCB colleague Arthur Mitchell in 1968. Soon thereafter he persuaded Tanaquil Le Clercq to begin teaching from her wheelchair.

To prepare, Wilde consulted teachers in the children's division at the School of American Ballet. Le Clercq, who had begun teaching DTH's beginners, had said SAB's faculty had been a valuable resource when she began teaching. Together, Wilde and Le Clercq coordinated their syllabuses and the principles they were intending to impart to their students.

Wilde's schedule for that year was delirious. She often taught ABT company class at ten in the morning, then class at its school. Then she would drive up to Harlem to teach her beginner's class. She was also teaching DTH company class once or twice a week, and teaching the Metropolitan Opera's resident ballet company on a weekly basis as well.

Wilde sometimes stayed overnight with Le Clercq in the apartment she and Balanchine had moved into before her paralysis. In the Apthorp building at Broadway and Seventy-Ninth Street, it had wide, Old World hallways that allowed Le Clercq to maneuver freely in her wheelchair. Her dexterity allowed her to be a fully functional hostess, although Wilde was delighted to run errands as needed.

In 1964, Le Clercq had written *Mourka: The Autobiography of a Cat*, a whimsical would-be memoir by the cat that Balanchine had trained to execute balletic leaps. In 1966 came *The Ballet Cook Book*, to which Wilde and many other dancers had contributed recipes. Cooking had become a favorite pastime of hers after her paralysis, perhaps at first a new link to Balanchine now that ballet was closed to her. But in 1969, Balanchine obtained a Mexican divorce, believing it would facilitate his marriage to Farrell. Instead Farrell had married Mejia. Mexican divorces are quick and no-fault; Wilde believed that by this time the decision was mutual. And Le Clercq enjoyed the independence she had never before had. Only at age forty was she "really making her own decisions; before it had been Mama and then Balanchine."

Le Clercq's always nimble mind assumed the mobility her body lacked. She read a lot and was now a crossword puzzle devotee who had composed one for the *New York Times*. At the same time, she retained the personal vanity of a star and a beautiful woman. Together the two former and present colleagues liked to buzz about how they were doing their hair and other such matters of adornment—a discretionary topic now rather than theatrically mandated. It sometimes did seem as though they were once again sharing a dressing-room table.

Le Clercq lived very definitely in the moment and never mentioned her tragedy to Wilde. The one regret Wilde heard her express was when Wilde once talked about her childhood on her mother's estate and the riding, climbing, exploring she'd done. How lucky she'd been to be able to do all that, Le Clercq commented. Edith Le Clercq, as Wilde well knew, had been so ambitious so early for her daughter that free outdoor play was out of the question.

ABT's staff began to ask Wilde to conduct more and more rehearsals. "You've got to come on tour with us," co-director Lucia Chase soon enjoined her. For several years, Wilde traveled with the company on its extensive tours across the United States, which might last months at a time, as long as the old Ballet Russe forays. When her children were very little, she brought them along as well, together with a nurse.

Although Balanchine had worked for ABT during the 1940s, he was prone to assailing Chase's taste. Wilde believed it was more discriminating than Balanchine would have admitted. Nevertheless, commercial considerations, sometimes imposed by board and backers, could dissuade Chase from her best instincts.

During the 1930s, after her husband's untimely death, Chase, a young society matron with two small children, began to study ballet seriously. She eventually became ballerina as well as patron of the small company formed by émigré Mikhail Mordkin, once a star of the Bolshoi in Moscow and Pavlova's partner on global tours. That company was eventually melded into (not yet "American") Ballet Theatre when it was formed in 1939. Some amount of cash subvention on Chase's part may have made her ballerina career possible; until she retired in 1980 at age eighty-three, Chase was still onstage at ABT performing roles like the Queen Mother in *Swan Lake*. But unlike Rebekah Harkness, Chase was not a dilettante. She was down in the trenches doing whatever she could to keep her company going. She gave millions of her own money and was indefatigably "bowing and scraping" to whomever could help the company. Often Wilde sat next to Chase on a plane trip from one tour city to another; invariably Chase would be writing thank-you notes to people in the city they had just left. Her passion for ballet extended beyond the interests of her own organization. "In her own way she was like Mr. B.," Wilde said. "Anything she could do to popularize and to make people appreciate the dance, that could bring people to it, that would help it to survive and grow—that's what she was all about."

Chase was open to Wilde's suggestions at casting meetings. Together with ballet masters Dimitri Romanoff and Enrique Martinez, long-term close advisers, the present and possible future capacity of individual company dancers was debated and recommendations proffered by each. But unlike NYCB, Chase's artistic policy was heavily dependent on importing already-perfected guest stars, who could be expected to show immediate results at the box office.

At NYCB, guests were treated less solicitously. During the early 1970s Wilde gave friendly counsel to Peter Martins, whom Balanchine had originally imported in 1967, to assuage his always-pressing problem of finding partners for his tall ballerinas: Martins started with Farrell and Mimi Paul, two of Balanchine's tallest. He joined as full company member in 1970. Like Erik Bruhn before him, Martins was both great partner and technician and, unlike Bruhn, Balanchine really wanted him in his company. Danish style informed Balanchine's, but the rigors of full immersion into Balanchine's technique, the caprices of the (now more than ever) czarlike choreographer, and the grueling responsibilities of NYCB's long seasons all weighed heavily on him.

"I just can't take it anymore," Martins told Wilde more than once over drinks at O'Neal's Balloon, NYCB's favorite hangout, across the street from the New York State Theater's stage door. Chase and ABT supporters were wooing him with an offer to virtually "defect," and he was seriously tempted. Wilde thought that he suited NYCB very well and urged him not to leave. Martins not only stayed with Balanchine, but also succeeded him as head of NYCB after Balanchine died in April 1983.

ABT performed several Balanchine ballets, and naturally it fell to Wilde to conduct many rehearsals. Kirov ballerina Natalia Makarova's defection in London in September 1970 brought her to ABT soon after. It was fascinating for Wilde to coach Makarova in Balanchine's *Theme and Variations*, which he'd created for ABT in 1947. The ballerina wasn't resistant, but its speed sometimes seemed to baffle her. "I felt like pushing her all the time. She was trying. It was not up her alley." But Makarova wound up dancing *Theme* creditably "at a decent tempo. It was still very fast."

Well before Wilde's children were born, her mother had come to Ninety-Fifth Street for a week-plus visit. She had her own room, but wasn't observing boundaries where her son-in-law was concerned. They rubbed each other the wrong way. "She wasn't about to let anything go by that she could pick on." When Bardyguine insisted that Eileen be transferred to a hotel, it fell to Wilde to tell her mother, sadly, "I think this isn't working out. We want you to visit, but you're being too bossy with George." Eileen was not happy about the move, but submitted to it, and tensions were alleviated for the balance of her stay.

Subsequent visits, both on Ninety-Fifth Street and in Tappan, were more successful. "I think she learned her lesson," Wilde said; nevertheless, "I don't think she had a lot of respect for men." Certainly Eileen had mellowed. A doer rather than a reader when raising her children, she now read "all kinds of things," Wilde recalled.

Wilde loved both of Bardyguine's parents, who for her exemplified the best and most generous elements of the Russian character, and the refinement of prerevolutionary intelligentsia. Wilde was prone to attribute her husband's ever-so-slight condescension toward America and Americans to his upbringing in France. His parents were not like that.

It was a "gruesome" experience to live through the death of her mother-in-law. In July 1971 Maria Nevelska was attacked by two unknown assailants in her Carnegie Hall ballet studio. Bardyguine was on tour;

Wilde was teaching a class when she was called to Roosevelt Hospital. Nevelska had been able to describe her attackers but was now barely conscious. After she was examined in the emergency room, five hours elapsed before she was treated by a neurosurgeon. She had been "just left in the hallway," Wilde complained to the *New York Times*. When *Dance Magazine* attempted to investigate, it claimed that the hospital was stonewalling, quoting a hospital representative who asked, "Why all this fuss for a ballet dancer?"

She lingered for two days before dying at age eighty. "She was so giving," Wilde said, "this little lady, always taking care of everybody. Her students paid what they could." Having lived through the Russian Revolution, Madame Nevelska was rather fearless, teaching regularly in a friend's studio in the suburbs and coming home alone late at night by train. Her murderers were never arrested; how anyone could have wanted to harm her was almost incomprehensible to Wilde.

It fell to Wilde, together with some émigré friends of her in-laws, to make all arrangements. Bardyguine's father was lost without his wife of fifty years. Eventually they moved him to the Tolstoy Foundation estate in Nyack, New York, on the Hudson River.

For two years, Wilde spent Mondays, ABT's day off, teaching in the dance department of the State University of New York at Purchase, which was then directed by William Bales. The college had just opened, and during Wilde's first year, portable barres and mirrors were set up in its art museum for classes. The next year they were held on the volleyball court, before proper studios were finally completed.

When Bales retired, college president Abbott Kaplan asked if she'd like to take over his job. Impossible, she said—she didn't have even a high school degree. That didn't matter, he assured her. But Wilde didn't want to deal with endless meetings and paperwork.

No longer directing the School of American Ballet, Diana Adams was now also teaching at City University of New York two days a week. Adams was, as always, moody. "Sometimes we'd have very good conversations, and sometimes she was—*blah*—flat." But after Wilde and Bardyguine moved to Tappan, they saw quite a bit of Adams and her husband, NYCB stage manager Ronald Bates. Anya and their daughter Georgina rode horses and studied ballet together.

Wilde didn't want her daughter to begin studying as early as she had. But when Anya at age six bloodied her toes standing in an old pair of her mother's pointe shoes, Wilde impressed upon her that if she wanted to really learn to stand in them it would take three years of preliminary work. Five years, training under several teachers including her mother, turned out to be enough to quench the young girl's interest.

The Bardyguines and the Bateses often celebrated Christmas or Thanksgiving together. A NYCB dancer had made a doll for Anya, which she brought with her to one holiday party chez Bates. Wilde and her husband believed in strict table manners for their children, but in the spirit of the occasion, Anya, Georgina, and Youri ran around the table and finished everything left in the wine glasses. "We got so sick in the car," Anya recalled. "Raggedy Ann was forever destroyed."

Virtually unknown in the West, the Shades scene from Petipa's 1877 *La Bayadère* created a sensation when the Kirov performed it during its Paris debut in June 1961. Its ranks of geometrically ordered corps de ballet women, spilling out of the opium-induced delirium of the ballet's hero, repeated a trancelike vision of continuum toward the infinite. The Shades was hailed as a forerunner of twentieth-century exercises in pure dance.

Two years after the Kirov's Paris debut, Rudolph Nureyev staged the Shades for London's Royal Ballet. In 1974, Wilde and ballet master Michael Lland worked closely with Makarova when she staged the Shades for ABT. Makarova was explicit about what she wanted: ABT needed to generate some of the quintessential Kirov virtues she herself exemplified. For the corps that meant more emphasis on the fluid expressiveness of the back, putting an additional respiratory pulse into movements, a particular coordination of all four limbs. The entire corps of twenty-four women has to do more than dance in strict unison; as Wilde notes, "everyone has to breathe together." It was as unfamiliar an aesthetic for them as *Theme and Variations* had been for Makarova. Her Shades was a triumph, and Wilde enjoyed the entire process.

That same summer saw the defection in Toronto of Makarova's ex-Kirov colleague Mikhail Baryshnikov. A month later, he was partnering her at ABT in *Giselle*. Baryshnikov took Wilde's company class, but "there was very little to correct. He really was a marvelous technician, and he was an artist."

With Baryshnikov's arrival, ballet may be said to have reached a peak, an unprecedented degree of popularity in this country. Three years after his ABT debut, much of the company, including Baryshnikov, participated in the film *The Turning Point*, brainchild of the director Herbert Ross and his wife, Nora Kaye, Wilde's former NYCB colleague.

Yet as always, without state support ballet's financial underpinnings were perpetually provisional. The ABT school's open admission policy actually generated a cash surplus, which meant it could also pay for scholarship students' tuition at the Children's Professional School. After Wilde succeeded Danelian as director on his retirement in 1979, she was pleased to turn over her reserves to the company as needed. She felt it was only fair, since the company's name supported the school.

Rehearsal time was at a premium at ABT, as in every American company, but Antony Tudor, now associate director, was always asking Wilde if she had as much time as she needed. He was pleasant to her as he had been when they worked together at NYCB twenty-five years earlier, but he could be brutal to dancers in rehearsal. Probably Tudor liked it when he struck a nerve, Wilde would tell furious and teary dancers who came to her for solace. Tudor's tactics did tend to pay off: in his way, as Balanchine did in his own more laconic way, Tudor ensured that no one did less than his or her best in his ballets.

Provoking a dancer wasn't a modus operandi that Wilde wanted to pursue, but coaching inevitably brings moments of sheer exasperation for coach and dancer. Wilde's flash point was reached when she believed that a dancer wasn't attacking a role with the same commitment that she had. "If you don't get it soon, you're never going to get it," Wilde might say when patience ran out. "Time is limited. You've got to dig in and think about it and really start working on it on your own. You can't wait for somebody to tell you everything!"

A ballet coach, like a teacher, is inevitably quasi-parental. To her children as well as to her students she wanted to impart a message that failure was acceptable, so long as it was a beginning rather than an end—a learning process to inform the next step toward achievement. "You can't give up on anything that you really want to do," she says today to her two grandchildren as she said to her own two children. She had learned that lesson early, trying to scale an apple tree or find her way back up a ski slope on her mother's estate. Goals had to be attacked with "every ounce that you can bring to it: ideas, physical strength, everything. Persevere and put a lot of sweat into it!"

35

PITTSBURGH

"Sure—me!" Wilde said, somewhat to her own surprise when Eugene Tanner, an ex-NYCB colleague, called in the spring of 1982 to ask if she had any suggestions about who could direct Pittsburgh Ballet Theatre. Artistic director Patrick Frantz was leaving to pursue choreography.

She had gradually been doing less and less coaching at ABT, where the rehearsal staff was increasingly Russian-dominated: ex-Kirov dancers Alexander Minz and Elena Tchernichova had begun working there in the late 1970s. "The Russians came in more and more, and they needed jobs," said Wilde tartly. But with both of her children now attending public elementary schools in Tappan, she could no longer take them with her on tour. In addition, her husband was still frequently on tour with various companies.

She had been happy and completely occupied with directing ABT's school. But Mikhail Baryshnikov, who replaced Lucia Chase as ABT director in 1980, had now decided to close it. He wanted a new model altogether, closer to the School of American Ballet or to the Rossi Street academy in Leningrad, where admission would be based solely on merit. "He didn't want anything to do with those open classes," Wilde said, but "Misha didn't understand that the school supported the company." Sometimes during the summer there could be as many as one hundred fee-paying students in class; at such times the center of the huge studio became a warren of portable ballet barres. Wilde admired Baryshnikov greatly, but he was never the consummate communicator, and it was executive director Charles Dillingham who told her that the school would be closed.

When Tanner called, Wilde was winding down ABT's scholarship program.

Now she was considering a two-month trip to New Zealand to teach for the national ballet there. Over the phone Wilde suggested to Tanner several other candidates besides herself. She was almost ready to remove herself from consideration the following day when she realized how urgently Pittsburgh needed to fill the position. She arrived at ABT to find Tanner waiting for her: "We've got to go out to lunch."

Before accepting, she made several trips to Pittsburgh. She met with five members of the board, who offered her the job and asked for an answer as soon as possible. She went again with her family on a warm day when passenger-balloon rides were being launched. Her two children were enchanted. The company assured her that they would help her family resettle. Bardyguine, too, could work for them.

Her friends were opposed: "Leave New York? Are you out of your mind? And you're going to make up your mind in a week?" But all her life she'd made quick decisions. As for leaving New York, Pittsburgh was no longer the begrimed industrial capital it was when she toured there with Ballet Russe in the 1940s. Furthermore, it had boasted a host of major cultural and educational institutions, some of them dating back to Andrew Carnegie's patronage. The city's natural setting is stunning, spanning three rivers and surmounting hills in all directions. It was participating in the cultural upgrading that had spread throughout America during the 1960s and '70s. Heinz Hall, a 1920s movie palace, had been restored for the symphony and reopened in 1971, one year after the Pittsburgh Ballet had been founded. The ballet performed at Heinz Hall as well, although in 1986 they would move to the Benedum Center, another restored 1920s movie palace with a stage better suited to ballet.

She'd been asked to watch the company perform on tour in West Virginia, but the board then decided that would be awkward. The company didn't know that Frantz was not going to remain as director. His wife was a principal dancer, who had actually been a student of Wilde's in New York.

Eventually, she went to see the company perform in eastern Pennsylvania, in a tent outdoors, accompanied by the Pittsburgh Symphony Orchestra. Balanchine's *Pas de Dix* "looked bad." The dancers "could do things," but the way they did them was "not classical at all. All these clunky feet."

A welcome was extended by Loti Falk, the company's finger-in-every-pie volunteer ombudsman. She was Italian, with grown sons from her first marriage, and was now in a second marriage, to Pittsburgh's wealthy Leon Falk. After the performance, Wilde went back to the Falks' country house, an old farmstead, and stayed overnight with some of the dancers. The vibes were good.

Wilde's appointment was announced toward the end of July. In November, Balanchine entered Roosevelt Hospital in Manhattan, where he died the following April. She went to visit him not long after he'd been admitted. "Oh, wonderful, wonderful," he said about her new position. Ultimately, she believed that he was "very pleased and proud that I was doing other things" than NYCB—even when she'd been working for ABT. "The more that everyone could do to keep the art alive and progressing and giving dancers opportunities—that's what he was all about."

Well before his death, the directorial landscape in the United States was dominated by ex-NYCB dancers, and they were a leadership presence in Europe as well. He was generous with all these companies. Perhaps surprisingly, given his omnipotent relationship with his ballerinas, he supported their taking power into their own hands. Balanchine had "very great faith in the ladies," Wilde said—"after he felt that he had created them."

Manipulative as Balanchine could be, Wilde also saw him manifest a "respect for dancers" that she wanted to perpetuate in Pittsburgh. "He was not like Tudor, screaming and putting people down," she said. She wanted to make everyone feel respected and important. Nevertheless, she was not satisfied with the dancers she had to work with for the upcoming season. She told them that they were on probation.

The full-length *Sleeping Beauty* had already been announced for the new season, a daunting challenge for any company. Ideally it requires a large ensemble and lavish scenery, as well as dancers with the most refined classical technique. Wilde cast *Beauty* as advantageously as she could.

Coaching the dancers herself, she elicited competent results. Nevertheless, she wanted "a much more classical type of company" than the ensemble she was working with.

Union rules dictated that midway through the season, the dancers be told whether they were going to be offered contracts for the following season. Early in 1983 she told about half the company that they were not going to be asked back. She spoke to each dancer individually. "I felt really bad more about the girls than the boys," who were cockier and more complacent. One person she thought worth retaining was Frantz's wife, but she soon left to join her husband in California.

Major dance companies had been touring Pittsburgh for years, but Wilde knew that with its own resident company only a decade old, it was her responsibility to develop her audiences and develop them the right way. Wilde did not completely approve of impresario Sol Hurok's influence on America ballet. Bardyguine had worked for him many times, and Wilde certainly enjoyed watching the glamorous, highly publicized foreign companies that Hurok imported. But she believed that they made the American public overly susceptible to the blandishments of celebrity and foreign allure. Hyped hysteria ensued, the "audience in competition with themselves about how many curtain calls it could reward them with." NYCB's audiences had been something else altogether—much more discerning and sophisticated.

Eventually she would greatly expand Pittsburgh's Balanchine repertory. When she first arrived, however, she wouldn't have dreamed of putting on an all-Balanchine evening. But for her first season in the spring of 1983, she could add one ballet to a mixed program, and she picked Balanchine's *Serenade*. The curtain went up on the corps de ballet, dressed in long sky-blue skirts, the stage lit low in matching half-light. "Ah!" several women behind her sighed. When she was told, "Oooh, I loved that. I got so involved," she felt almost as pleased for Balanchine's sake as if she'd choreographed it herself.

Victoria Simon, who staged several Balanchine works for Wilde in Pittsburgh, found her commitment to his work heartening. Many smaller companies around the United States were of the opinion that fund-raising and attendance prospects mandated an ever-revolving repertory. "A lot of companies if they do *Serenade* say, 'Oh, I can't do *Serenade* again for five years.'" But Simon "was always very happy that she kept those ballets going," giving audience and dancers the chance to grow with them and in them.

Wilde wanted ballets to be prepared in a bit more orderly and methodical way than had been done at City Ballet. She could afford to sustain longer and longer rehearsal periods, and now preferred to have works new to the company staged during the very beginning of the season, following their late-summer performances in city parks. For one thing, it was easier to secure the stager she wanted. Learning something in September that they would not be doing until the following April "used to drive people crazy," but Wilde was determined. "You've got in your head now; you've got it in your body," she told dancers when they balked. "Don't lose it." The work would be rehearsed several times a month over the course of the season; a few weeks before its premiere they would come back to it full force.

Wilde was eventually able to enlarge the company by a third, until it numbered thirty-five; she was able to augment the ranks with apprentices when needed. She traveled around the country auditioning dancers. On one audition tour she reached the North Carolina School of the Arts in Winston-Salem. Melissa Hayden was teaching there. "Oh, you have to teach a class!" Hayden cried when Wilde appeared in her studio. "You can teach this class!" She insisted that Wilde take over the class she was teaching, and, as usual where Hayden was concerned, "I couldn't fight it." She did as she was told.

Several times Wilde conducted auditions at Yvonne Mounsey's studio in Santa Monica, California, the Westside School of Ballet. Mounsey was gutsy and independent-minded. Born in South Africa in 1919, she supported liberalization there. Wilde enjoyed staying with Mounsey and her third husband, a retired businessman, in their comfortable home in the hills overlooking the Santa Monica beach.

It is all too easy for a director to take everything personally, to view a dancer's potential through the lens of personal preference—it happens all the time. As Wilde said, it's too tempting to believe that "if I don't see something likable, how will the audience?" Nevertheless, if the dancer has something valuable to contribute, ignoring that potential works to a company's peril. Talent has to be recognized, even if that recognition is accompanied by the sentiment "What a shame you're so talented!"

When a dancer was having a particularly good season under her direction, Wilde was tempted to say, "Enjoy it, because the next one's probably not going to be as good." It might then be somebody else's turn. That's what life had been like at NYCB. Balanchine would make new things for her, and then there'd be a season where she was recycling the same repertory and other ballerinas were having glorious new roles.

"Oh, it's hard," Wilde said. "You're miserable. You think, What have I done?" and subject yourself to more self-criticism and scrutiny than is healthy. Yet in those situations it is rarely about the dancer. In Balanchine's case particularly it was a matter of how his creative stimulus functioned. In every case it was about the needs of pleasing an audience with varied repertory, and a diverse mix of performance qualities. "Artistic directors cannot do everything for everybody."

When commissioning new works, Wilde didn't like to impose too many prerequisites apart from the all-important limitations of expense. "You can't do something that's going to need ten rehearsals of the orchestra. It's better to do it straight off, because otherwise they come up with all kinds of ideas."

"Once it was set, she got out of the way and got very excited about what was going to happen," recalled Bruce Wells, who was resident choreographer in Pittsburgh from 1990 to 1995. In his mind's eye he sees her in her customary rehearsal uniform of chiffon skirt over tights—perhaps indebted to Danilova's—sitting "like a little girl, with her feet pulled up," absorbing the steps he was creating, marking them out on her fingers, the way dancers customarily do.

These were years when crossover between modern dance and ballet was occurring all the time—no longer the novelty it had been when Wilde danced in Valerie Bettis's *Virginia Sampler* in 1947. Paul Taylor's *Airs*, for example, had originally been commissioned by ABT; when Taylor didn't like their rehearsal limitations, he finished it on his own company in 1978. Two years later, Baryshnikov had taken it into ABT's repertory. Wilde also included several Taylor works in Pittsburgh's repertory. In 1986, she commissioned modern dance choreographer Ohan Naharin's first work using ballet dancers, *Tabula Rasa*.

The company and school worked in a building downtown. It had one excellent studio. Another studio contained a low ceiling and a structural pillar, which meant it was hazardous for leaping adult bodies and thus could only house children's classes. A third studio was minuscule, appropriate only for the very youngest beginners. Soon after she became director, Wilde told the board that it was mandatory they have a new place to work. Leon Falk led the search for a new building.

He located a former warehouse on Twenty-Ninth Street, purchased it, and totally renovated for the company. In a voluntary capacity, his wife Loti did everything from stuffing envelopes to hiring outside publicity firms. She was also good at fund-raising. Falk "worked like a dog," wearing her many hats. After Eugene Tanner left, Falk became the de facto general manager. She never tried to encroach on Wilde's artistic bailiwick, but her interfering everywhere else made it impossible for the administrative staff to do their jobs well or happily. They were in a state of "totally continuous turmoil," Wilde said. The financial situation remained shaky.

Mrs. Falk was finally asked to pull back, which was difficult for all concerned but propitious for the company. Stephen Richard, whose background was with theater companies in California, was hired in 1987 as general manager. Richard came in on a three-year contract and over that time "got everything shipshape." It became a much more settled staff and was on a stronger financial foundation. Wilde, too, learned how to fund-raise, an essential component—perhaps, given the lack of government funding, the most important—of any American artistic director's life. She went to prospective funders' homes and took them to lunch. She learned how to sell an idea, sell a ballet: "We need to do this ballet: It would be fabulous for the company. The dancers really need that kind of challenge."

Wilde and Bardyguine bought a home in Mount Lebanon, a pleasant suburb south of the city with one of the country's best school systems. The house's big stone fireplace and chimney reminded her of Ottawa. Enclosed in a round tower, the stairway had a touch of Gothic stage set—perhaps Balanchine's *La Sonnambula*. Her pride and joy was an Alaskan cedar she planted on the front lawn. The tree grew and grew, its limbs drifting down to the ground almost like the tulle layers of a tutu. Cars would stop and passengers ring her bell to ask what that tree was. ("Don't drive by the house," her son told her recently—the current owners had cut down the tree.)

Wilde was out of the house at eight o'clock every morning to make the forty-minute drive downtown. She never stayed overnight in town, which meant a very late night after a performance—virtually the same hours she'd worked all her life.

She watched every single performance, sitting on the aisle toward the rear of the orchestra section, so that if a disaster occurred onstage she could get backstage easily. If something in performance didn't go to her liking, the back of the seat in front of her bore the brunt of her agitated foot. "Be careful, you're in a very dangerous seat," she said to whoever sat directly in front of her.

One time, the woman performing Wilde's own role in *Square Dance* tore her Achilles tendon onstage, but short of a disaster in public were the many near-misses and by-the-skin-of-their-teeth episodes that the profession makes inevitable. In September 1991, she wrote Anya, who was then living in Europe, about a fraught run of Bruce Wells's *Romeo and Juliet*. "My two Mercutios were off this past week, Kip with a not too bad sprained ankle and Alex had a rib in his back pop out which pressed on a nerve so he couldn't breathe. It went out 3 times so he has to stop and let it heal but it makes me a nervous wreck as that role is really big and there's no one else & with the sword fights you can't just send someone on—it's too dangerous, and we are giving 6 performances of it. I pray they hold up as do my Romeos, as they both have other roles when they aren't Romeo."

"I ALWAYS FELT a lack of knowledge of certain things, which is why I was always reading and trying to do something about it." Wilde would have liked having more formal education than she'd gotten, but she realized that education comes in many forms. Frugal living in New York had allowed the Bardyguines to take their young children driving through Europe most summers, visiting sundry historical sites, museums, monuments, gardens. Most important to her was that with luck her children would find something they really wanted to do, the same way she had. It didn't bother her that her two children chose not to go to college.

Between horseback riding and ballet, Anya had long ago decided she preferred the horses. After graduating from high school a year early, she went to work for a trainer in eastern Pennsylvania. There she met a Dutch horse dealer who invited her to work for him in Holland. From there she went to stables in Belgium and Germany. Eventually she became an airline stewardess as a way to make possible frequent trips between the United States and Frankfurt, a center of horse-trading where she kept an apartment.

Youri had inherited his father's ability to build things, and construction, plumbing, and electrical repair interested him as a teenager. After graduating from high school, he worked in home construction for two years, then enrolled in a one-year program in deepwater commercial diving at a school in Maryland.

As her children were coming of stage, Wilde saw the strong, sophisticated, and dryly ironic man she had married ebb away. Still working as technical director of Pittsburgh Ballet Theatre, he suffered a stroke—his second. (During the 1970s, Bardyguine had been working at the New York State Theater and gone out for coffee with some of the technical crew when he had a slight stroke.) Now he went back to work in Pittsburgh but was increasingly difficult and demanding with stage crews.

Bardyguine was "never one to mince words," his wife recalled, and "never a patient person," and certainly a display of irascibility could sometimes prove effective with lighting and stage technicians. But his fuse became shorter and shorter. Eventually it was Wilde herself who had to tell him he was being let go. "You're just too difficult," she told him. "I appreciate what you're doing, but it disrupts anything when you can't get along with people at all."

He still worked sometimes for Heinz Hall, but most of the time he was at home and drinking heavily. Once a heavy smoker, he never touched another cigarette after his first stroke. But now he seemed to lack the willpower to make any reforms. Mutual recrimination between husband and wife flared up. Wilde sent her husband to visit her sister and brother-in-law, who were now living in Vermont. "I know she just wants to get rid of me," he told them. An expensive tricycle enabled him to exercise, but perhaps was an all too telling symbol of regression. Wilde wrote her daughter: "I made Dad promise to ride here on our street for a while, but I don't trust him, he is so determined about the wrong things, the exercise would be fine if he just would stay on quiet streets but he's got to have a destination. He shops so much we end up fighting about it just because I hate all the waste. . . . Well, honey, sorry to complain to you, I know no one else can do anything with him."

Bardyguine's son, who was living at home while working, bore the brunt of his father's frustrations. "Youri couldn't come through the door right," said his sister, who was glad that she was far away in Europe. Youri was a responsible young man who tended his sister's horse after she moved to Europe; to Wilde's eye he had become the son his father had wanted to raise. "He was always cleaning up like his father had taught him: everything in his place." But his father couldn't take pleasure in seeing him thrive. Trivial disputes escalated to the point where Wilde began to worry that they would come to blows. "I'm not an angel, but I wouldn't put up with that. One day I said, 'That's it,' and I went out and put him in a nursing home." He continued to drink. After taking a fall, he went to a facility to dry out. His former nursing home wouldn't take him back, and he tried another and then another. "It was grim," Wilde said. But she went to visit him every day. At that point it was duty, not love, but the imperatives of duty had ruled much of Wilde's behavior over the course of her lifetime.

Bardyguine died of vascular disease in September 1994. Wilde had no intention of remarrying, but now, after a decade of directing, and having celebrated her sixty-fifth birthday in 1993, she was thinking of retiring. She met the dancer Ib Andersen and immediately thought that he might be her perfect successor. He had an illustrious pedigree. Andersen had been a star of the Royal Danish Ballet almost from the moment he entered the company. In 1980 at twenty-five he joined New York City Ballet. He danced with them for a decade before retiring following an injury. She told Andersen that she could see him succeeding her. She couldn't make the board's decision for them, but she could position him advantageously. In 1994 she hired him as ballet master and also gave him an opportunity to choreograph. Over the years Andersen spent in Pittsburgh, Wilde remained convinced of his artistic qualifications. But he failed on the crucial criterion of being able to make nice with board members and potential funders. At a party after a performance, he would stay enmeshed in a clutch of dancers. She arranged a dinner with a board member and his wife, who were NYCB admirers. That went well, but Andresen remained generally aloof.

Eventually it proved futile. In May, Wilde called Andersen and told him that the board was no longer considering him. Instead they selected Terence Orr, who had danced, then coached at ABT for many years. With him came his wife, ex-ABT ballerina Marianna Tcherkassky, who became ballet mistress there as well.

Andersen returned to work in Pittsburgh in July 1996, intending to stay for a third and final season. However, a contretemps with Wilde hastened his departure. In an interview published August 4, she said, "I think he's very negative."

"And then she went on and said some things that were kind of nice," Andersen later related to Alexandra Tomalonis of the quarterly *Dance View.* "So I called her, and I asked her to retract it in the paper, and also in front of the dancers. And she agreed to that. And then she called me the next day and said she had been in front of the dancers doing what I had asked—which I found out she had not done, and, on the other hand, she had actually rubbed it in. Then she called me and said she couldn't retract it because that was actually something that she said."

Andersen resigned at that point: "She had taken my credibility away. So in that way, I feel I was fired." Interviewed in *Dance Magazine*, Wilde credited Andersen with generating "a new, higher level of confidence" among the company's dancers.

She came to believe that his personality issues were due to his being psychologically in too much of a postperforming limbo in Pittsburgh. In 2001 he became director of Ballet Arizona, which he continues to lead. She was pleased when he asked her to teach company class during a recent trip to Phoenix.

36

SILVER

SNEAKER

A week after her eighty-seventh birthday in July 2015, Wilde was waiting in
Pittsburgh for a friend from Paris, formerly a dancer with Pittsburgh Ballet
Theatre, to arrive for an annual visit. Together they would drive into Ohio
to visit mutual friends over the weekend. On Monday, she would get up at
four in the morning to drive her friend back to the Pittsburgh airport. She
was also planning a trip to Vermont for her sister Nora's ninetieth birthday
in August. Over Labor Day she would attend the annual New York City
Ballet reunion hosted by Robert Barnett and Virginia Rich at their home
in Asheville, North Carolina.

Wilde decided to stay in Pittsburgh after retiring from Pittsburgh Ballet
Theatre in 1997. For one thing, her son, Youri, continues to live there. The
city has a great deal to offer, and she can live there much more comfortably
on a fixed income than she could in New York City.

Her son works on diving projects all around the United States. Wherever he is, he checks in with her by phone once or twice a week. He keeps
her abreast of his sons' hockey games, which she'll attend with him or
even by herself. His two boys, Nicholas, thirteen, and Alexei, eleven, are
not interested in her balletic celebrity, but "they're impressed that I've
been everywhere!" Her daughter staffs flights between the United States

and Europe. She lives with her husband in rural Virginia, a historic area of nineteenth-century towns and Civil War battlegrounds. Wilde visits frequently.

Pittsburgh Ballet Theatre retained her on a ten-year consultancy contract after she retired in 1997, and her advice continues to be solicited. Wilde shows up to any event or rehearsal that PBT asks her to attend. Indeed, living as long as she has also means enjoying the experience of being virtually rediscovered. In 2013 she was recipient of the *Dance Magazine* Award; the selection committee cited her lifetime of achievement. Fifteen years earlier, the Balanchine Foundation had taped her coaching dancers in roles she'd created in *Square Dance* and *Raymonda Variations.* Recently they called and asked if there were any other works about which she'd like her coaching perspective similarly preserved for posterity.

In 2014, Video Artists International began issuing on DVD NYCB's Montreal telecasts from the 1950s through the 1970s. Some dancers withheld permission, preventing certain performances from being released. Wilde gave her approval without hesitation, but that didn't mean she wasn't going to scrutinize herself ruthlessly. The first disc in the series included the 1957 *Serenade* she danced with Adams, Mounsey, Bliss, and d'Amboise. She watched not at home but at a friend's because her own TV "makes everyone look fat." As employed by any present or former ballet dancer, the word "fat" should, of course, be treated advisedly.

Weight no longer became an issue, however, the moment she stopped dancing. Today she stands five foot two, two and three-quarter inches shorter than at her tallest, and weighs ninety-three pounds, far thinner than she ever was during her dancing years. Muscle mass disappeared. But scores of roles and hundred of performances remain embedded in muscle memory. She can still not only visualize certain steps and passages but almost recapture what it felt like to perform them. For example, the first entrance of the second ballerina in *Concerto Barocco*, which she danced first in 1945. "Off-balance *effacé* and back and then pull into back *passé*: I can feel myself running in, taking a breath and starting."

But in old age, Wilde continues to manifest new movement possibilities.

"It's incredible how many muscles are unused," she says. "It's very danger-ous, actually." Although any type of ballet practice is just too onerous for her today, by studying yoga, learning movements and positions she never attempted in ballet, she has discovered muscles she never knew she had.

A decade ago she joined a senior citizens walking group, Silver Sneakers, that gets her out of her Highland Park apartment first thing in the morning. Conducted by a coach, the seniors' peregrinations vary day to day. "Some days we're just marching, which I hate, but whatever they tell us to do," she and her fellow enrollees do. In addition, a friend sometimes drives her to the higher reaches of the park so she can do two turns on foot around the reservoir.

Living as long as she has increasingly also means being one of a dwin-dling epoch. In 2004, the Joffrey Ballet, now based in Chicago, invited Wilde to watch and comment on *Square Dance*, part of a mixed bill that also included *Apollo*, which they asked Tallchief to inspect. Wilde hadn't seen her in years. "She was still Maria in that everything was centered on Maria," but for the first time in her life, Wilde felt sorry for her. Tallchief died in 2013, but to Wilde, the former go-getter had already reached the point of "What am I still doing here?" She couldn't drive anymore because of failing eyesight. She was living in a senior facility outside Chicago. "I just lie in bed all day with the television," Tallchief told her. And her grandson? "Oh, he comes and jumps on the bed. I mean, God!"

After Balanchine and Le Clercq divorced, he ceded to her their Man-hattan apartment as well as their house in Weston, Connecticut. But it was primarily in Florida that Wilde continued to see her. For a substantial sum, Le Clercq had leased New York City Ballet the performance rights to the enormous catalogue of Balanchine ballets to which he'd willed her ownership. Le Clercq bought a house in Windermere, Florida, next door to a friend who lived with his sister and brother-in-law. Most winters, Wilde spent a long weekend there. Above Le Clercq's garage was an apartment. "This is *your* garage!" Le Clercq would say. "When are you going to come and really stay?"

There was nothing of ballet in the house. Beauty for her was concentrated in the natural world. "She loved the flowers and the birds," Wilde said. One of her final memories of her stays there is driving out to buy "a big, big bag of bird feed" for waterfowl that congregated on the property.

Le Clercq was "a free spirit" deadlocked by others' ambitions, by fate. "She enjoyed life up to the end," Wilde said, "but she was always afraid of getting a cold because her lungs were so weak." Finally, Le Clercq did die of pneumonia after a long hospitalization—on New Year's Eve 2000, forty-eight years to the day since her marriage to Balanchine. Wilde came to New York for her funeral. Part of her was relieved that Le Clercq had finally been released from what was in so many ways an oppressed existence.

In the final years of her life, Diana Adams seemed to Wilde less guarded, less defensive. Her last job had been starting and heading the school of the St. Louis Ballet during the 1980s. Adams's husband Ronald Bates and she had a messy divorce, and he died soon after of a heart attack. Their daughter had proved very difficult. Adams now moved to California to be near her. Not long before she died in January 1993, Adams talked by phone to Wilde. Adams was in a very good mood. Georgina had just been to visit her. "Georgie just left and we had a really nice time. You must come out." Adams didn't divulge that she was undergoing treatment for cancer; she died suddenly soon thereafter.

Like Le Clercq, Yvonne Mounsey was a free spirit, and Wilde received some vicarious satisfaction seeing the way they each approached life—a bit less straitlaced than she, less concerned with fulfilling duty and obligation. Diagnosed with cancer in her late eighties, Mounsey refused traditional treatment and flew from Los Angeles home to South Africa for a course of alternative medicine. Returning to the United States, she seemed to be cured but eventually suffered a recurrence. Wilde was relieved when Mounsey died in her sleep in 2012 before any more treatment was attempted, shortly after turning ninety-three.

"I'm reading the *New York Times* and a book on elephants," Wilde said one day in November 2014. She subscribes not only to the *Times* (print edition) but also to the *New Yorker* and *National Geographic.* Current events frequently distress her. In July 2013, a City Center Encores revival of Marc Blitzstein's socially conscious *The Cradle Will Rock* played for a limited run of five performances in Manhattan. One left City Center elated and optimistic. "Optimistic?" she said. "In this day and age? It should have run for five *weeks*!"

Age changes perceptions, habits, patterns of behavior. Once she reached decisions quickly; now more often "I have problems making up my mind what I'm going to do." She is more aware of mitigating factors, prone to reflect that, Oh, well, nothing is *that* important anymore. No octogenarian, even the most vital, is immune to health issues. Trooper that she remains, Wilde has attended functions and fulfilled family and official duties while in severe physical pain.

But for Wilde, it was ever thus. Today her daughter wonders how in the world her mother could have done things like dance with a broken rib—as she did during a performance of Balanchine's *Gounod Symphony* in the early 1960s. Her partner André Prokovsky lifted her exactly as he'd done many times before, but this time the lift went awry. She was in terrible pain but continued the ballet. Two years ago I watched her teach in Saratoga, New York, in a summer program run by Melinda Roy and Roberto Muñoz. She didn't dance in class, but demonstrated as fully as she possibly could. It was no wonder that she subsequently decided teaching had just become too exhausting.

Wilde's zeal was shared by her colleagues. Today the life of NYCB dancers is dramatically different. It is much easier for them to enroll in college programs while they are still performing. Wilde thinks it's all to the good—to the benefit of their personal development, to their future well-being and career prospects. Still, she is certain that it leaves the dancer divided.

The work ethic of Wilde and her colleagues was stringent. She is perfectly aware that Balanchine would adjust things to suit an individual ballerina. But wonderful steps that made his ballets unusual seem to have evaporated for no reason at all. When emendation is done to make a step easier, Wilde is not sympathetic. Those "goddamned hops on pointe" in her *Sylvia* solo should be performed as Balanchine intended—traveling from upstage right to downstage left. Wilde is not pleased when today ballerinas opt to stay much less spectacularly and strenuously in one place, not having to push the supporting leg forward an inch with each hop, while the working leg bends and stretches in *ballonné*. Wilde as well as Tallchief, the role's creator, had very strong feet, but even they didn't find the hops easy; today's pointe shoes are much more individually tailored to the ballerina's foot.

Wilde was a very young woman during the years she danced for Balanchine. In maturity, she might have approached him a little differently. "I did what I was told, but I didn't question," Wilde said ruefully. She wouldn't have questioned his authority, but rather his artistic motivations and intentions. Wilde admired NYCB soloist Barbara Millberg's ability to draw him out on subjects like music; Millberg herself played piano. Wilde listened when Balanchine recommended a particular conductor's recording, but "I never thought of questioning him about something like music."

"I was there as an instrument of whatever he wanted to do," she said. "I never kind of said, '*Why* am I supposed to do this step that way?,'" let alone ask him what he was trying to express in a particular ballet. But she knows that in all likelihood Balanchine "wouldn't have told me anyway." He rarely verbalized those kinds of intentions. Back in the 1930s, the American Ballet's Elise Reiman had tried asking him things like that only to be told, "Whatever it means to you, dear." First and foremost, Balanchine was inspired by music. Wilde tried to find her way into his ballets that same way. By listening to the music, she could put herself into his creative impulse but also unlock her own vision, her own fantasy.

Popular representations of ballet bother Wilde when they strike her as superficial. A librarian friend sends her books for children written on the subject. Some are more successful than others. "It's not wrong to do," she says. "It does create interest in the dance. I'm all for that." But she'd like the perspective to be broader and deeper, "to get away from its strictly being tiaras and magic wands.

"So often I think they're giving the wrong impression. Ballet is the joy of learning and moving," its aim, as she practiced it, "to give out to people and make something exciting and memorable for them."

ACKNOWLEDGMENTS

Patricia Wilde entered into the process of recollecting her life with the same unqualified commitment that she applied to living her life. She probably never dreamed that she'd be spending months verbalizing a lifetime of experiences and emotions to a stranger, but she answered indefatigably and thoughtfully my thousands of questions. It was also a great pleasure to discuss with Nora White Shattuck her recollections of her sister, their upbringing and their family. Youri Bardyguine and Anya Bardyguine Davis's dedication to their mother and father's achievements and legacy ensured that important materials were preserved and freely made available to me.

At the University Press of New England, editor Stephen P. Hull grasped the book from speculative proposition to manifest reality. He was always helpful in a pinch, and rigorous about queries. Between this book and my last for him, he has learned more about ballet than he ever cared to know, and taken it with good cheer. Agent Kathleen Anderson put together a good contract. I appreciated the precision of UPNE production editor Susan A. Abel and my proofreader John Morrone.

One of the best things about New York City is its public library system, and for me the best part of it is the Library for the Performing Arts. Its Dance Collection contains clippings, periodicals, oral histories, and vintage footage, all allowing me not simply to amass material but to saturate myself in the ballet world of Wilde's era. It was a treat to watch there with Wilde in 2012 footage of herself with Ballet Russe de Monte Carlo and New York City Ballet. The Dance Collection's holdings are so vast and interesting that at times I had to absent myself to concentrate on actually writing the book.

Dale Stinchcomb at Harvard University's Houghton library, Amy Bordy at the School of American Ballet, as well as the Canadian National Research Council, and the press office of the Royal Opera House in Copenhagen all supplied important data. Joy Williams Brown pulled out her scrapbooks to establish details concerning Balanchine's trip to Mexico City in 1945.

Marvin Hoshino, editor and designer of *Ballet Review*, published my interviews with Wilde, which sparked my decision to write this book, and, as always, gave expert advice and assistance about dealing with ancient visuals.

At Pittsburgh Ballet Theatre, Robert Vickrey and Lisa Auel did everything they could to be of any assistance.

I thank Nicholas Lobenthal and Alexandra von Ferstel for their hospitality

Once again, thank you to Ralph Gleason for wireless facilitation and Kevan Croton for computer troubleshooting.

And once again, my father displayed his literary and lawyerly precision, reading every word and commenting. My mother was highly interested in this book, which took her back to her days as an undergraduate watching Wilde and colleagues at City Center. It was lovely synchronization that my finishing writing this book coincided with my tremendously supportive sister Lydia finishing her first novel.

The Soka Gakkai International and its members are always a source of wisdom and energy.

NOTES

Unless otherwise noted, all quotes from Patricia Wilde
are from author's interviews with her, 2009–2015. Author's interview
sources are mentioned only the first time they appear in text.

INTRODUCTION

x "beautiful Veronese grandeur": Denby, *Dancers, Buildings and People in the Streets*, 48.

xi "Mozartean precision": author's interview with Bruce Wells, August 2015.

xi "a force of nature": author's interview with Violette Verdy, September 2015.

1. EILEEN SIMPSON

1 "very wealthy": author's interview with Nora White, July 2014.

6 "a daily spectator": author's interview with Joy Williams, April 2015.

3. DEPRESSION AND WORLD WAR

21 "a picturesque Robin Hood": *Ottawa Evening Citizen*, May 28, 1940.

4. LEAVING OTTAWA

27 "Dolin would swish me around": author's interview with Irina Baronova, January 1981.

5. BIG CITY AND BARN

30 "a very dramatic character": Martha Ullman West, "Todd Bolender and American Ballet Caravan," *Ballet Review*, Winter 2010.

31 "lovely girls": author's interview with Jacqueline Kilgore, December 2014.

31 "how impressed he was": author's interview with Robert Barnett, June 2011.

31 "very, very special": author's interview with Carol Harriton, December 2014.

33 "very good dancers": author's interview with Elise Reiman, February 1989

7. SCHOOLING AMERICAN BALLET

44 "The school was much smaller": author's interview with Natalie Molo, December 1981.

46 "great thing about lifting up": author's interview with Pat McBride, February 1983.

46 "didn't have a musical sense": author's interview with Muriel Stuart, December 1981.

47 "I knocked on the door": author's interview with Betty Nichols, February 1983.

49 "had suggested a divorce": Mason, *I Remember Balanchine*, 185.

8. MEXICO CITY, 1945

54 "one of my problems": Patricia Wilde 1976 interview with Tobi Tobias, Oral History Archive, Oral History Project, Dance Collection, New York Public Library.

9. OPENING NIGHT

63 "most beautiful I ever saw": author's interview with Barbara Walczak, December 2012.

64 "nervous opening night": *Dance News*, October 1945.

64 "fine clean style": *New York Herald-Tribune* [henceforth *NYHT*], November 1, 1945.

10. ON TOUR

67 "we fended for ourselves": author's interview with Frederic Franklin, August, 2010.

11. BALANCHINE'S BALLET RUSSE

73 "The leading dancers are excellent": *NYHT*, February 24, 1946.
73 "She was different": author's interview with Vida Brown, January 1985.
75 "talked about boys": author's interview with Helen Kramer, October 2013.
76 "just about every Russian dancer": Jack Anderson, *The One and Only: The Ballet Russe de Monte Carlo*, 110.
78 "Whether you stage a classic ballet": *Dance News*, April 1946.
78 "generous cuts": *NYHT*, February 24, 1947.

12. NO SAFETY NET

87 "a lot of laughing": author's interview with Sonia Tyven, April 2015.

13. NEW VOICES

89 "legs like Mary Ellen Moylan": author's interview with Mimi Paul, November 2008.

14. ANNIVERSARY SEASON

91 "speaking to you": Records of the Ballet Russe de Monte Carlo, Dance Collection, New York Public Library.
92 "you are a very ambitious girl": Ibid.
94 "heavy, farcical and styleless": *New York Times* [henceforth *NYT*], September 20, 1948.
94 "I must go in front": Leslie Norton with Frederic Franklin, *Frederic Franklin: A Biography of the Ballet Star*, 117.
96 "made do with a warm-up": author's interview with John Taras, December 1999.

15. PARIS, 1949

101 "wanted to bring Egorova": Peter Anastos, "A Conversation with George Skibine," *Ballet Review*, Spring 1982.

103 "very sorry to let you go": Records of the Ballet Russe, Dance Collection, New York Public Library.

16. ROYAL OPERA HOUSE

114 "To Laugh or Not to Laugh": *NYT*, March 19, 1950.

114 "muttered furiously": author's interview with Walter Georgov, November 1981.

116 "sleep with Mr. B.": author's interview with Marian Horosko, May 2009.

17. PUTTING NEW YORK CITY BALLET ON THE MAP

118 "The eyes take care of themselves": Tallchief, *Maria Tallchief: America's Prima Ballerina*, 264.

119 "palpable shudders": Joel Lobenthal, "*Symphonie Concertante* Revived," *Ballet Review*, Summer 1983.

119 "a carload of crooners": Chujoy, *The New York City Ballet*, 263.

121 "I was my own dancer": Emily Hite, "Yvonne Mounsey: Encounters with Mr. B," *Ballet Review*, Spring 2012.

121 "A single choreographer": Kirstein, "Ballet: Record and Augury," *Theatre Arts*, September 1940.

124 "liked Tudor a lot": Mason, *I Remember Balanchine*, 349.

125 "a coruscant dream": *Chicago Daily Tribune*, April 25, 1951.

18. EAST SIDE, WEST SIDE

129 "feel for her plight": Bocher, *The Cage*, 121.

131 "pranced and bounced": *NYHT*, June 13, 1951.

131 "romp like vaudevilleans": *Dance Magazine*, August 1951.

132 "created a sensation": *New York Journal-American*, November 21, 1951.

134 "incomparable bravura": Martin, *NYT*, February 20, 1952.

19. GRAND TOUR, 1952

135 "it suddenly became clear": *Life*, May 12, 1952.

138 "threw bunches of flowers": Le Clercq to Fizdale and Gold, no date [Spring 1952], Dance Collection, New York Public Library.

142 "sensuous splendor": *Dance News*, August 1952.

142 "tired old swans": Caryl Brahms, "I Blame Balanchine," *Ballet Today*, September 1952.

142 "a way to make some money": September 30, 1952, MS Thr 411 (2778), Houghton Library, Harvard University.

20. IN THE DRESSING ROOM

145 "always a nervous wreck": *Milwaukee Journal*, July 22, 1956.

148 "He told Kai": author's interview with Una Kai, January 2015.

148 "you can't put your heels down": Mason, *I Remember Balanchine*, 174.

149 "spurs the ground": *Dance News*, December 1952.

21. BY THE SEAT OF HER TUTU

154 "look at that!": author's interview with Allegra Kent, August 2014.

22. THE POODLE

156 "the fundamental force": Hubert Saal, *Town and Country*, October 1952.

157 "stylistic and dramatic areas": *NYHT*, May 7, 1953.

157 "qualities of youth": *NYT*, May 7, 1953.

159 "dancing like dreams": *NYT*, May 16, 1953.

160 "rejoicing under the stars": *Denver Post*, July 3, 1953.

160 "a large turnout of balletomanes": *Los Angeles Daily News*, July 28, 1953.

160 "a beautiful dancer": *Los Angeles Mirror*, July 28, 1953.

160 "wonderful meals": author's interview with Jonathan Watts, March 2014.

23. WEDDING NIGHT

165 "wonders today": author's interview with Anya Bardyguine Davis, May 2014.

167 "carried out": author's interview with Jillana Zimmerman, September 2015.

168 "Balanchine weirdie": Robert Sylvester, *New York Daily News*, January 22, 1954.

169 "very popular with the audience": *Ballet Annual*, vol. 9, p. 131.

171 "a seven-acre parcel": Barry Katz, "Weston Arabesque: George Balanchine and Tanaquil Le Clercq in Weston," *Weston Magazine*, Fall 2002.

24. EXPANDING HORIZONS

174 "a mistake": author's interview with Maria Tallchief, December 1981.

178 "not yet free": *New York Times*, December 5, 1954.

180 "glaring and muttering": *Chicago Daily Tribune*, November 9, 1954.

180 "ballet technicians": *Chicago American*, unsigned, November 7, 1954.

25. MOVING ALL OVER

181 "one of the best dancers": *Cue*, February 1955.

184 "was more musical": *The Nation*, June 23, 1956.

185 "described by the *Times*": S.J.C., *NYT*, June 1, 1956.

27. ZENITH

195 "visibly moved": Gruen, *The Private World of Ballet*, p. 95.

198 "stricken with stage fright": author's interview with Mollie Keeler James, May 2015.

198 "mouths were hanging open": author's interview with Virginia Rich, November 2015.

198 "brings to mind the elegance": Goldner, *Balanchine Variations*, 67.

199 "ballerina of the barn": P. W. Manchester, *Dance News*, January 1958.

201 "was becoming anxious": Kent, *Once a Dancer*, 120.

28. THE FAR EAST

203 "didn't want to see any of us": Gruen, *The Private World of Ballet*, 96.

203 "thin and dancing beautifully": Le Clercq to Fizdale and Gold, undated [Fall 1958], Dance Collection, New York Public Library.

205 "a super-human performing burden": *Dance Magazine*, November 1958.

206 "skim across the stage": Nancy Reynolds, *Repertory in Review*, 190.

206 "jumps, turns, lifts": *Dance News*, February 1959.

29. A BALANCHINE SWAN

214 "highly impressive": *NYT*, March 18, 1961.
214 "soft and lyrical": *NYHT*, March 18, 1961.

30. *RAYMONDA VARIATIONS*

222 "putting her safety in jeopardy": P. W. Manchester, *Dance News*, December 1954.
224 "helped you to understand": author's interview with John Prinz, April 2009.
225 "I'm so small": Mason, *I Remember Balanchine*, 363.
226 "nervous as all hell": author's interview with Victoria Simon, November 2015.
226 "had moved a few paces": *New York World-Telegram and Sun*, December 8, 1961.
226 "what a lyric dancer": *New York Journal-American*, December 8, 1961.
226 "dancing enchantingly": *NYT*, January 15, 1962.

31. THE USSR

228 "seemed to have been made for her": *NYT*, April 25, 1962.
228 "anti-Stalinist": Prevots, *Dance for Export*.
230 "fairly indifferent": *NYT*, October 10, 1962.
232 "Martin tabulated": *NYT*, November 10, 1962.

32. "YOU CAN ALWAYS COME BACK"

237 "I learned how to pace myself": Mason, *I Remember Balanchine*, 331.
237 "There aren't *real* fifth positions anymore": Gruen, *The Private World of Ballet*, 97.
238 "She's playing with fire": Davie Lerner, "Remembering Tanaquil Le Clercq," *Ballet Review*, Summer 2001.
238 "warm, caring, and attentive": d'Amboise, *I Was a Dancer*, 282.
239 "at her greatest": Denby, *Dancers, Buildings and People in the Streets*, 228.
239 "great female trouper": *New Yorker*, May 9, 1964.
240 "at least four classes": Patricia Wilde, Adjudicator's Report, Southeastern Regional Ballet Association, 1965.

241 "gained enormously in authority": *Dancing Times*, August 1965.

242 "lacks now in line": *Dance and Dancers*, October 1965.

243 "perfect person": Rebekah Harkness diary, Dance Collection, New York Public Library.

243 "applauded the ballerina": *NYHT*, December 2, 1965.

244 "anyone over 23": *New York Post*, December 24, 1965.

34. AMERICAN BALLET THEATRE

258 "just left in the hallway": *NYT*, July 30, 1971.

258 "all this fuss": *Dance Magazine*, Obituaries, September 1971.

35. PITTSBURGH

272 "I think he's very negative": Jane Vranish, "Top Choices Emerge in Search for PBT's New Artistic Director," *Pittsburgh Post-Gazette*, August 4, 1996.

272 "some things that were kind of nice": Alexander Tomalonis, "A Conversation with Ib Andersen," *Dance View* 14, no. 1 (1996–97).

272 "a new, higher level of confidence": Karen Dacko, "Patricia Wilde Passes the Torch," *Dance Magazine*, November 1996.

BIBLIOGRAPHY

Amberg, George. *Ballet in America: The Emergence of an American Art.* New York: Duell, Sloan and Pearce, 1949.

Anawalt, Sasha. *The Joffrey Ballet: Robert Joffrey and the Making of an American Dance Company.* New York: Scribner's, 1996.

Anderson, Jack. *The One and Only: The Ballet Russe de Monte Carlo.* New York: Dance Horizons, 1981.

Anderson, Jack, and Janet Light. *The Ballet Russe de Monte Carlo: The Golden Age of Costume and Set Design.* Manchester, VT: Hudson Hills, 2002.

Ashley, Merrill. *Dancing for Balanchine.* New York: Dutton, 1984.

Banes, Sally. *Dancing Women: Female Bodies on Stage.* New York: Routledge, 1998.

Baronova, Irina. *Irina: Ballet, Life and Love.* Gainesville: University Press of Florida, 2005.

Beaton, Cecil. *Ballet.* London: Wingate, 1951.

Bentley, Toni. *Costumes by Karinska.* New York: Harry N. Abrams, 1995.

———. *Winter Diary: A Dancer's Journal.* New York: Random House, 1982.

Bird, Dorothy. *Bird's Eye View: Dancing with Martha Graham and on Broadway.* Pittsburgh, PA: University of Pittsburgh Press, 1997.

Bocher, Barbara. *The Cage: Dancing for Jerome Robbins and George Balanchine, 1949–1954.* Createspace, 2012.

Brady, Joan. *The Unmaking of a Dancer: An Unconventional Life.* New York: Harper & Row, 1982.

Braunsweg, Julian. *Braunsweg's Ballet Scandals: The Life of an Impresario and the Story of Festival Ballet.* London: Allen and Unwin, 1973.

Buckle, Richard. *Diaghilev*. New York: Atheneum, 1979.

———. *In Search of Diaghilev*. London: Sidgwick and Jackson, 1955.

———. *Nijinsky*. New York: Simon & Schuster, 1971.

Buckle, Richard, in collaboration with John Taras. *George Balanchine, Ballet Master*. New York: Random House, 1988.

Chazin-Bennahum, Judith. *René Blum and the Ballets Russes*. New York: Oxford University Press, 2011.

Chujoy, Anatole. *The New York City Ballet*. New York: Alfred A. Knopf, 1953.

Clarke, Mary, and Clement Crisp. *Ballerina: The Art of Women in Classical Ballet*. London: BBC Books, 1987.

Cohen, Selma Jeanne, ed. *International Encyclopedia of Dance*. New York: Oxford University Press, 1998.

Contreras, Gloria. *What I Learned from Balanchine: Diary of a Choreographer*. New York: Jorge Pinto Books, 2008.

Conyn, Cornelius. *Three Centuries of Ballet*. New York: Elsevier Press, 1953.

Croce, Arlene. *Afterimages*. New York: Alfred A. Knopf, 1977.

———. *Going to the Dance*. New York: Alfred A. Knopf, 1982.

———. *Sight Lines*. New York: Alfred A. Knopf, 1987.

Croft, Clare. *Dancers as Diplomats: American Choreography in Cultural Exchange*. New York: Oxford University Press, 2015.

Dalrymple, Jean. *From the Last Row: A Personal History of the New York City Center of Music and Drama, Inc.* Clifton, NJ: J. T. White, 1975.

d'Amboise, Jacques. *I Was a Dancer*. New York: Alfred A. Knopf, 2011.

Danilova, Alexandra. *Choura*. New York: Alfred A. Knopf, 1986.

De Mille, Agnes. *And Promenade Home*. Boston: Little, Brown, 1958.

———. *Dance to the Piper*. Boston: Little, Brown, 1952.

———. *Russian Journals*. New York: Dance Perspectives Foundation, 1970.

Denby, Edwin. *Dancers, Buildings and People in the Streets*. New York: Horizon Press, 1965.

———. *Looking at the Dance*. New York: Pellegrine & Cudahy, 1968.

Dolin, Anton. *Alicia Markova: Her Life and Art*. New York: Hermitage House, 1953.

———. *Autobiography*. London: Oldborne, 1960.

———. *Divertissement*. London: Sampson Lowe, Marston & Co., 1931.

———. *Last Words: A Final Autobiography*. London: Century, 1985.

Duberman, Martin. *The Worlds of Lincoln Kirstein*. New York: Alfred A. Knopf, 2007.

Dunning, Jennifer. *But, First a School.* New York: Elizabeth Sifton Books / Viking, 1985.

Easton, Carol. *No Intermissions: The Life of Agnes de Mille.* Boston: Little, Brown, 1996.

Eliot, Karen. *Dancing Lives: Five Female Dancers from the Ballet D'Action to Merce Cunningham.* Urbana: University of Illinois Press, 2007.

Ewing, Alex C. *Bravura! Lucia Chase and the American Ballet Theatre.* Gainesville: University Press of Florida, 2009.

Farrell, Suzanne. *Holding On to the Air.* New York: Summit Books, 1990.

Fisher, Barbara Milberg. *In Balanchine's Company: A Dancer's Memoir.* Waterbury, CT: Wesleyan University Press, 2006.

Fokine, Michel. *Memoirs of a Ballet Master.* Edited by Anatole Chujoy. Translated by Vitale Fokine. Boston: Little, Brown, 1961.

Fonteyn, Margot. *Autobiography.* New York: Alfred A. Knopf, 1976.

———. *The Magic of Dance.* New York: Alfred A. Knopf, 1979.

Garafola, Lynn. *Dance for a City: Fifty Years of the New York City Ballet.* New York: Columbia University Press, 1999.

———. *Diaghilev's Ballets Russes.* New York: Oxford University Press, 1989.

Garcia-Marquez, Vicente. *The Ballets Russes: Colonel de Basil's Ballets Russes de Monte Carlo, 1932–1952.* New York: Alfred A. Knopf, 1990.

———. *Massine: A Biography.* New York: Alfred A. Knopf, 1995.

Garis, Robert. *Following Balanchine.* New Haven, CT: Yale University Press, 1995.

Geva, Tamara. *Split Seconds: A Remembrance.* New York: Harper & Row, 1972.

Goldner, Nancy. *Balanchine Variations.* Gainesville: University Press of Florida, 2008.

———. *More Balanchine Variations.* Gainesville: University Press of Florida, 2011.

Gottlieb, Robert. *George Balanchine: The Ballet Maker.* New York: Atlas Books / HarperCollins, 2004.

———, ed. *Reading Dance: A Gathering of Memoirs, Reportage, Criticism, Profiles, Interviews, and Some Uncategorizable Extras.* New York: Alfred A. Knopf, 2008.

Gruen, John. *Erik Bruhn, Danseur Noble.* New York: Viking Press, 1979.

———. *The Private World of Ballet.* New York: Viking Press, 1973.

Haggin, B. H. *Ballet Chronicle.* New York: Horizon, 1970.

———. *Discovering Balanchine.* New York: Horizon, 1981.

Homans, Jennifer. *Apollo's Angels: A History of Ballet*. New York: Random House, 2010.

Huckenpahler, Victoria. *Ballerina. A Biography of Violette Verdy*. New York: Audience Arts, 1978.

Hurok, Sol. *Sol Hurok Presents: A Memoir of the Dance World*. New York: Hermitage House, 1953.

Jacobs, Laura. *Landscape with Moving Figures: A Decade on Dance*. New York: Dance and Movement Press, 2006.

Jowitt, Deborah. *Jerome Robbins: His Life, His Theater, His Dance*. New York: Simon & Schuster, 2004.

———. *Time and the Dancing Image*. Berkeley: University of California Press, 1989.

Karthas, Ilyana. *When Ballet Became French: Modern Ballet and the Cultural Politics of France, 1900–1939*. Chicago: McGill-Queen's University Press, 2015.

Kavanaugh, Julie. *Secret Muses: The Life of Frederick Ashton*. New York: Pantheon, 1996.

Kendall, Elizabeth. *Balanchine and the Lost Muse*. New York: Oxford University Press, 2013.

Kent, Allegra. *Once a Dancer . . . An Autobiography*. New York: St. Martin's, 1997.

Kirkland, Gelsey, with Greg Lawrence. *Dancing on My Grave*. New York: Doubleday, 1986.

Kirstein, Lincoln. *Movement and Metaphor: Four Centuries of Ballet*. New York: Praeger, 1970.

———. *The New York City Ballet*. New York: Alfred A. Knopf, 1973.

Krokover, Rosalyn. *The New Borzoi Book of Ballets*. New York: Alfred A. Knopf, 1956.

Lawrence, Greg. *Dance with Demons: The Life of Jerome Robbins*. New York: G. P. Putnam's Sons, 2001.

Lawrence, Robert. *The Victor Book of Ballets and Ballet Music*. New York: Simon & Schuster, 1950.

Lee, Carol. *Ballet in Western Culture: A History of Its Origins and Evolution*. Boston: Allyn and Bacon, 1999.

Levinson, André. *Marie Taglioni*. Translated by Cyril W. Beaumont. London: Dance Books, 1977, reprint of 1930 ed.

Lewin, Yaël. *Night's Dancer: The Life of Janet Collins*. Middletown, CT: Wesleyan University Press, 2011.

Maiorano, Robert. *Worlds Apart: The Autobiography of a Dancer from Brooklyn*. New York: Coward, McCann & Geoghegan, 1980.

Maiorano, Robert, with Valerie Brooks. *Balanchine's* Mozartiana: *The Making of a Masterpiece*. New York: Freundlich Books, 1985.

Makarova, Natalia. *A Dance Autobiography*. New York: Alfred A. Knopf, 1979.

Markova, Alicia. *Giselle and I*. London: Barrie and Rockliff, 1960.

——. *Markova Remembers*. Boston: Little, Brown, 1986.

Martins, Peter, with Robert Cornfield. *Far from Denmark*. Boston: Little, Brown, 1982.

Mason, Francis. *I Remember Balanchine: Recollections of the Ballet Master by Those Who Knew Him*. New York: Doubleday, 1991.

Massine, Léonide. *My Life in Ballet*. New York: St. Martin's, 1968.

Maynard, Olga. *The American Ballet*. Philadelphia: Macrae Smith, 1959.

——. *Bird of Fire: The Story of Maria Tallchief*. New York: Dodd, Mead, 1961.

Nabokov, Nicholas. *Old Friends and New Music*. Boston: Little, Brown, 1951.

Newman, Barbara. *Grace under Pressure: Passing Dance through Time*. New York: Proscenium, 2003.

——. *Striking a Balance: Dancers Talk about Dancing*. Boston: Houghton Mifflin, 1982.

Nijinska, Bronislava. *Early Memoirs*. Translated from the Russian by Jean Robinson. New York: Holt, Rinehart and Winston, 1981.

Nikitina, Alice. *Nikitina by Herself*. Translated by Baroness Budberg. London: A. Wingate, 1959.

Norton, Leslie. *Léonide Massine and the 20th Century Ballet*. Jefferson, NC: McFarland, 2004.

Norton, Leslie, with Frederic Franklin. *Frederic Franklin: A Biography of the Ballet Star*. Jefferson, NC: McFarland, 2007.

Ohman, Frank, and Emily Berkowitz. *Balanchine's Dancing Cowboy*. ePUBit, 2013.

Page, Ruth. *Class: Notes on Dance Classes around the World, 1915–1980*. Princeton, NJ: Princeton University Press, 1984.

——. *Page by Page*. Brooklyn, NY: Dance Horizons, 1978.

Prevots, Naima. *Dance for Export: Cultural Diplomacy and the Cold War*. Middletown, CT: Wesleyan University Press, 1998.

Reynolds, Nancy. *No Fixed Points: Dance in the Twentieth Century*. New Haven, CT: Yale University Press, 2003.

——. *Repertory in Review: 40 Years of the New York City Ballet*. New York: Dial, 1977.

Robert, Grace. *The Borzoi Book of Ballets*. New York: Alfred A. Knopf, 1946.

Robinson, Harlow. *The Last Impresario: The Life, Times and Legacy of Sol Hurok*. New York: Viking, 1994.

Roné, Elvira. *Olga Preobrajenska: A Portrait*. New York: Marcel Dekker, 1978.

Scholl, Tim. *From Petipa to Balanchine: Classical Revival and the Modernization of Ballet*. New York: Routledge, 1994.

Schorer, Suki. *Balanchine's Pointework*. Madison, WI: Society of Dance History Scholars, A-R Editions, 1995.

———. *Suki Schorer on Balanchine Technique*. New York: Alfred A. Knopf, 1999.

Shearer, Moira. *Balletmaster: A Dancer's View of George Balanchine*. New York: G. P. Putnam's Sons, 1987.

Sorell, Walter. *The Dance through the Ages*. New York: Grosset & Dunlap, 1967.

———. *Dance in Its Time*. Garden City, NY: Anchor Press/Doubleday, 1981.

Souritz, Elizabeth. *Soviet Choreographers in the 1920s*. Translated from the Russian by Lynn Visson. Edited, with additional translation, by Sally Banes. Durham, NC: Duke University Press, 1990.

Steele, Valerie, ed. *Dance and Fashion*. New Haven, CT: Yale University Press, 2014.

Sutton, Tina. *The Making of Markova: Diaghilev's Baby Ballerina to Groundbreaking Icon*. London: Pegasus, 2013.

Tallchief, Maria, with Larry Kaplan. *Maria Tallchief: America's Prima Ballerina*. New York: Henry Holt, 1997.

Taper, Bernard. *Balanchine: A Biography*. Rev. and updated. New York: Macmillan, 1974.

Tchernichova, Elena, with Joel Lobenthal. *Dancing on Water: A Life in Ballet from the Kirov to the ABT*. Boston: Northeastern University Press, 2013.

Teachout, Terry. *All in the Dances: A Brief Life of Balanchine*. Orlando, FL: Harcourt, 2004.

Tennant, Victoria. *Irina Baronova*. Chicago: University of Chicago Press, 2014.

Tracey, Robert, with Sharon Delano. *Balanchine's Ballerinas: Conversations with the Muses*. New York: Linden Press / Simon & Schuster, 1983.

Twysden, Gertrude. *Alexandra Danilova*. New York: Kamin Dance, 1947.

Unger, Craig. *Blue Blood*. New York: William Morrow, 1988.

Vaill, Amanda. *Somewhere: A Life of Jerome Robbins*. New York: Broadway Books, 2006.

Villella, Edward. *Prodigal Son: Dancing for Balanchine in a World of Pain and Magic*. New York: Simon & Schuster, 1992.

Volkov, Solomon. *Balanchine's Tchaikovsky: Interviews with George Balanchine.* New York: Simon & Schuster, 1985.

Walczak, Barbara, and Una Kai. *Balanchine the Teacher: Fundamentals That Shaped the First Generation of New York City Ballet Dancers.* Gainesville: University Press of Florida, 2008.

Walker, Katherine Sorley. *De Basil's Ballets Russes.* New York: Atheneum, 1982.

Wood, Roger. *The New York City Ballet—in Action.* With critical notes by P. W. Manchester. Mitcham, UK: Saturn, 1953.

Zorina, Vera. *Zorina.* New York: Farrar, Straus and Giroux, 1986.

Zoritch, George. *Ballet Mystique: Behind the Glamour of the Ballet Russe.* Cynara Editions, 2000.

INDEX

Photographs are indicated by "P" followed by
the page number in the photo section.

Kramer, Helen, 74–75
Krassovska, Nathalie, 83, 93–95
Kschessinskaya, Mathilde, 99

Laing, Hugh, 123–24, 158, 184, 216
Lanese, Lillian, 32
Last Flower (Dollar), 41
Lavrovsky, Leonid, 208
Lazovsky, Yurek, 46, 74
Le Clercq, Edith, 5–6, 44, 117, 191–94, 197, 232, 255
Le Clercq, Tanaquil: Balanchine marriage, 116–17, 144–45, 147, 171–73, 191–92, 200, 254–55; Farrell as Balanchine muse and, 238; Molo relationship, 44; as NYCB dancer, 114, 123, 125, 130, 133, 138, 156, 159, 160, 167, 168, 177, 178–79, 182–85, 189, P9; Paris visit, 103; performing experiences, 142, 144–45, 222; polio diagnosis, 186–87, 192–94, 195–97, 203, 216, 232; retirement, 275–76; style and technique of, 128, 156; as teacher, 254; writing career, 254–55
Leonidoff, Leon, 137, 139, 232
Leporsky, Zoya, 36, 65
Lester, Keith, 93
Lewis, Emory, 157
Lichine, David, 41
Lieberson, Goddard, 49
Liebeslieder Walzer (Balanchine), 229
Lifar, Serge, 85, 98
Life for the Czar, A (Balanchine), 122, 225
Lilac Garden (Tudor), 156, 226
Lincoln Center, 63, 234
Lindgren, Robert, x, 67, 92

Littlefield, Carl, 33
Littlefield, Catherine, 33
Littlefield, Dorothie, 33–34, 36, 53
Littlefield Ballet, 33–34
Lland, Michael, 259
London, George, 219
Loren, Sophia, 251
Loring, Eugene, 47
Low, Betty, 26
Lowry, McNeil, 236
Ludlow, Conrad, 228, 229, 234
Lyric Opera of Chicago, 179

Madroños (Cobos), 87
Magallanes, Nicholas: Balanchine relationship, 56–57; as Ballet Russe dancer, 61–62, 70, 75–76, 78; as Ballet Society dancer, 98; Mexico City tour, 50; as NYCB dancer, 116, 120, 125, 133–34, 153, 167, 178, 197, 215–16, 230, P10
Mailer, Norman, 127
Makarova, Natalia, 257, P14
Manchester, P. W., 178, P6
Marchand, Colette, 100–101
Marie-Jeanne: as American Concert Ballet dancer, 32; on Balanchine, 148; as Ballet International dancer, 36, 41; as Ballet Russe dancer, 63, 73, 76–77, 87, 91; as Ballet Society dancer, 89, 98; Mexico City tour, 49–50, 55, 57; as NYCB dancer, 89, 161; as School of American Ballet dancer, 48–49
Mariinsky Ballet, 33, 37, 44–45, 78, 99, 114, 182, 231
Markova, Alicia, 93, 95–96, 99, 140

Preobrajenska, Olga, 99, 101–2, 104–5

Présages, Les (Massine), 96

Prinz, John, 224

Prodigal Son (Balanchine), 122–23, 139–40, 211

Prokofiev, Sergei, 169, 208

Prokovsky, André, 244, 277

Pugni, Cesare, 93

Quartet (Robbins), 168–69

Quelques Fleurs (Boris), 93

Ravel, Maurice, 124–26

Raven, Seymour, 180

Raymonda (Balanchine), 71–73, 76–78, 189, 224–26, 243

Raymonda (Bolshoi), 219

Raymonda Variations (Balanchine), 78, 224–26, 231, 236, 274

Reed, Janet, 113–14, 130, 153–54, 160, 169, 177, 196, P9

Rehner, Bernice, 50

Reiman, Elise, 33, 278

Reynolds, Nancy, 206

Riabouchinska, Tatiana, 41–42

Rich, Virginia, 187, 198, 273

Richard, Stephen, 268

Rieti, Vittorio, 71, 207

Rigoletto (Verdi), 52

Rimbaud, Arthur, 121–22

Robbins, Jerome, 121, 124, 129–30, 133, 139–41, 144–45, 168–69, 183, 193, P6

Rodeo, 75, 80, 82, 98–99

Rogers, Buddy, 92–93

Roma (Balanchine), 182–83

Romanoff, Boris, 37

Romanoff, Dimitri, 256

Romantic ballet, 93–95, 130–32, 147

Romeo and Juliet (Lavrovsky), 208

Romeo and Juliet (Wells), 269

Rosenthal, Jean, 137, 170

Ross, Bertram, 210

Ross, Herbert, 260

Rossini, Gioachino, 159

Rossi Street academy (Leningrad), 208, 231, 234, 262

Rouge et Noir (Massine), 96–98, 140

Roy, Melinda, 277

Royal Academy of Dance, 114

Royal Ballet (London), 101, 105, 106, 259

Royal Danish Ballet, 119, 215, 271

Rudolph, Norman, 27–28

Ruslan and Lyudmila (Fokine), 181–82

Russian Imperial Ballet, 33, 72, 77, 99, 101–2, 132

Saal, Hubert, 131, 156

SAB. *See* School of American Ballet (SAB)

Samson et Dalila (Saint-Saëns), 52, 53

Scheherazade (Fokine), 82

Schoenberg, Arnold, 167–68

School of American Ballet (SAB): ABT closing and, 262; Balanchine and, 23, 47–48, 148; as Ballet Society feeder, 98; Danilova as teacher, 69; Ford Foundation grant of 1963, 236; foundation funding for, 221; *Giselle* production, 38; Nora as student, 6, 23, 25, 28, 29, 46; as NYCB feeder, 120; overview of, 44–46; Wilde as student, 6, 22–24, 29, 32–33, 43–49, 109, 239

Schorer, Suki, 226